"Chock-full of systematic strategies for the treatment of a wide variety of psychological problems. Eminently readable and helpful for professionals as well as patients."

> —Aaron T. Beck, MD, president of the Beck Institute for Cognitive Therapy and Research Psychopathology

"An outstanding book. I recommend it without reservation for both general readers and therapists. It stands apart from other similar books in its reliance on scientific data, not fad, hype, or mysticism."

> —Jacqueline B. Persons, PhD, director of the San Francisco Bay Area Center for Cognitive Therapy and clinical professor in the Department of Psychology at the University of California, Berkeley

"An excellent resource, reference tool, treatment manual, therapy coach, and compendium of techniques."

> —Arthur Freeman, EdD, ABPP, HSPP, president of the Freeman Institute for Cognitive Therapy and director of clinical training and supervision for the Center for Brief Therapy in Fort Wayne, IN

"One of the most comprehensive and empirically sound guidebooks in all of self-help literature. All of the major problems in living are covered."

> —Cory F. Newman, PhD, clinical director of the Center for Cognitive Therapy and associate professor of psychology in psychiatry at the University of Pennsylvania

"For professionals and the public, this wonderful workbook, like a wise teacher, can help make a positive difference."

> —Thomas F. Cash, PhD, professor emeritus of clinical psychology at Old Dominion University in Norfolk, VA

"A jewel of a book: supportive and empathetic, short on platitudes and long on practical applications. A must-buy for all cognitive behavioral therapists."

> —Thomas E. Ellis, PsyD, ABPP, professor of psychology at Marshall University in Huntington, WV

Thoughts &Feelings

Taking Control of Your Moods & Your Life

FOURTH EDITION

MATTHEW M^CKAY, PhD
MARTHA DAVIS, PhD
PATRICK FANNING

New Harbinger Publications, Inc.

Publisher's Note

This publication is designed to provide accurate and authoritative information in regard to the subject matter covered. It is sold with the understanding that the publisher is not engaged in rendering psychological, financial, legal, or other professional services. If expert assistance or counseling is needed, the services of a competent professional should be sought.

Distributed in Canada by Raincoast Books

New Harbinger Publications, Inc.
5674 Shattuck Avenue
Oakland, CA 94609
www.newharbinger.com

Acquired by Melissa Kirk; Cover design by Amy Shoup; Text design by Tracy Marie Carlson; Edited by Jasmine Star

Library of Congress Cataloging-in-Publication Data

McKay, Matthew.
  Thoughts and feelings : taking control of your moods and your life / Matthew McKay, Martha Davis, and Patrick Fanning. -- 4th ed.
    p. cm.
  Includes bibliographical references and index.
  ISBN 978-1-60882-208-9 (pbk.) -- ISBN 978-1-60882-209-6 (pdf e-book) -- ISBN 978-1-60882-210-2 (epub)
  1. Cognitive therapy--Popular works. I. Davis, Martha, 1947- II. Fanning, Patrick. III. Title.
  RC489.C63M34 2011
  616.89'1425--dc23

        2011035736

21 20 19

20 19 18 17 16 15 14

Dedicated to all the researchers and clinicians who have shown us what works.

Contents

Preface to the Fourth Edition vii

Acknowledgments ix

How to Use This Book xi

1: Making Your Own Treatment Plan 1

2: Uncovering Automatic Thoughts 15

3: Changing Patterns of Limited Thinking 27

4: Changing Hot Thoughts 47

5: Relaxation 59

6: Worry Control 69

 7: Coping with Panic. 85

 8: Coping Imagery 105

 9: Mindfulness 115

10: Defusion. 127

11: Getting Mobilized 137

12: Putting Values into Action 153

13: Brief Exposure. 165

14: Prolonged Exposure 181

15: Testing Core Beliefs 195

16: Changing Core Beliefs with Visualization 207

17: Stress Inoculation for Anger Control 219

18: Covert Modeling 233

19: Covert Sensitization 243

20: Problem Solving 253

21: When It Doesn't Come Easy 273

References and Resources .281

Index. 287

Preface to the Fourth Edition

The first edition of *Thoughts and Feelings* appeared in 1981. It was an introduction to cognitive behavioral therapy that was used by general readers and therapists alike. It provided simple, step-by-step instructions for a dozen specific techniques.

Over the years we came to realize the book's limitations. To begin with, some of the techniques had not stood the test of time. Later studies had shown them to be less effective than newer, more powerful interventions. In addition, although cognitive behavioral therapists were developing multistep protocols to treat many disorders, the original edition of *Thoughts and Feelings* didn't show how to link a series of techniques together into an integrated treatment plan for problems like depression, panic disorder, or anger.

With the second, third, and now fourth editions of *Thoughts and Feelings*, the book has been revised to include more effective methodologies and reflect changes in modern practices. *Thoughts and Feelings* now offers multistep treatment plans for many mood-based problems. These plans are outlined in chapter 1 to show you a sequence of relevant chapters and techniques for each disorder. This is consistent with the way cognitive behavioral treatments are conducted during therapy: You take a series of steps to acquire skills that serve as building blocks in coping with problems.

For this edition, we have removed the chapter on thought stopping, a technique that in recent years has been shown to be of little value. We replaced it with a new chapter on defusion, a powerful technique now used in the third wave of behavior therapies as a core treatment. Defusion has impressive research support for helping manage anxiety, depression, and anger. We have also removed the chapter on coping during exposure, because experience has shown that relaxation techniques and coping thoughts work best when used before and after exposure, not during exposure.

Two chapters have been significantly revised and renamed in light of current research: "Flooding" has become "Prolonged Exposure," and "Stress Inoculation" has become "Brief Exposure." Finally, the chapter "Getting Mobilized" is now followed by a new chapter, "Putting Values into Action," which stresses the consistent application of values to life goals.

In the second and third editions of *Thoughts and Feelings*, we sacrificed a bit of logic in order to keep the chapter numbering system consistent with the first edition, and thus reduce confusion in classrooms where students were using various editions. However, the cumulative changes since 1981 have finally necessitated a complete rearrangement of the table of contents so that the most basic skills are taught first, the more widely used interventions appear earlier, and the less common techniques or treatments for rarer diagnoses appear later in the book.

Our intention is still for both the general reader and the therapist to use this book. The general reader will find that each treatment protocol has clear, easy-to-follow steps that provide tools for genuine self-help. Therapists will find the book to be a resource for the most effective treatment methods, as well as a helpful take-home manual for clients.

Thoughts and Feelings was written because life is hard. To cope, all of us have been given a random set of tools and instructions by parents, family, friends, teachers, bosses, and others. Some of this has been helpful, some not. *Thoughts and Feelings* is about tools that work. It is a guide for changing old patterns of responding in order to take control of your moods and your life.

—Matthew McKay

—Patrick Fanning

—Martha Davis

Acknowledgments

Grateful acknowledgment is made to Norman Cavior, PhD, our teacher, and the one who first introduced us to cognitive behavioral techniques. He continues to be a source of wisdom and inspiration.

We also wish to acknowledge three fine writers who made significant contributions to the second edition: Mary Hills Hoffman, Dana Landis, and Susan Johnson.

How to Use This Book

We've chosen to present cognitive behavioral techniques in a workbook format so you can practice them as self-help steps toward change. People in the helping professions—therapists, doctors, nurses, social workers, even teachers and supervisors—will find many of these techniques useful in their personal lives, and also of value to clients, patients, students, or employees.

In chapter 1 you'll find a list of twelve major problems and a specific, step-by-step treatment plan for each of them. The treatment plan will give you the sequence in which to work through relevant chapters and techniques. At the end of chapter 1 is the Treatment Planner chart, which gives an overview of which chapters you should read to treat these and a few other problems.

In most cases you'll find it helpful to read chapters 2, 3, and 4 first, because they represent the foundation of cognitive behavioral therapy. You'll learn how thoughts influence feelings and how habitual negative thoughts can impact your mood. You'll also find tools for changing your thoughts in order to relieve anxiety, depression, and anger.

The full benefits of cognitive behavioral therapy can be realized only through regular practice over time. Simply understanding a technique is of little value without firsthand experience. In other words, this is not a book for passive reading. You have to do the exercises, fill in the worksheets, and carry out real changes in how you think and behave.

The length of time required to practice a particular technique will vary. See the "Time to Mastery" sections for an idea of the time required to develop each new skill. Because regular practice is the key to successful change, practice the exercises daily. Some of the techniques will need to be "overlearned" so they become automatic responses. The goal is to be able to use the techniques wherever and whenever you need to, without having to refer to the book.

If you feel you have limited self-discipline or are not highly motivated, try these two alternatives:

1. Make a contract with another person, as described in chapter 21, to reinforce your commitment to learning and using the relevant techniques in this book.

2. Seek a consultation with a cognitive behavioral therapist to help you develop and monitor your treatment program.

Before undertaking any cognitive behavioral treatments for anxiety, you should get a complete physical checkup. Have your doctor rule out thyroid problems, hypoglycemia, mitral valve prolapse, and other cardiac arrhythmia problems. If you experience any prolonged physical effects while doing exercises in this book, consult your physician.

CHAPTER 1

Making Your Own Treatment Plan

You're probably reading this book because you're feeling bad. You may be depressed, anxious, angry, worried, confused, frustrated, upset, ashamed... Unfortunately, the list is very long. Please remember that you are not alone or unusual in your struggle with painful feelings and experiences. Everybody experiences emotional distress sometimes. It's normal.

When the pain becomes too strong and too enduring, it's time to do something about it. By reading this book, you are taking an important first step toward feeling better.

When you feel bad, you don't have the time and patience to wade through simplistic pep talks, unrealistic success stories, needless horror stories, or long-winded and obscure discussions of theory. Therefore, we have made this book as clear and as brief as possible.

On the other hand, when you feel bad you don't have the energy to seek out partial fragments of the solution to your problem in widely scattered locations. So we've also made this book as complete as possible. Everything you need to learn the techniques in this book is presented in detail, proceeding logically, step-by-step.

If you are in pain, you also don't have any time to waste on unproven remedies of doubtful utility. Therefore, we have included only techniques that have been proven to have strong therapeutic benefits in many well-designed studies with many different types of people, and over a long period of time.

Over the past thirty years, many new cognitive behavioral techniques have been developed and refined to relieve anxiety, lift depression, and calm anger. The best of these techniques are presented in this book. They offer you real promise that help is on the way. With patience and a little effort, you can start to feel better soon.

WHY COGNITIVE BEHAVIORAL THERAPY WORKS

Many people believe that painful feelings are caused by forgotten childhood experiences and that the only way to relieve these feelings is through long, difficult analysis to root out unconscious memories and associations.

There is undoubtedly some connection between your distant past and painful feelings in the present. But modern cognitive behavioral therapists have discovered a much more immediate and accessible source of emotions: your current train of thought. It has been demonstrated over and over again that most painful emotions are immediately preceded by some kind of interpreting thought.

For example, a new acquaintance doesn't telephone when he said he would. If your interpreting thought was "He doesn't like me after all," you would feel sad at being rejected. If your thought was "He's been in a car crash," you would feel anxiety for his well-being. If you thought, "He deliberately lied to me about calling," you might feel anger at his falsehood.

One simple insight forms the heart of cognitive behavioral therapy: You can change your feelings by changing your thoughts. Hundreds of studies over the last thirty years have proved that this simple insight can be applied to relieve a large variety of problems more easily and quickly than any other therapeutic technique.

DESIGNING YOUR TREATMENT PLAN

This is not the kind of book that you must read cover to cover. This chapter will help you assess your problem and plan which chapters to work through to solve your problem.

Twelve major emotional problems and the plans to treat them are summarized below. The treatment plans follow a definite sequence, beginning with the most useful or general technique and proceeding to more specialized interventions.

For each problem below, we begin by discussing characteristic symptoms. Then the pertinent chapters are listed in the order in which they should be read. Each section concludes with a brief description of the steps and rationale for the protocol.

If you'd like an overview of all the problems this book treats, see the Treatment Planner chart at the end of this chapter. It shows, at a glance, all of the treatment for each of the problems discussed below.

Worry

Worry is the main symptom of generalized anxiety disorder. You have a problem with worry if you have been excessively apprehensive more days than not for at least six months. Seriously anxious people find it difficult to control their worry and typically experience these symptoms:

- Restlessness

- Fatigue

- Difficulty concentrating

- Irritability

- Muscle tension

- Sleep disturbance

> **Treat worry by working through the following chapters in order:**
> Chapter 5, "Relaxation"
> Chapter 6, "Worry Control"
> Chapter 20, "Problem Solving"

Begin at chapter 5, "Relaxation" and emphasize practicing cue-controlled relaxation. In chapter 6, "Worry Control," you'll learn how to make an accurate risk assessment, do worry exposure, and achieve worry behavior prevention. Because some worries can be addressed by searching for alternative solutions, chapter 20, "Problem Solving," will be helpful, as it teaches skills for finding new answers. If worry persists due to deeply held negative beliefs, read chapter 15, "Testing Core Beliefs." Chapter 9, "Mindfulness," may help you focus on the here and now, which can also help ease worry, and chapter 10, "Defusion," will help you detach from worry-provoking thoughts.

Panic Disorder

Panic is a period of intense fear. When you experience a panic attack, you feel some of the following symptoms very intensely, and they'll reach a peak quickly—within ten minutes:

- Pounding heart and fast heart rate

- Sweating

- Trembling

- Shortness of breath

- A feeling of choking

- Chest pain

- Stomach pain or nausea

- Feeling spacey

- Fear of losing control or "going crazy"

- Fear of dying

- Numbness or tingling

- Chills or suddenly feeling hot or flushed

Treat panic disorder by working through the following chapter:

Chapter 7, "Coping with Panic"

Follow all of the steps outlined in chapter 7, "Coping with Panic." You'll need to master breath control training, learn how to use a Probability Form, and practice interoceptive desensitization.

If you haven't developed agoraphobia (fear of being away from a safe place) or significant avoidance because of the fear of panicking, chapter 7 will be sufficient. However, if you've reached a point where you are avoidant or agoraphobic, you'll need to develop a fear hierarchy as explained in chapter 13, "Brief Exposure," and work through chapter 14, "Prolonged Exposure," so you can begin exposing yourself to your feared situations in gradual steps.

Chapter 9, "Mindfulness," can help you observe your symptoms, moment to moment, as transitory, nonfatal phenomena.

Perfectionism

When you struggle with perfectionism, nothing is ever good enough. Shades of gray disappear and you see only black and white—mostly black. You are your own harshest critic, constantly upbraiding yourself for failing to come up to the mark. You may spend hours checking and rechecking calculations, revising a paper, or sanding and polishing a craft project. Yet all of this striving for perfection doesn't please you; it only makes you all the more anxious about making mistakes and being criticized for them.

Treat perfectionism by working through the following chapters in order:

Chapter 2, "Uncovering Automatic Thoughts"

Chapter 3, "Changing Patterns of Limited Thinking"

Chapter 4, "Changing Hot Thoughts"

Chapter 6, "Worry Control" (worry behavior prevention only)

Chapter 15, "Testing Core Beliefs"

Begin with chapters 2, 3, and 4 to develop skills in using the Thought Journal. Pay attention to limited thinking patterns, particularly polarized thinking, catastrophizing, magnifying, and shoulds. In chapter 4 you'll also learn how to confront hot thoughts (the thoughts that trigger emotion) about the seemingly dire consequences of making mistakes.

The program for worry behavior prevention in chapter 6 is critical for limiting the excessive checking and overworking that grow out of fears of making mistakes or being criticized. Chapter 15, "Testing Core Beliefs," will give you tools to identify and change deeply held beliefs about unworthiness and incompetence that may fuel your perfectionism.

If you still have serious problems with perfectionism after working through chapter 15, see chapter 13, "Brief Exposure," to develop a hierarchy of feared mistakes, then expose yourself through imagery to each step of your hierarchy. You will also need to expose yourself to mistakes in real life by deliberately making mistakes in a series of planned experiments (see "Step 6: Test Your Rules," in chapter 15).

Obsessional Thinking

Obsessional thinking consists of recurrent thoughts, impulses, or images that intrude on your consciousness. Obsessional thinking is not ordinary worry over a current problem; it's a disturbing, unwelcome train of thought that is excessive, unreasonable, and time-consuming. You try to stop obsessing, but the thoughts soon start up again. Obsessional thinking can significantly interfere with your normal routine at home, school, or work.

Treat obsessional thinking by working through the following chapters in order:

Chapter 10, "Defusion"

Chapter 14, "Prolonged Exposure"

Chapter 6, "Worry Control" (worry behavior prevention only)

The protocol for obsessional thinking starts with chapter 10, "Defusion," because it's simple and easy to learn. This technique will allow you to detach from many unwanted thoughts. But there will be some thoughts—usually those that trigger very high anxiety—that will require a more powerful strategy. Chapter 14, "Prolonged Exposure," shows you how to bombard yourself with images derived from your obsessional thoughts and in so doing take away their power.

The section on worry behavior prevention in chapter 6 completes the treatment by helping you stop any checking or avoidance behaviors that reinforce your obsessions.

Phobia

Phobias are generally classified into three main categories: specific phobias, agoraphobia, and social phobia. Specific phobias include excessive or unreasonable fear of such things as flying, heights, animals, injections, blood, and so on. You avoid the object of your fear as much as possible. If you must fly, ascend heights, or approach feared animals, it causes you intense anxiety, perhaps a full-blown panic attack. Specific phobias go beyond normal caution in risky situations. They seriously interfere with your relationships, daily routine, schooling, or career.

Agoraphobia is anxiety about or avoidance of public places. People with agoraphobia fear leaving a safe place, such as their home. They don't want to be in a situation in which escape would be difficult or embarrassing. They are often concerned about having a panic attack someplace where help isn't available. People with agoraphobia typically fear being outside their home alone, being in a crowd, standing in line, crossing a bridge, traveling in a bus or train, and so on.

Social phobia is a strong, persistent fear of being with unfamiliar people. If you have social phobia, you try to avoid situations in which you must meet new people, interact with those you don't know well, or face the scrutiny of strangers. You're afraid you may behave awkwardly or embarrass yourself by showing how anxious you are. When you must be in social situations, you're very anxious, even though you realize your fear is excessive. Social phobia seriously interferes with your life.

Treat phobia by working through the following chapters in order:

Chapter 7, "Coping with Panic" (only if you have agoraphobia)

Chapter 5, "Relaxation"

Chapter 13, "Brief Exposure"

The basic treatment protocol for all phobias is the same, with the exception of agoraphobia. Agoraphobia usually starts with untreated panic disorder. The panic disorder must be resolved first by working through chapter 7, "Coping with Panic." Then you can continue with the regular phobia protocol.

To use the regular phobia protocol, initially work through chapter 5, "Relaxation." Then work with chapter 13, "Brief Exposure," to develop a fear hierarchy, expose yourself to those situations using visualization, and then practice brief exposure in real-life situations.

If brief exposure doesn't completely resolve the phobia, move on to chapter 14, "Prolonged Exposure," which emphasizes long periods of visualized or real-life exposure. If you're working through this protocol for a social phobia, you might also wish to explore chapter 9, "Mindfulness," chapter 18, "Covert Modeling," or chapter 8, "Coping Imagery," to develop and practice a specific plan for handling novel social situations.

Depression

When you're depressed, your mood is sad and nothing seems interesting or pleasurable. It can affect your appetite, causing you to lose or gain weight. You might sleep a lot more or less than usual. You feel restless and yet tired at the same time. It's hard to concentrate or make decisions, especially the decision to get up and do something. You feel worthless. Life seems hopeless. Thoughts of death are common, and you may even think about suicide. One very important note: If you have serious thoughts of suicide, this book is not enough. You need to see a mental health professional as soon as possible.

> **Treat depression by working through the following chapters in order:**
>
> Chapter 11, "Getting Mobilized"
>
> Chapter 2, "Uncovering Automatic Thoughts"
>
> Chapter 3, "Changing Patterns of Limited Thinking"
>
> Chapter 4, "Changing Hot Thoughts"
>
> Chapter 12, "Putting Values into Action"
>
> Chapter 20, "Problem Solving"

Since a major feature of depression is feeling tired and passive, start by reading chapter 11, "Getting Mobilized," so you can begin using activity scheduling. The next step is to read chapters 2, 3, and 4 to become skilled in using the Thought Journal, a structured journal that allows you to explore, confront, and change patterns of negative thinking. Pay particular attention to limited thinking patterns, particularly filtering, polarized thinking, overgeneralization, and magnifying.

Chapter 12, "Putting Values into Action," will give you motivation to act according to your values, and chapter 20, "Problem Solving," will provide a method for developing alternative solutions to interpersonal, job, financial, and other problems.

If depression persists after you work through these chapters, you may need to change specific core beliefs about your competence, worth, and so on. Work through chapter 15, "Testing Core Beliefs," and then chapter 16, "Changing Core Beliefs with Visualization," to identify and change depression-generating core beliefs. Chapter 9, "Mindfulness," may also help stop rumination by helping you focus on the present moment.

Low Self-Esteem

When you suffer from low self-esteem, you feel worthless, flawed, and incompetent. You are blind to your strong points and exaggerate your weak points. Your accomplishments in life seem trivial, and your failures loom large. Your mood may be sad and depressed, or you may be irritable and aggressive to cover your feelings of low self-worth. You expect people to see through to your unworthy core and are surprised and incredulous if someone claims to like you. Low self-esteem keeps you from setting and achieving goals, forming meaningful relationships, trying for promotions, and taking other kinds of risks.

> **Treat low self-esteem by working through the following chapters in order:**
>
> Chapter 2, "Uncovering Automatic Thoughts"
>
> Chapter 3, "Changing Patterns of Limited Thinking"
>
> Chapter 4, "Changing Hot Thoughts"
>
> Chapter 15, "Testing Core Beliefs"
>
> Chapter 16, "Changing Core Beliefs with Visualization"

Begin with chapters 2, 3, and 4 to develop skills in using the Thought Journal. Pay close attention to limited thinking patterns, particularly filtering, polarized thinking, overgeneralization, and magnifying.

Next, work through chapter 15, "Testing Core Beliefs," to identify and change deep beliefs about your worthiness, and then chapter 16, "Changing Core Beliefs with Visualization," which provides a way to strengthen this work by restructuring your memories in regard to childhood situations in which these core beliefs were formed.

You may still have to work on remaining hot thoughts (thoughts that immediately precede a painful emotion). If one or two hot thoughts persist that undermine your self-esteem, try working through chapter 10, "Defusion."

Shame and Guilt

People who suffer from shame and excessive guilt often feel worthless and to blame for anything that goes wrong. Early sexual or physical abuse frequently contributes to a feeling of being "damaged goods," unworthy of any love or happiness in life. When tragedy strikes, pervasive shame and guilt make it seem like well-deserved punishment rather than simple bad luck.

Treat shame and guilt by working through the following chapters in order:

Chapter 2, "Uncovering Automatic Thoughts"

Chapter 3, "Changing Patterns of Limited Thinking"

Chapter 4, "Changing Hot Thoughts"

Chapter 10, "Defusion"

Chapter 15, "Testing Core Beliefs"

Start your program by reading chapters 2, 3, and 4 to develop skills in using the Thought Journal. Pay special attention to limited thinking patterns, particularly magnifying, polarized thinking, overgeneralization, and shoulds.

You'll need the skills from chapter 10, "Defusion," to detach from habitual thoughts that trigger shame or guilt. Most importantly, you'll need to work through chapter 15, "Testing Core Beliefs," to identify and change deep beliefs about your worthiness, acceptability, and so on.

If your shame seems to arise out of childhood experiences of abuse, you should also work through the exercises in chapter 16, "Changing Core Beliefs with Visualization."

Anger

You have a problem with anger if you frequently react to stress or frustration by yelling, hitting, or throwing or breaking things. You have a problem with anger when your temper negatively affects your intimate relationships, your family life, your work, or your friends and acquaintances.

> **Treat anger by working through the following chapters in order:**
> Chapter 2, "Uncovering Automatic Thoughts"
> Chapter 3, "Changing Patterns of Limited Thinking"
> Chapter 4, "Changing Hot Thoughts"
> Chapter 5, "Relaxation"
> Chapter 17, "Stress Inoculation for Anger Control"

The first step toward anger control is to read chapters 2, 3, and 4 to develop skill in using the Thought Journal. This will help you identify thoughts that trigger anger, and then develop strategies to evaluate and challenge them. Next, learn all of the relaxation skills in chapter 5, particularly cue-controlled relaxation.

Chapter 17, "Stress Inoculation for Anger Control," will show you how to put your cognitive and relaxation skills together as you practice them in visualized anger-provoking situations.

If anger persists in specific, predictable situations, work through chapter 18, "Covert Modeling," to develop a specific plan to change your behavior and practice a sequence of new, more effective responses. And if you still tend to dwell on angry thoughts, read chapter 9, "Mindfulness," to learn to shift your awareness to more neutral observations.

Bad Habits

Bad habits range from excessive television watching to compulsive spending, from nail biting to driving too fast, from eating too much to letting the laundry and dishes pile up too long. A bad habit is any recurrent behavior that you can't seem to stop doing even though you realize it has a negative impact on your life.

This book doesn't offer a strong treatment plan for addictive bad habits such as smoking, alcoholism, or drug abuse. However, less severe habits like those mentioned above can be improved significantly with the techniques offered here.

> **Treat bad habits by working through the following chapters in order:**
>
> Chapter 5, "Relaxation"
> Chapter 18, "Covert Modeling"
> Chapter 20, "Problem Solving"

Since many bad habits occur in response to stress, your first step is to read and master chapter 5, "Relaxation." You should be prepared to use cue-controlled relaxation whenever stress or anxiety begins to trigger your habit.

Next, work through chapter 18, "Covert Modeling," to develop alternative responses to replace your old habitual patterns. Finally, use chapter 20, "Problem Solving," to develop alternative solutions to difficult situations that have triggered the habit in the past.

Some persistent habits can be treated with a technique outlined in chapter 19, "Covert Sensitization," where you pair the habit with unpleasant stimuli to extinguish it.

Mild Avoidance

Mild avoidance is a persistent fear of certain situations, people, or things. The fear is strong enough that you tend to avoid the feared situation when possible, but not so strong that you can't force yourself to deal with the situation if you must. For example, mild avoidance of flying might mean you go by train or car when possible but fly when there's no other option. Mild avoidance interferes moderately with your relationships, work, or education.

> **Treat mild avoidance by working through the following chapters in order:**
>
> Chapter 5, "Relaxation"
> Chapter 8, "Coping Imagery"
> Chapter 9, "Mindfulness"

Because your avoidance is more on the level of procrastination and putting off rather than full phobia, you probably won't have to develop a hierarchy and do brief exposure to feared situations to overcome it. Start with chapter 5, "Relaxation," and work to become skilled at deep breathing and cue-controlled relaxation. Then work through chapter 8, "Coping Imagery," to practice relaxing and coping while imagining yourself handling the stressful situation. Finally, chapter 9, "Mindfulness," will help you stay in the moment so that you'll be less prone to anxiety-driven avoidance.

Procrastination

In its most debilitating form, procrastination combines poor time-management and problem-solving skills with perfectionism and performance anxiety. You put off what you should be doing, waste time on low-priority distractions, let impossibly high standards keep you from starting, and fear failure or criticism once you do get started.

Treat procrastination by working through the following chapters in order:

Chapter 2, "Uncovering Automatic Thoughts"

Chapter 3, "Changing Patterns of Limited Thinking"

Chapter 4, "Changing Hot Thoughts"

Chapter 20, "Problem Solving"

Your first step should be working through chapters 2, 3, and 4 to develop skills in using the Thought Journal. Since procrastination often comes from a fear of failure or mistakes, pay special attention to limited thinking patterns, particularly catastrophizing, magnifying, and filtering. You'll need to confront and change trigger thoughts that define average performance or getting criticized as failure. Next, work through chapter 20, "Problem Solving," to develop a plan to accomplish goals you've been avoiding.

If procrastination persists, it is often due to deep beliefs about unworthiness or incompetence. You can identify and begin to change such beliefs by working through chapter 15, "Testing Core Beliefs."

TREATMENT PLANNER

The following chart presents every treatment plan in the book at a glance. To use it, locate a problem in the left column. Reading to the right, the number 1 appears in the column corresponding to the chapter you should work through first. The number 2 indicates the chapter teaching skills you should acquire second, and so on.

For some problems you may find columns marked with an X. These chapters aren't part of the core treatment plan for the problem but do contain additional procedures that may be applicable and useful if symptoms persist.

As you'll see, a few problems don't have a specific treatment plan, just chapters marked with an X to indicate suggested treatment options. A final note: If you're working with aggression, see the treatment program for anger; if you're working with obsessions, follow the program for anxiety disorders; and if you're working on self-criticism, follow the program for low self-esteem.

Don't be daunted—the chart only *looks* complicated. Take your time and work step-by-step. You can do it. Congratulations on embarking on this challenging voyage of self-discovery and healing!

Treatment Planner

Problem	Chapter 2 Uncovering Automatic Thoughts	Chapter 3 Changing Patterns of Limited Thinking	Chapter 4 Changing Hot Thoughts	Chapter 5 Relaxation	Chapter 6 Worry Control	Chapter 7 Coping with Panic	Chapter 8 Coping Imagery	Chapter 9 Mind-fulness	Chapter 10 Defusion
Anxiety Disorders									
Worry				1	2			X	X
Panic disorder						1		X	
Perfectionism	1	2	3		4				
Obsessional thinking					3				1
Phobia Specific				1			X	X	
Agoraphobia				2		1	X	X	
Social				1			X	X	
PTSD			2	1				X	
Performance anxiety			2	1				X	
Depressive Disorders									
Depression	2	3	4					X	
Low self-esteem	1	2	3						X
Shame and guilt	1	2	3						4
Anger	1	2	3	4				X	
Physical Stress									
Muscular tension				X					
Fight-or-flight Symptoms				X		X			
Behavioral Problems									
Bad habits				1					
Mild avoidance				1			2	3	
Procrastination	1	2	3						
Immobilization									
Interpersonal Conflict								**X**	
Negative Core Beliefs									

Chapter 11 Getting Mobilized	Chapter 12 Putting Values into Action	Chapter 13 Brief Exposure	Chapter 14 Prolonged Exposure	Chapter 15 Testing Core Beliefs	Chapter 16 Changing Core Beliefs with Visualization	Chapter 17 Stress Inoculation for Anger Control	Chapter 18 Covert Modeling	Chapter 19 Covert Sensitization	Chapter 20 Problem Solving
				X					3
		X	X						
		X		5					
			2						
		2	X				X		
		3	X				X		
		2	X				X		
		3	4						
							3		
1	5			X	X				6
				4	5				
				5	X				
						5	X		
							2	X	3
				X					4
X	X								X
							X		X
				X	X				

CHAPTER 2

Uncovering Automatic Thoughts

Thoughts cause feelings. This is the essential insight of cognitive therapy. All of the cognitive techniques that have been developed and refined in the last six decades flow out of this one simple idea: that thoughts cause feelings, and many emotions are preceded and caused by a thought, however abbreviated, fleeting, or unnoticed that thought may be.

In other words, events by themselves have no emotional content. It is your interpretation of an event that causes your emotions. This is often represented as the ABC model of emotions, where A stands for activating event, B stands for belief, or thought, and C stands for consequence, or feeling:

$$\text{A. Event} \rightarrow \text{B. Thought} \rightarrow \text{C. Feeling}$$

Here's an example:

A. Event: You get into your car and turn the key, and nothing happens.

B. Thought: You interpret the event by saying to yourself, "Oh no! My battery's dead. This is awful! I'm stuck, and I'll be late."

C. Feeling: You experience an emotion appropriate to your thoughts. In this case, you feel depressed and anxious about being late.

But if you change the thought, you change the feeling. If you had thought, "My son must have left the lights on all night again," you might have felt anger. If you had thought, "I'll have an extra cup of coffee, relax, and wait for a jump from the tow truck," you would have felt mild annoyance at most.

In this chapter you will learn how to uncover the automatic thoughts in this cycle using a Thought Journal, which we've provided. This is the basic skill you need to master in order to use cognitive therapy to reduce painful feelings.

SYMPTOM EFFECTIVENESS

By itself, uncovering automatic thoughts is not considered a full-scale treatment. It is just the first step in many different cognitive behavioral treatments. However, as a result of exploring how you react to upsetting situations, you may feel some immediate reduction in anxiety, depression, anger, perfectionism, low self-esteem, shame and guilt, or procrastination. This is a good sign that cognitive therapy is likely to help you quickly.

That said, it is more likely that you will *not* experience any improvement in symptoms by the end of this chapter. In fact, some feelings may actually intensify as a result of exploring them. Don't worry. Remember that this is an early step along the way.

TIME TO MASTERY

Most people make significant progress during the first week of faithfully keeping a Thought Journal. The longer you practice tuning in to your automatic thoughts, the better you get at it. It's a skill like knitting, skiing, writing, or singing on key: Practice makes perfect.

INSTRUCTIONS

As you begin to uncover your automatic thoughts, it will be helpful for you to have an understanding of their nature and how they work, including how they can form complex feedback loops, so we'll discuss this first. Then we'll help you learn to hear your own automatic thoughts so you can begin to record them in a Thought Journal. This is an extremely useful approach for exploring, confronting, and changing patterns of negative thinking.

Understanding Feedback Loops

The event-thought-feeling sequence is the basic building block of emotional life. But the building blocks can become very jumbled and confusing. In real life, people typically don't experience a simple series of ABC reactions, each with its discrete activating event, thought, and resultant feeling. More often, a series of ABC reactions join to form a feedback loop in which the ending feeling from one sequence becomes the starting event for another sequence.

In the case of painful feelings, a negative feedback loop can occur, in which an uncomfortable feeling itself becomes an activating event: the subject of further thoughts, which produce more painful feelings, which become a larger event inspiring more negative thoughts, and so on. The loop can continue until you work yourself into a rage, anxiety attack, or deep depression.

Feelings have physiological components. When you experience emotions such as fear, anger, or joy, your heart speeds up, you breathe faster and less deeply, you sweat more, and blood vessels in different parts of your body contract or dilate. Conversely, "quiet" emotions, such as depression, sadness, or grief, involve a slowing down of some of your physiological systems. Either way, both the emotion and the accompanying bodily sensations trigger an evaluation process in which you start trying to interpret and label what you feel.

Feedback Loop

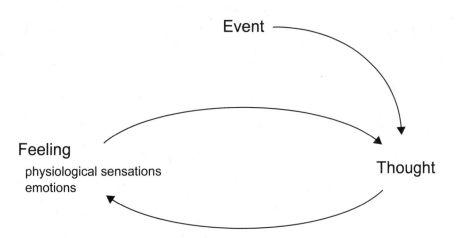

For example, if your car wouldn't start late at night when you were in a bad neighborhood, the negative feedback loop might go like this:

A. **Event:** Car doesn't start.

B. **Thought:** "Oh no! This is awful. I'll be late—and this is a dangerous street."

C. **Feelings:** Heart beating fast, feeling hot and sweaty, irritation, anxiety.

B. **Thought:** "I'm scared. I could get mugged—this is really bad!"

C. **Feelings:** Stomach clenching, hard to breathe, dizzy, fear.

B. **Thought:** "I'm freaking out. I'll lose control. Can't move. Can't get safe."

C. **Feelings:** Strong adrenaline rush, panic.

The Nature of Automatic Thoughts

You are constantly describing the world to yourself, giving each event or experience some label. You automatically make interpretations of everything you see, hear, touch, and feel. You judge events as good or bad, pleasurable or painful, safe or dangerous. This process colors all of your experiences, labeling them with private meanings.

These labels and judgments are fashioned from the unending dialogue you have with yourself, a waterfall of thoughts cascading down the back of your mind. These thoughts are constant and rarely noticed, but they are powerful enough to create your most intense emotions. This internal dialogue is called "self-talk" by rational emotive therapist Albert Ellis, and "automatic thoughts" by cognitive theorist Aaron Beck. Beck prefers the latter term "because it more accurately describes the way thoughts are experienced. The person perceives these thoughts as though they are by reflex—without any prior reflection or reasoning; and they impress him as plausible and valid" (Beck 1976, 237).

Automatic thoughts usually have the following characteristics, which we'll discuss in detail below:

- They often appear in shorthand.

- They are almost always believed.

- They are experienced as spontaneous.

- They are often couched in terms of "should," "ought," or "must."

- They tend to "awfulize."

- They are relatively idiosyncratic.

- They are persistent and self-perpetuating.

- They often differ from the person's public statements.

- They repeat certain themes.

- They are learned.

AUTOMATIC THOUGHTS APPEAR IN SHORTHAND

Automatic thoughts often appear in shorthand, composed of just a few essential words phrased in telegraphic style: "lonely…getting sick…can't stand it…cancer…no good." One word or a short phrase functions as a label for a group of painful memories, fears, or self-reproaches.

An automatic thought needn't be expressed in words at all. It can be a brief visual image, an imagined sound or smell, or a physical sensation. For example, a woman who was afraid of heights had a half-second image of the floor tilting and felt herself sliding down toward the window. This momentary fantasy triggered acute anxiety whenever she ascended above the third floor.

Sometimes an automatic thought is a brief reconstruction of an event in the past. For instance, a depressed woman kept seeing the stairway in Macy's where her husband first announced his plan to leave her. The image of the stairway was enough to unleash all the feelings associated with that loss.

Occasionally an automatic thought can take the form of intuitive knowledge, without words, images, or sense impressions. For example, a chef who was plagued with self-doubt "just knew" that it was useless to try to get promoted to head chef.

AUTOMATIC THOUGHTS ARE ALMOST ALWAYS BELIEVED

Automatic thoughts typically seem very believable, no matter how illogical they appear upon analysis. For example, a man who reacted with rage to the death of his best friend actually believed for a time that his friend deliberately died to punish him.

Automatic thoughts have the same believable quality as direct sense impressions. You attach the same truth value to automatic thoughts as you do to sights and sounds in the real world. If you see a man getting into a Porsche and have the thought "He's rich. He doesn't care about anyone but himself," the judgment is as real to you as the color of the car.

AUTOMATIC THOUGHTS ARE EXPERIENCED AS SPONTANEOUS

You believe automatic thoughts because they are automatic. They seem to arise spontaneously out of ongoing events. They just pop into your mind, and you hardly notice them, let alone subject them to logical analysis.

AUTOMATIC THOUGHTS ARE COUCHED IN TERMS OF "SHOULD," "OUGHT," OR "MUST"

A woman whose husband had recently died thought, "You ought to go it alone. You shouldn't burden your friends." Each time the thought popped into her mind, she felt a wave of hopelessness. People torture themselves with shoulds, such as "I should be happy, more energetic, creative, responsible, loving, generous…" Each ironclad should precipitates a sense of guilt or a loss of self-esteem.

Shoulds are hard to eradicate, since their origin and function is actually adaptive. They are simple rules to live by that have worked in the past. They are templates for survival that you can access quickly in times of stress. The problem is that they become so automatic that you don't have time to analyze them, and so rigid that you can't modify them to fit changing situations.

AUTOMATIC THOUGHTS TEND TO AWFULIZE

Automatic thoughts predict catastrophe, see danger in everything, and always anticipate the worst. A stomachache is a symptom of cancer, or a look of distraction on a lover's face is the first sign of withdrawal. These catastrophic thoughts are the major source of anxiety.

Like shoulds, they are also hard to eradicate because of their adaptive function. They help you predict the future and prepare for the worst-case scenario.

AUTOMATIC THOUGHTS ARE IDIOSYNCRATIC

Here's an example of how different automatic thoughts can arise for different people in response to the same event. In a crowded theater, a woman suddenly stood up, slapped the face of the man next to her, and hurried up the aisle and out the exit. One woman who witnessed this event was frightened because she thought, "She's really going to get it when they get home." She imagined the details of a brutal beating and recalled times when she had been physically abused. A teenager was angry because he thought, "That poor guy. He probably just wanted a kiss, and she humiliated him. What a bitch." A middle-aged man, seeing his ex-wife's face set in angry lines, told himself, "Now he's lost her, and he'll never get her back," and felt depressed. A social worker felt a sense of righteous pleasure as she thought, "Serves him right. I wish some of the timid women I know had seen that."

Each response was based on a unique way of viewing the stimulus event and resulted in a different strong emotion.

AUTOMATIC THOUGHTS ARE PERSISTENT AND SELF-PERPETUATING

Automatic thoughts are hard to turn off or change because they are reflexive and plausible. They weave unnoticed through the fabric of your internal dialogue and seem to come and go with a will of their own. One automatic thought tends to act as a cue for another and then another and another. You may have experienced this chaining effect as one depressing thought triggers a long chain of associated depressing thoughts.

AUTOMATIC THOUGHTS OFTEN DIFFER FROM PUBLIC STATEMENTS

Most people talk to others very differently from the way they talk to themselves. To others they usually describe events in their lives as logical sequences of cause and effect. But to themselves they may describe the same events with self-deprecating venom or dire predictions.

One executive calmly explained aloud, "Since I got laid off, I've been a little depressed." This matter-of-fact statement differed sharply from the actual thoughts that unemployment triggered in him: "I'm a failure. I'll never work again. My family will starve. I can't make it in this world." These thoughts left him with an image of himself spiraling down into a bottomless black pit.

AUTOMATIC THOUGHTS REPEAT CERTAIN THEMES

Chronic anger, anxiety, or depression results from a focus on one particular group of automatic thoughts to the exclusion of all contrary thoughts. The theme of anxious people is danger. They are preoccupied with the anticipation of dangerous situations, forever scanning the horizon for future threats or pain. Depressed people often focus on the past and obsess on the theme of loss. They also focus on their own failings and flaws. Chronically angry people repeat automatic thoughts about the seemingly deliberate hurtful behavior of others.

Preoccupation with these themes creates a kind of tunnel vision in which you think only one kind of thought and notice only one aspect of your environment, resulting in one predominant and usually quite painful emotion. Aaron Beck has used the term "selective abstraction" to describe this type of tunnel vision in which you look at one set of cues in your environment to the exclusion of all others.

AUTOMATIC THOUGHTS ARE LEARNED

Since childhood, people have been telling you what to think. You have been conditioned by family, friends, teachers, the media, and others to interpret events a certain way. Over the years, you have learned and practiced habitual patterns of automatic thoughts that are difficult to detect, let alone change. That's the bad news. The good news is, what has been learned can be unlearned and changed.

Listening to Your Automatic Thoughts

Hearing your automatic thoughts is the first step in gaining control of unpleasant emotions. Most of your internal dialogue is harmless. The automatic thoughts that cause harm can be identified because they almost always precede a persistent painful feeling.

To identify the automatic thoughts that are causing an ongoing painful feeling, try to recall the thoughts you had just prior to the start of the emotion and those that go along with the sustained emotion. You can think of it as listening in on an intercom. The intercom is always on, even when you're conversing with others and going about your life. You are functioning in the world and are also talking to yourself at the same time.

Listen in on your internal dialogue and hear what you're telling yourself. Your automatic thoughts are assigning private, idiosyncratic meanings to many external events and internal sensations and making judgments and interpretations of your experience.

Automatic thoughts are often lightning fast and very difficult to catch. They flash on as a brief mental image or are telegraphed in a single word. Here are two methods for coping with the swiftness of these thoughts:

- Reconstruct a problem situation, going over it again and again in your imagination until the painful emotion begins to emerge. What are you thinking as the emotion comes up? Regard your thoughts as a slow-motion film. Look at your internal dialogue frame by frame. Notice the millisecond it takes to say, "I can't stand it" or the half-second image of a terrifying event. Notice how you're internally describing and interpreting the actions of others: "She's bored." "He's putting me down."

- Stretch out the shorthand statement into the original statement from which it was extracted. "Feeling sick" might stand for "I'm feeling sick and I know I'm going to get worse. I can't stand it." "Crazy" might mean "I feel like I'm losing control, and that must mean I'm going crazy. My friends will reject me." Hearing the shorthand isn't enough. It is necessary to identify with your entire interior argument in order to understand the distorted logic from which many painful emotions bloom.

Recording Your Thoughts

To appreciate the power of your automatic thoughts and the role they play in your emotional life, use the following form to keep a Thought Journal. As soon as possible after you experience an unpleasant feeling, record it on the form, which is self-explanatory except for how to rate your feelings. To assess your distress level, use a scale of 0 to 100 in which 0 means the feeling causes no distress and 100 is the most distressing emotion you have ever felt.

Make several copies of the form and carry one with you at all times for at least one week, making an entry only when you feel a painful emotion. You may find that concentrating on your automatic thoughts makes the feelings worse for a while. Keep working on it—it's normal to feel worse before you start to feel better. Also, be aware that you'll use the material you generate in your Thought Journal in the next two chapters. (If you need a little help getting started, an example from Antonio, a bookkeeper who was stressed-out at tax time, follows the blank form.)

The process of uncovering automatic thoughts may make you begin to distrust these thoughts and start questioning and disputing them as they pop up. The next chapter, on changing patterns of limited thinking, will give you specific tools for disputing automatic thoughts.

At this point, it's important for you to recognize that thoughts create and sustain emotions. To reduce the frequency of painful emotions, you need to listen to what you think, then ask how true your thoughts are. Remember, what you think ultimately creates what you feel.

Thought Journal

Situation When? Where? Who? What happened?	Feelings One-word summaries Rate 0-100	Automatic thoughts What were you thinking just before and during the unpleasant feeling?

Antonio's Thought Journal

Situation When? Where? Who? What happened?	Feelings One-word summaries Rate 0-100	Automatic thoughts What were you thinking just before and during the unpleasant feeling?
Stuck on freeway.	anger 80	Late. Boss angry. Last one in. Have to rush all day.
Given extra work.	anxiety 90	I'll be here all night. I can't stand it. Jenny will be mad if I'm late.
	resentment 75	They always dump on me. It's not fair.
Have to work through lunch.	anxiety 85	I'm hungry. I'm tired. I can't stand this.
	anger 65	Why don't they get enough staff to help? This is ridiculous.
Working late, have to call wife.	anxiety 75	She's really going to blow up.
Driving home.	depression 80	This is my whole life. There's no way out of this.
Watching TV with kids.	depression 90	They never talk to me. They hardly know me. They don't care.
Wife goes to bed early.	depression 85	She's really mad. She's disgusted with me.

SPECIAL CONSIDERATIONS

Sometimes automatic thoughts come so quickly and in such abbreviated form that you can't identify them, even though you know you just had some. In that case, you can simply count your thoughts. Carry an index card with you, and each time you notice that you've had an automatic thought, make a mark on the card. You can also keep a count of your episodes of automatic thoughts on a golf wrist counter or a knitting stitch counter.

Counting your automatic thoughts will help you get some distance from them, as well as a feeling of control. Rather than assuming that your automatic thoughts are an accurate assessment of events, you can note them and let them go. Once you've counted a thought, you needn't dwell on it.

This process will eventually slow your thoughts and sharpen your attention so the content of the thoughts starts to become clear. When that happens, you may want to continue counting but also start categorizing your thoughts and counting how many you have of various types: catastrophic thoughts, thoughts about loss, insecure thoughts, and so on.

If you forget to count your thoughts, set your phone or watch alarm or a timer to go off every twenty minutes. When the alarm goes off, stop what you're doing, look inside yourself, and count any negative thoughts you notice.

CHAPTER 3

Changing Patterns of Limited Thinking

A man walks up to a drugstore counter and asks for a particular brand of dental floss. The clerk says it's out of stock. The man concludes that the clerk has the dental floss but just wants to get rid of him because she doesn't like his looks. This logic seems obviously irrational and paranoid.

But consider the case of a woman whose husband comes home with a cloudy look on his face. She immediately concludes that he's angry because she was too tired to make love the previous night. She expects to be hurt by some sort of retaliation and quickly responds by becoming peevish and defensive. This logic makes perfect sense to her, and she doesn't question her conclusion until she learns that her husband had a minor auto accident on the way home.

The progression of logic she used goes like this:

1. My husband looks upset.

2. My husband often gets upset when I disappoint him.

3. Therefore, he's upset with me for disappointing him.

The problem with this logic lies in her assumptions that her husband's moods always relate to her and that she is the prime cause of his ups and downs. This pattern of limited thinking, called personalization, is the tendency to relate all the objects and events around you to yourself. Personalization limits you and causes pain because you consistently misinterpret what you see and then act on that misinterpretation.

This chapter will examine eight limited thinking patterns and give you practice in identifying them. Then it will teach you to analyze the automatic thoughts you recorded in chapter 2 and identify which of the limited thinking patterns you habitually employ in difficult situations. You'll learn how to compose balanced alternative self-statements that will become more believable than your painful automatic thoughts, and how to start making action plans based on your new, balanced thoughts.

SYMPTOM EFFECTIVENESS

Challenging automatic thoughts is a powerful way to counter perfectionism, curb procrastination, and relieve depression and anxiety. It is also helpful in treating low self-esteem, shame and guilt, and anger.

The techniques in this chapter are based on the cognitive therapy of Aaron Beck (1976), who pioneered this method of analyzing automatic thoughts and composing rational comebacks to refute and replace distorted thinking. This approach works well for abstract thinkers—people who can analyze their automatic thoughts to find thematic patterns of limited thinking.

TIME TO MASTERY

You should begin to get results after one to four weeks of analyzing your automatic thoughts. If you try all of the exercises in this chapter and still have difficulty picking out your limited thinking patterns, don't give up hope. Go on to the next chapter, which will help you accomplish the same thing—creating more balanced thoughts—by compiling the evidence for and against the thoughts that trigger painful emotions.

INSTRUCTIONS

In order to change patterns of limited thinking, it's helpful to recognize and identify them, so we'll start by explaining some of the most common types. The remainder of the chapter is devoted to explaining how to use your Thought Journal to identify the patterns you tend to use and develop more balanced thoughts to counter them.

Learning to Identify Eight Patterns of Limited Thinking

Here are eight of the most common patterns of limited thinking. It helps to study them separately, one at a time. However, in your ongoing stream of consciousness these patterns often occur in rapid succession, overlapping and blending into each other.

FILTERING

Filtering is characterized by a sort of tunnel vision: looking at only one element of a situation to the exclusion of everything else. A single detail becomes the focus, and the whole event or situation is colored by this detail. For example, a computer draftsman who was uncomfortable with criticism was praised for the quality of his recent detail drawings and asked if he could get the next job out a little more quickly. He went home depressed, having decided that his employer thought he was dawdling. He filtered out the praise and focused only on the criticism.

Each person looks through his or her own particular tunnel. Depressed people are hypersensitive to loss and blind to gain. For anxious people, the slightest possibility of danger seems like a bomb threat even though the scene might otherwise be safe and secure. People who experience chronic anger look through a tunnel that highlights evidence of injustice and screens out fairness and equity.

Memory can also be very selective. You may remember only certain kinds of events from your entire life history. When you filter your memories, you often pass over positive experiences and dwell on memories that leave you angry, anxious, or depressed.

Filtering "awfulizes" your thoughts by pulling negative events out of context and focusing on them while ignoring your good experiences. Your fears, losses, and irritations become exaggerated in importance because they fill your awareness to the exclusion of everything else. Key words for the filtering pattern are "terrible," "awful," "disgusting," "scary," and so on. A key phrase is "I can't stand it."

POLARIZED THINKING

Polarized thinking is sometimes called black-and-white thinking. In this limited thinking pattern, no shades of gray are allowed. You insist on either-or choices, perceiving everything at the extremes with very little room for a middle ground. People and things are good or bad, wonderful or horrible, delightful or intolerable. Since your interpretations are extreme, your emotional reactions are extreme, fluctuating from despair to elation to rage to ecstasy to terror.

The greatest danger in polarized thinking is its impact on how you judge yourself. You could believe that if you aren't perfect or brilliant, then you must be a failure or an imbecile. There's no room for mistakes or mediocrity. For example, a charter bus driver told himself he was a real loser when he took the wrong freeway exit and had to drive two miles out of his way. One mistake meant that he was incompetent and worthless. Similarly, a single mother with three children was determined to be strong and in charge. The moment she felt tired or nervous, she began thinking of herself as weak and falling apart, and she often criticized herself in conversations with friends.

OVERGENERALIZATION

In overgeneralization, you make broad conclusions based on a single incident or piece of evidence. One dropped stitch leads you to conclude, "I'll never learn how to knit." You interpret a rejection on the dance floor as "Nobody would ever want to dance with me."

This pattern can lead to an increasingly restricted life. If you got sick on a train once, you decide never to take a train again. If you got dizzy on a sixth-floor balcony, you never go out on balconies again. If you felt anxious the last time your husband took a business trip, you'll be a wreck every time he leaves town. One bad experience means that whenever you're in a similar situation, you will repeat the bad experience.

Overgeneralizations are often couched in the form of absolute statements, as if there were some immutable law that governs and limits your chances for happiness. Some of the cue words that indicate you may be overgeneralizing are "all," "every," "none," "never," "always," "everybody," and "nobody." For example, you are overgeneralizing when you make sweeping conclusions such as the following: "Nobody loves me," "I'll never be able to trust anyone again," "I will always be sad," "I've always had lousy jobs," "No one would stay friends with me if they really knew me."

Another hallmark of overgeneralization is applying global labels to people, places, and things you don't like. Somebody who refused to give you a ride home is labeled a "total jerk." A quiet guy on a date is a "dull clam." Democrats are "knee-jerk liberals." New York City is "hell on earth." Television is an "evil, corrupting influence." You're "stupid" and "totally wasting your life." Each of these labels may contain a grain of truth, but it generalizes that grain into a global judgment that ignores all contrary evidence, making your view of the world stereotyped and one-dimensional.

MIND READING

When you mind read, you assume you know how others are feeling and what motivates them, which can lead to snap judgments: "He's just acting that way because he's jealous," "She's only interested in your money," "He's afraid to show he cares."

If your brother, who recently broke up with his girlfriend, visits a new woman acquaintance three times in one week, there are any number of conclusions you might arrive at; for example, that he's in love, angry at his old girlfriend and hoping she'll find out, on the rebound, or afraid of being alone again. Without asking, you have no way of knowing which is true. Mind reading makes one conclusion seem so obviously correct that you assume it's true, act on it inappropriately, and get into trouble.

With mind reading, you also make assumptions about how people are reacting to you. You might assume what your boyfriend is thinking and say to yourself, "This close, he sees how unattractive I am." If he's mind reading too, he may be saying to himself, "She thinks I'm really immature." You may have a casual encounter with your supervisor at work and come away thinking, "She's getting ready to fire me." These assumptions are born of intuition, hunches, vague misgivings, or a couple of past experiences. They are untested and unproven, but you believe them nonetheless.

Mind reading arises from a process called projection. You imagine that people feel the same way you do and react to things the same way you do. Therefore, you don't watch or listen closely enough to notice that others are actually different. If you get angry when someone is late, you imagine everyone feels that way. If you feel excruciatingly sensitive to rejection, you expect that most people are the same. If you are very judgmental about particular habits and traits, you assume others share your beliefs.

CATASTROPHIZING

If you catastrophize, a small leak in the sailboat means it will surely sink. A contractor whose estimate gets underbid concludes he'll never get another job. A headache suggests that brain cancer is looming. Catastrophic thoughts often start with the words "what if." You read a newspaper article describing a tragedy or hear gossip about some disaster befalling an acquaintance, and you start wondering, "What if it happens to me?" "What if I break my leg skiing?" "What if they hijack my plane?" "What if I get sick and have to go on disability?" "What if my son starts taking drugs?" The list is endless. There are no limits to an active catastrophic imagination.

MAGNIFYING

When you magnify, you emphasize things out of proportion to their actual importance. Small mistakes become tragic failures. Minor suggestions become scathing criticism. A slight backache becomes a ruptured disk. Minor setbacks are cause for despair. Slight obstacles seem like overwhelming barriers. Words like "huge," "impossible," and "overwhelming" are magnifying terms. This pattern creates a tone of doom and hysterical pessimism.

The flip side of magnifying is minimizing. When you magnify, you view everything negative and difficult in your life through a telescope that enlarges your problems. But when you view your assets, such as your ability to cope and find solutions, you look through the wrong end of the telescope, so everything positive is minimized.

PERSONALIZATION

There are two kinds of personalization. One involves directly comparing yourself with other people: "He plays piano so much better than I do," "I'm not smart enough to go with this crowd," "She knows herself a lot better than I do," "He feels things so deeply, while I'm dead inside," "I'm the slowest person in the office." Sometimes the comparison is actually favorable to you: "He's dumb (and I'm smart)," "I'm better looking than she is." The opportunities for comparison never end. And even when the comparison is favorable, the underlying assumption is that your worth is questionable. Consequently, you must continue to test your value, constantly measuring yourself against others. If you come out better, you have a moment's relief. If you come up short, you feel diminished.

This chapter began with an example of the other kind of personalization: the tendency to relate everything around you to yourself. A depressed mother blames herself when she sees any sadness in her children. A businessman thinks that every time his partner complains of being tired, he means he's tired of being in business with him. A man whose wife complains of rising prices hears her complaints as attacks on his ability as a breadwinner.

SHOULDS

You may operate from a list of inflexible rules about how you and other people should act and view these rules as right and indisputable. You see any deviation from your values or standards as bad, and as a result, you often judge others and find fault. People irritate you. They don't act correctly, and they don't think correctly. They have unacceptable traits, habits, and opinions that make them hard to tolerate. They should know the rules, and they should follow them.

One woman felt that her husband should want to take her on Sunday drives. She decided that a man who loves his wife ought to take her to the country and then out to eat at a nice place. The fact that he didn't want to meant he only thought about himself. Cue words indicating the presence of this pattern are "should," "ought," and "must." In fact, therapist Albert Ellis dubbed this thinking pattern "musterbation" (Ellis and Harper 1961).

Your shoulds are just as hard on you as they are on other people. You feel compelled to be or act a certain way, but you never ask objectively if it really makes sense. Psychiatrist Karen Horney (1939) called this the "tyranny of shoulds." Here is a list of some of the most common and unreasonable shoulds:

- I should be the epitome of generosity, consideration, dignity, courage, and unselfishness.

- I should be the perfect lover, friend, parent, teacher, student, or spouse.

- I should be able to endure any hardship with equanimity.

- I should be able to find a quick solution to every problem.

- I should never feel hurt. I should always be happy and serene.

- I should know, understand, and foresee everything.

- I should always be spontaneous but also always control my feelings.

- I should never feel certain emotions, such as anger or jealousy.

- I should love all of my children equally.

- I should never make mistakes.

- My emotions should be constant. Once I feel love, I should always feel love.

- I should be totally self-reliant.

- I should assert myself but never hurt anybody else.

- I should never be tired or get sick.

- I should always be at peak efficiency.

Summary of the Eight Limited Thinking Patterns

- **Filtering.** You focus on the negative details while ignoring all the positive aspects of a situation.

- **Polarized thinking.** Things are black or white, good or bad. You have to be perfect or you're a failure. There's no middle ground, no room for mistakes.

- **Overgeneralization.** You reach a general conclusion based on a single incident or piece of evidence. You exaggerate the frequency of problems and use negative global labels.

- **Mind reading.** Without their saying so, you know what people are feeling and why they act the way they do. In particular, you have certain knowledge of how people think and feel about you.

- **Catastrophizing.** You expect, even visualize, disaster. You notice or hear about a problem and start asking, "What if?" What if tragedy strikes? What if it happens to you?

- **Magnifying.** You exaggerate the degree or intensity of a problem. You turn up the volume on anything bad, making it loud, large, and overwhelming.

- **Personalization.** You assume that everything people do or say is some kind of reaction to you. You also compare yourself to others, trying to determine who is smarter, more competent, better looking, and so on.

- **Shoulds.** You have a list of ironclad rules about how you and other people should act. People who break the rules anger you, and you feel guilty when you violate the rules.

Exercises

The following exercises are designed to help you notice and identify limited thinking patterns. Work through the exercises one after another, referring back to the preceding summary as needed to analyze how each statement or situation is based on one or more of the limited thinking patterns.

Matching Exercise

Draw a line connecting the sentence in the first column to the pattern it exemplifies in the second column.

Statement	Pattern
1. Ever since Lisa, I've never trusted a redhead.	Filtering
2. Quite a few people here seem smarter than me.	Polarized thinking
3. You're either for me or against me.	Overgeneralization
4. I could have enjoyed the picnic, but the chicken was burnt.	Mind reading
5. He's always smiling, but I know he doesn't like me.	Catastrophizing
6. I'm afraid the relationship's over, because he hasn't called for two days.	Magnifying
7. You should never ask people personal questions.	Personalization
8. These tax forms are impossible. They're too much to deal with.	Shoulds

Multiple Choice

In this exercise, circle the limited thinking patterns present in each example. There may be more than one right answer.

1. The washing machine breaks down. A mother with twins in diapers says to herself, "This always happens. I can't stand it. The whole day's ruined."

    a. Overgeneralization

    b. Polarized thinking

    c. Shoulds

    d. Mind reading

    e. Filtering

2. A woman who had gone out to breakfast with a friend later said, "He looked up from across the table and said, 'That's interesting.' I knew he was dying for breakfast to be over so he could get away from me."

    a. Magnifying

    b. Polarized thinking

    c. Shoulds

    d. Mind reading

    e. Personalization

3. A man was trying to get his girlfriend to be warmer and more supportive. He got irritated every night when she didn't ask him how his day was or failed to give him the attention he expected.

   a. Shoulds

   b. Personalization

   c. Overgeneralization

   d. Catastrophizing

   e. Magnifying

4. A driver feels nervous on long trips because he's afraid of having car trouble or getting sick and being stranded far from home. Faced with having to drive five hundred miles to Chicago and back, he tells himself, "It's too far. My car has over sixty thousand miles on it—it will never make it."

   a. Overgeneralization

   b. Catastrophizing

   c. Filtering

   d. Magnifying

   e. Mind reading

5. Getting ready for the prom, a high school student thinks, "I've got the worst hips in my homeroom, and the second-worst hair. If this French twist comes undone, I'll just die. I'll never get it back together, and the evening will be ruined. I hope Ron gets his dad's car. If only he does, everything will be perfect."

   a. Personalization

   b. Polarized thinking

   c. Filtering

   d. Mind reading

   e. Catastrophizing

Answer Key

1. a, e

2. d

3. a

4. b, d

5. a, b, e

Circle the Pattern and Quote the Phrase

This exercise requires a little more work on your part. Read the statement and circle the applicable patterns in the list following the statement. Next to each pattern, write the phrase that contains it. As we mentioned earlier in the chapter, there are overlaps between some of these thinking patterns. You may identify limited thinking patterns that don't appear in the answer key. That's probably okay. The main thing is to develop skill in recognizing automatic, habitual ways of seeing things.

1. Jim's so easily upset, you just can't talk to him. He blows up at everything. He just doesn't have my patience. What if he blows up at work? He'll lose his job and we'll be homeless in about two weeks.

Pattern	Phrase Containing the Pattern
Filtering	
Polarized thinking	
Overgeneralization	
Mind reading	
Catastrophizing	
Magnifying	
Personalization	
Shoulds	

2. One time she came up to me and said, "This nursing station looks like a cyclone hit it. Better clean up the mess before the shift is over." "Well," I said, "this was a mess when I got here. It's not my fault. The night shift shouldn't be allowed to punch out unless all the charts are filed." She knew it wasn't my mess. She wants to fire me and she's just looking for an excuse.

Pattern	Phrase Containing the Pattern
Filtering	
Polarized thinking	
Overgeneralization	
Mind reading	
Catastrophizing	
Magnifying	

Personalization _____

Shoulds _____

3. A lot of the time I feel nervous when I'm out with Ed. I keep thinking how smart and sophisticated he is, and that I'm just a hayseed by comparison. He cocks his head and looks at me, and I know he's thinking how dumb I am. He's really sweet and we have a good time talking. But when he cocks his head, I feel like I'll be dumped. One time he kind of wrinkled up his face when I said something a little critical about his jacket. Now I'm afraid to say anything for fear of hurting him.

   Usually I think Ed is completely wonderful. But last week he made me take the bus to his house instead of picking me up. I suddenly felt he didn't give a damn, that he was just another jerk. That was a passing thing, and now he's wonderful again. My only problem is this business of being nervous when he cocks his head.

Pattern	Phrase Containing the Pattern
Filtering	_____
Polarized thinking	_____
Overgeneralization	_____
Mind reading	_____
Catastrophizing	_____
Magnifying	_____
Personalization	_____
Shoulds	_____

4. There are three ways to make a magazine succeed: work, work, and more work. If you have to work sixteen hours a day to get it out, then that's what you have to do. These kids today want to go home at five o'clock. If they're too lazy to work, I say get rid of them. Profits get slimmer every year because of total laziness. It's the way they're raised—the way the whole damn country is falling apart. In five years it will drive me under. There are just two kinds of editors: the ones who get the job done and the nine-to-fivers. It's the nine-to-fivers who will put me under. I can't fight the whole world.

Pattern	Phrase Containing the Pattern
Filtering	_____
Polarized thinking	_____
Overgeneralization	_____
Mind reading	_____

Catastrophizing _____

Magnifying _____

Personalization _____

Shoulds _____

Answer Key

1. Overgeneralization: "He blows up at everything."
   Catastrophizing: "He'll lose his job and we'll be homeless."
2. Mind reading: "She knew... She wants... She's just looking..."
   Shoulds: "The night shift shouldn't..."
3. Mind reading: "I know he's thinking how dumb I am."
   Personalization: "I keep thinking how smart and sophisticated he is, and that I'm just a hayseed by comparison."
   Polarized thinking: "I felt he was just another jerk... Now he's wonderful again."
4. Shoulds: "That's what you have to do."
   Filtering: "Total laziness" (sees laziness only).
   Polarized thinking: "There are just two kinds of editors."
   Magnifying: "I can't fight the whole world."

Composing Balanced or Alternative Thoughts

Listed below are alternative responses to the eight patterns of limited thinking discussed in this chapter. It isn't necessary to read through the list from beginning to end. You can just use it as a reference when you're having problems with a particular pattern.

FILTERING

Pattern summary	Key balancing statement
Focusing on the negative	Shift focus.
Filtering out the positive	

You have been stuck in a mental groove, focusing on things from your environment that typically frighten, sadden, or anger you. In order to conquer filtering, you will have to deliberately shift focus. You can shift focus in two ways: One approach is to place your attention on coping strategies for dealing with the problem rather than obsessing about the problem itself. The other is to focus on the opposite of your primary mental theme. For example, if you tend to focus on the theme of loss, instead focus on what you still have that is of value. If your theme is danger, focus instead on things in your environment that represent comfort and safety. If your theme is injustice, stupidity, or incompetence, shift your focus to what people do that does meet with your approval.

POLARIZED THINKING

Pattern summary	Key balancing statements
Seeing everything as awful or great, with no middle ground	Don't make black-or-white judgments. Think in percentages.

The key to overcoming polarized thinking is to stop making black-or-white judgments. People are not either happy or sad, loving or rejecting, brave or cowardly, smart or stupid. They fall somewhere along a continuum between these extremes. Human beings are just too complex to be reduced to either-or judgments.

If you have to make these kinds of ratings, think in terms of percentages: "About 30 percent of me is scared to death, and 70 percent is holding on and coping," "About 60 percent of the time he seems terribly preoccupied with himself, but 40 percent of the time he can be really generous," "About 5 percent of the time I'm an ignoramus, but the rest of the time I do all right."

OVERGENERALIZATION

Pattern summary	Key balancing statements
Making sweeping statements based on scanty evidence	Quantify. Consider the evidence. Avoid absolutes. Don't use negative labels.

Overgeneralization is exaggeration—the tendency to take a button and sew a vest on it. Fight it by quantifying instead of using words like "huge," "awful," "massive," "minuscule," and so on. For example, if you catch yourself thinking, "We're buried under massive debt," rephrase with a quantity: "We owe $47,000."

Another way to avoid overgeneralization is to examine how much evidence you really have for your conclusion. If the conclusion is based on one or two cases, a single mistake, or one small symptom, throw it out until you have more convincing proof. This is such a powerful technique that most of the next chapter is devoted to amassing evidence for and against your hot thoughts.

Stop thinking in absolutes by avoiding words such as "every," "all," "always," "none," "never," "everybody," and "nobody." Statements that include these words ignore the exceptions and shades of gray. Replace absolutes with words such as "may," "sometimes," and "often." Be particularly sensitive to absolute predictions about the future, such as "No one will ever love me." They are extremely dangerous because, as you behave in accordance with them, they can become self-fulfilling prophecies.

Pay close attention to the words you use to describe yourself and others. Replace frequently used negative labels with more neutral terms. For example, if you call your habitual caution "cowardice," replace it with "care." Think of your excitable mother as vivacious instead of ditzy. Instead of blaming yourself for being lazy, call yourself laid-back.

MIND READING

Pattern summary	Key balancing statements
Assuming you know what others are thinking and feeling	Check it out. Generate alternative interpretations.

In the long run, you are probably better off making no inferences about people at all. Either believe what they tell you or hold no belief about their thoughts and motivations until conclusive evidence comes your way. Treat all of your notions about people as hypotheses to be tested and checked out by asking them.

Sometimes you can't check out your interpretations. For instance, you may not be ready to ask your daughter if her withdrawal from family life means she's pregnant or taking drugs. But you can allay your anxiety by generating alternative interpretations of her behavior. Perhaps she's in love, premenstrual, studying hard, depressed about something, deeply engrossed in a project, or worrying about her future. By generating a string of possibilities, you may find a more neutral interpretation that's as likely to be true as your direst suspicions. This process also underlines the fact that you really can't know accurately what others are thinking and feeling unless they tell you.

CATASTROPHIZING

Pattern summary	Key balancing statement
Assuming the worst will happen	Assess the odds.

Catastrophizing is the royal road to anxiety. As soon as you catch yourself catastrophizing, ask yourself, "What are the odds?" Make an honest assessment of the situation in terms of odds or percent of probability. Are the chances of disaster 1 in 100,000 (0.001 percent), 1 in 1,000 (0.1 percent), or 1 in 20 (5 percent)? Looking at the odds helps you realistically evaluate whatever is frightening you.

MAGNIFYING

Pattern summary	Key balancing statement
Enlarging difficulties	Get things in proportion.
Minimizing the positive	

To combat magnifying, stop using words like "terrible," "awful," "disgusting," "horrendous," and so on. In particular, banish phrases like "I can't stand it," "It's impossible," and "It's unbearable." You can stand it, because history shows that human beings can survive almost any psychological blow and can endure incredible physical pain. You can get used to and cope with almost anything. Try saying phrases such as "I can cope" and "I can survive this" to yourself instead.

PERSONALIZATION

Pattern summary	Key balancing statements
Assuming the reactions of others always relate to you	Check it out.
	We all have strong and weak points.
Comparing yourself to others	Comparison is meaningless.

If you assume that the reactions of others are often about you, force yourself to check it out. Maybe the reason your boss is frowning isn't that you're late. Make no conclusion unless you are satisfied that you have reasonable evidence and proof.

When you catch yourself comparing yourself to others, remind yourself that everyone has strong and weak points. By matching your weak points to the corresponding strong points of others, you're just looking for ways to demoralize yourself.

The fact is, human beings are too complex for casual comparisons to have any meaning. It would take you months to catalog and compare all the thousands of traits and abilities of two people.

SHOULDS

Pattern summary	Key balancing statements
Holding arbitrary rules for the behavior of self and others	My rules are flexible. Values are personal.

Reexamine and question any personal rules or expectations that include the words "should," "ought," or "must." Flexible rules and expectations don't use these words, because there are always exceptions and special circumstances. Think of at least three exceptions to your rule, and then imagine all the exceptions there must be that you can't think of.

You may get irritated when people don't act according to your values. But your personal values are just that—personal. They may work for you, but as missionaries have discovered all over the world, they don't always work for others. People aren't all the same. The key is to focus on each person's uniqueness—his or her particular needs, limitations, fears, and pleasures. Because it is impossible to know all of these complex interrelations, even with intimates, you can't be certain whether your values apply to another. You are entitled to an opinion, but allow for the possibility that you may be wrong. Also, allow other people to find different things important.

Using Your Thought Journal to Combat Limited Thinking Patterns

Now that you've learned to identify limited thinking patterns, it's time to apply your new skill to the Thought Journal you started in the previous chapter. We've added three columns to the blank form that follows, giving you space to fill in your limited thinking patterns, balanced or alternative thoughts, and a new rating of your feelings after generating balanced or alternative thoughts. As before, make copies of the blank form and carry one with you at all times for at least the next week.

Start by analyzing your most distressing automatic thoughts to see which limited thinking pattern is most characteristic of each. You may find evidence of more than one limited thinking pattern. Write down all that apply.

In the next column, rewrite your automatic thoughts in a more balanced way, or compose an alternative thought that refutes the automatic thought. You can refer to the section that follows for help in countering the limited thinking patterns.

In the last column, rate your feeling again after you've worked on countering your automatic thoughts, using the same scale of 0 to 100, in which 0 means the feeling causes no distress and 100 is the most distressing emotion you have ever felt. The feeling should be less intense as a result of your work. Again, an example from Antonio follows the blank form.

Thought Journal

Situation When? Where? Who? What happened?	Feelings One-word summaries Rate 0-100	Automatic thoughts What were you thinking just before and during the unpleasant feeling?	Limited thinking pattern	Balanced or alternative thoughts Circle possible action plans	Rerate feelings 0-100

Based on the "Thought Record," developed by Dennis Greenberger and Christine Padesky (1995).

Antonio's Thought Journal

Situation When? Where? Who? What happened?	Feelings One-word summaries Rate 0-100	Automatic thoughts What were you thinking just before and during the unpleasant feeling?	Limited thinking pattern	Balanced or alternative thoughts Circle possible action plans	Rerate feelings 0-100
Given extra work.	anxiety 90	I'll be here all night. I can't stand it. Jenny will be mad if I'm late.	Magnifying	Of course I can stand it. I've been standing it for twelve years. I can prioritize the work and concentrate on one thing at a time.	50
Watching TV with kids.	depression 90	They never talk to me. They hardly know me. They don't care.	Filtering Overgeneralizing	They talk to me about baseball, trading cards, and school stuff. It's the TV—they're engrossed in it and I'm not, so I sit there obsessing.	25
Wife goes to bed early.	depression 85	She's really mad. She's disgusted with me.	Mind reading	I have no evidence that she's mad or disgusted. I should check it out.	30

In Antonio's example Thought Journal, he started with the thought that he couldn't stand his work situation. After identifying his limited thinking patterns and composing his alternative thoughts, he felt better. He realized that he had magnified his workload to the point that he had collapsed emotionally and was working inefficiently at low-priority tasks. He went on to examine the depression he felt at home and found that he had been filtering and mind reading. This alone helped him feel much better, as he realized that there was no factual basis for his assumptions about how his wife and kids felt about him.

Keep this new Thought Journal for one to four weeks, identifying your automatic thoughts and analyzing them for limited thinking patterns. After one week you should be adept at recognizing your habitual patterns of limited thinking. You'll begin to notice your automatic thoughts popping up in stressful situations, and eventually you'll be able to recognize limited thinking patterns in real life and correct them with balanced or alternative thoughts as you go.

If you keep this new Thought Journal for a full week and still have trouble spotting limited thinking patterns, go on to the next chapter and try the approach there, which involves considering and weighing the evidence. It may be a better alternative for you.

Action Plans

Your balanced or alternative thoughts may suggest actions you can take, such as checking out assumptions, gathering information, making an assertive request, clearing up misunderstandings, making plans, changing your schedule, resolving unfinished business, or making commitments. Circle those items and plan when you'll put them into action.

For example, Antonio circled "I can prioritize the work" as an action plan to reduce anxiety on the job. He also circled "I should check it out" as an action plan to relieve the depression he felt when he assumed his wife was mad at him. It took him several days to work up the courage to ask his wife how she felt. It turned out that she was angry, but she was mostly worried about him turning into a workaholic and getting an ulcer or having a heart attack.

It may be difficult, time-consuming, or embarrassing to follow your action plan. You may have to break your plan down into a series of easier steps and schedule each step. But it's worth doing. Behavior that is inspired by your balanced or alternative thoughts will greatly reduce the frequency and power of your negative automatic thoughts. For more on action plans, see the next chapter.

CHAPTER 4

Changing Hot Thoughts

If the techniques in chapter 3, "Changing Patterns of Limited Thinking," worked well for you, it may not be necessary for you to work through this chapter. If, however, you had difficulty identifying your patterns of limited thinking, this chapter presents an alternative approach based on evidence gathering and analysis, which provides a powerful weapon against automatic thoughts.

This chapter is to be used in conjunction with chapter 2, "Uncovering Automatic Thoughts." It will give you skills to do three things: identify the evidence that supports your hot (or trigger) thoughts; uncover evidence that contradicts your hot thoughts; and synthesize this information to create a healthier, more realistic perspective.

Gathering evidence on both sides of the question is crucial to reaching a clearer, more objective understanding of your experience. Psychologist Albert Ellis was the first to develop a method to evaluate evidence for and against key beliefs, as a component of rational emotive therapy (Ellis and Harper 1961). But because his approach assumes that hot thoughts are always irrational and focuses mostly on the evidence against them, it may not always feel objective. It also may alienate people who have solid evidence to support certain hot thoughts.

Psychologist Christine Padesky (Greenberger and Padesky 1995), building on the work of Aaron Beck (1976) and Albert Ellis, developed strategies for gathering and analyzing evidence used in this chapter. Padesky didn't assume that hot thoughts are totally irrational. She focused instead on looking at all the evidence and working toward a balanced position.

SYMPTOM EFFECTIVENESS

Various thought journals have been used effectively to treat depression, anxiety, and related problems such as perfectionism, low self-esteem, shame and guilt, procrastination, and anger. Numerous studies over the past twenty years have demonstrated the usefulness of this technique.

TIME TO MASTERY

Using the Thought and Evidence Journal described in this chapter, you can make significant changes in your moods in as little as one week. However, it will take from two to twelve weeks to consolidate your gains, as your new, more balanced thoughts gain strength through repetition.

INSTRUCTIONS

In this chapter, we provide a new form that will allow you to record and analyze the evidence for and against your hot thoughts. As before, make copies of the blank form and carry one with you at all times for at least the next week. Because this technique varies from the approach in chapter 3, here's a brief outline of the process and how to use the form. These steps are described in detail below.

1. Select a hot thought.

2. Identify evidence that supports your hot thought.

3. Uncover evidence against your hot thought.

4. Write your balanced or alternative thoughts.

5. Rate your mood again.

6. Record and save alternative thoughts.

7. Practice your balanced thoughts

8. Develop an action plan

Thought and Evidence Journal

Situation *When? Where? Who? What happened?*	Feelings *One-word summaries* *Rate 0-100*	Automatic thoughts *What were you thinking just before and during the unpleasant feeling?*	Evidence for	Evidence against *Circle possible action plans.*	Balanced or alternative thoughts *Rate believability 0-100%*	Rerate feelings *0-100%*

Step 1: Select a Hot Thought

Return to the Thought Journal that you began keeping in chapter 2 to select a hot thought from your record of automatic thoughts. Choose several thoughts that had a major impact on your mood because of either their power or their frequency. Rate how strongly each thought contributed to your painful feelings using a scale of 0 to 100, in which 100 indicates that the thought was solely responsible for your feelings. Circle the thought with the highest score; that's the one you'll work on now.

To help illustrate this approach, we'll take some examples from Len, a rep for a large printing company whose customers are mostly publishers and advertising companies. When Len rated all of his automatic thoughts using the scale of 0 to 100 outlined above, "I'm a first-class failure" turned out to be his hottest thought by far. By itself, the thought could hit Len hard enough to stir up strong feelings of inadequacy and depression.

Len's Thought Journal

Situation When? Where? Who? What happened?	Feelings One-word summaries Rate 0-100	Automatic thoughts What were you thinking just before and during the unpleasant feeling?
Sales figures for December were posted. I'm second from the bottom in sales out of nine reps.	depression 85	I'm a stinko salesman. 70 They all think something's wrong with me. 40 Print buyers probably don't like me. 40 I'm a first-class failure. 95 Commissions will be way down. It's going to hurt. 65 I'm not working hard enough. 20

Step 2: Identify Evidence That Supports Your Hot Thought

Once you've identified your hot thought, record it on a blank copy of the Thought and Evidence Journal, filling in the first three columns, including your ratings of the feeling and associated thoughts. Then, in the fourth column, write down the experiences and facts that seem to support your hot thought. This is not the place to put your feelings, impressions, assumptions about the reactions of others, or unsupported beliefs. In the "Evidence for" column, stay with the objective facts. Confine yourself to exactly what was said, what was done, how many times, and so on.

While it's important to stick with the facts, it's also important to acknowledge all of the past and present evidence that supports and verifies your hot thought.

Len identified five pieces of evidence that seemed to support the hot thought "I'm a first-class failure." Here's what he wrote in his "Evidence for" column:

- *Only $24,000 in sales for December.*

- *Couldn't close that big account when they seemed almost ready to give me the contract.*

- *Boss asked if I had any problems.*

- *This is the third time in twelve months I've been below $30,000 in sales.*

- *Had a disagreement with Randolph, and he pulled his job.*

Notice that Len doesn't talk about conjectures, assumptions, or a "feeling" that he's doing a bad job. He confines himself to the facts and an objective description of events.

Step 3: Uncover Evidence against Your Hot Thought

Coming up with evidence against your hot thought will probably be the hardest part of the technique. It's easy to think of things that support your hot thought, but you're likely to draw a blank when it's time to explore evidence against it, and you may need some help.

To assist you in the search for evidence against your hot thought, there are ten key questions you need to ask. Go through all ten questions for every hot thought you're analyzing. Each will help you explore new ways of thinking:

1. Is there an alternative interpretation of the situation, other than your hot thought?

2. Is the hot thought really accurate, or is it an overgeneralization? Is it true that the situation means your hot thought is true? In Len's case, for example, do low sales figures in December necessarily mean he's a failure?

3. Are there exceptions to the generalizations made by your hot thought?

4. Are there balancing realities that might soften negative aspects of the situation? In Len's case, for example, are there other things besides sales that he can feel good about in his job?

5. What are the more probable consequences and outcomes of the situation? This question helps you differentiate what you fear might happen from what you can reasonably expect will happen.

6. Are there experiences from your past that would lead you to a conclusion other than your hot thought?

7. Are there objective facts that would contradict items in the "Evidence for" column? Is it really true, for example, that Len lost that big contract because he was a failure as a salesman?

8. What are the real odds that what you fear will actually occur? Think like a bookie. Are the odds 1 in 2, 1 in 50, 1 in 1,000, 1 in 500,000? Think of all the people right now in this same situation; how many of them will end up facing the catastrophic outcome you fear?

9. Do you have the social or problem-solving skills to handle the situation differently?

10. Could you create a plan to change the situation? Is there someone you know who might deal with this differently? What would that person do?

On a separate piece of paper, write your answers to all of the questions relevant to your hot thought. It may take some thinking to find exceptions to the generalization created by your hot thought, to objectively evaluate the odds of something catastrophic happening, or to recall balancing realities that can give you confidence and hope in the face of problems. Don't be tempted to take shortcuts or rush through this step in the evidence-gathering process. The work you put in is key in developing the ability to challenge hot thoughts.

Len spent more than half an hour answering the ten questions. Here's what they helped him come up with for the "Evidence against" column:

- *December's normally a low month. That might explain most of my drop-off in sales. (Question 1)*

- *To be accurate, for the year overall I ranked fourth of the nine reps. That's not great, but it's not being a failure. (Question 2)*

- *Some months have been good. I did $68,000 in August and $64,000 in March. (Question 3)*

- *I have good relationships with many customers. In some cases I've really helped them with major decisions. Most know they can trust me as an advisor. (Question 4)*

- *My sales are good enough at number four in the company that they wouldn't fire me. (Question 5)*

- *Five years ago I was ranked number two, and I'm always in the top half of the pack. Over the years, there have been a lot of months when I got the best salesman award. (Question 6)*

- *I was just outbid on that big account. It wasn't my fault. (Question 7)*

- *Randolph said he wanted recycled paper and pulled the job when he didn't like the price. That's not my fault. (Question 7)*

- *I need to think more about my relationship with each customer and less about the dollar worth of each contract. From experience, I know that works better for me. (Question 10)*

Len found it particularly useful to look for objective facts that either counterbalanced or contradicted each item in the "Evidence for" column. He kept asking himself, "What in my experience balances out this piece of evidence?" and "What objective facts contradict this piece of evidence?" Len was surprised at how much he discovered to write in the "Evidence against" column. This helped him realize that he tended to shut a lot of things out of his awareness when he was feeling depressed.

Step 4: Write Your Balanced or Alternative Thoughts

Now it's time to synthesize everything you've learned in both the "Evidence for" and "Evidence against" columns. Read over both columns slowly and carefully. Don't try to deny or ignore evidence on either side. Then write new, balanced thoughts that incorporate what you learned as you gathered the evidence. In your balanced thoughts it's okay to acknowledge important items in the "Evidence for" column, but it's equally important to summarize the main things you learned in the "Evidence against" column.

Here's what Len wrote in the "Balanced or alternative thoughts" column in his Thought and Evidence Journal:

My sales are down and I've lost two deals, but I have a solid sales record over the years and have had a lot of good months. I just need to focus on my customer relationships and not the money.

Notice that Len didn't ignore or deny that sales were down, but he was able to use items from his "Evidence against" column to develop a clear, balanced statement that acknowledged his track record as a competent salesman.

Synthesizing statements don't have to be long, but they do need to summarize the main points on both sides of the question. Don't hesitate to rewrite your new, balanced thought several times until the statement feels strong and convincing.

When you're satisfied with the accuracy of what you've written, rate your belief in this new balanced thought as a percentage ranging from 0 to 100. Len, for example, rated his belief in his new balanced thought at 85 percent. If you don't believe your new thought more than 60 percent, you should revise it further, perhaps incorporating more items from the "Evidence against" column. It's also possible that the evidence you've gathered isn't yet convincing enough, so you need to develop more ideas for the "Evidence against" column.

Step 5: Rate Your Mood Again

It's time to find out where all of this work has gotten you. As part of your Thought Journal from chapter 2, you identified a painful feeling and rated its intensity on a scale of 0 to 100. Now rate the intensity of that same feeling again to see if it has changed as a result of the evidence you gathered and the new, balanced thought you developed.

Len found that his depression was much less intense after he went through this process, declining from 85 to 30 on the scale of 0 to 100. Most of the remaining depression seemed to be based on a realistic concern about reduced income due to his low December sales.

Seeing your mood change can be a strong reinforcement for continuing to work with the Thought and Evidence Journal, as you confront powerful hot thoughts and make positive changes in how you feel.

Step 6: Record and Save Alternative Thoughts

We encourage you to record what you learn each time you examine the evidence and develop balanced or alternative thoughts. It's helpful to put this information on index cards that you can keep with you and read whenever you wish. On one side of the card, write a description of the problem situation and your hot thought. On the other side, write your alternative or balanced thought. Over time, you may create a number of these cards. They can be a valuable resource for reminding you of your new, healthier thoughts when upsetting circumstances might cause you to forget them.

Step 7: Practice Your Balanced Thoughts

You can use your index cards in a simple exercise that will give you practice with your balanced thoughts. Start by reading the side of the card that describes the triggering situation and your hot thought. Then work at forming a clear visualization of the situation: Picture the scene, see the shapes and colors, and be aware of who is there and what they look like. Hear the voices and other sounds that are part of the scene. Notice the temperature. Notice if you're touching anything and what it feels like. Using all five senses makes your scene much more vivid. (See "Special Considerations" in chapter 16, "Changing Core Beliefs with Visualization," for more help with creating vivid imagery.)

When the image of the scene is very clear, read your hot thought. Try to focus on it to the point of having an emotional reaction. When you can picture the scene clearly and feel some of the emotions that go with it, turn the card over and read your balanced thoughts. Think of the balanced thoughts while continuing to visualize the scene, and continue to pair the balanced thoughts with the scene until your emotional reaction subsides.

Len did this exercise by picturing the monthly sales notice while thinking his hot thought "I'm a first-class failure." After feeling a small surge of depression, he paired the image of the sales report with the balanced thoughts described earlier. It took several minutes of focusing on the balanced thoughts before his depression started to subside. One of the important things Len learned from this exercise was that he could both increase and decrease his depression by focusing on key thoughts.

Step 8: Develop Your Action Plan

As with the Thought Journal in chapter 3, you can use the Thought and Evidence Journal to help you develop action plans. Study the "Evidence against" column and look for an item that involves using coping skills or implementing a plan to handle the situation differently. Circle any items that suggest a plan of action. In the space below, write three specific steps you could take to implement your action plan in the problem situation:

1. _____

_____

2. _____

_____

3. _____

_____

Len's action plan focused on his decision to think about customer relationships rather than the dollar value of each contract. Here's what he decided to do:

1.   *Send New Year's greetings to all of my regular customers.*

2.   *Call each customer with a request for feedback about how I and my company could improve service.*

3.   *Focus on enjoying my customers as people; for example, taking the time to chat instead of pushing quickly to business.*

Example

To give you an idea of how the whole process looks in action, let's consider an example from Holly, a modern dance teacher. Her classes were offered on a drop-in basis, and she was paid per student. Attendance at one of her seven classes had recently declined sharply. To make matters worse, after class one night, one of the remaining students in that class had criticized Holly for not giving much attention or feedback to individual dancers.

Holly felt like she'd been slapped. She went home wondering if she should continue teaching—or would even be allowed to. Here's how she completed her Thought and Evidence Journal.

Holly's Thought and Evidence Journal

Situation When? Where? Who? What happened?	Feelings One-word summaries Rate 0-100	Automatic thoughts What were you thinking just before and during the unpleasant feeling? Rate 0-100	Evidence for	Evidence against Circle possible action plans.	Balanced or alternative thoughts Rate believability 0-100%	Rerate feelings 0-100%
Class dwindling. Criticized for not giving individual attention.	depressed 65 anxious 80	I'm turning off the class. 30 I'm no good at this. 50 I'm a fraud. 85 I'll lose my job. 85 Stupid me; I never notice what's happening until it's too late. 50 I'll have to cancel the class. 20	Class size dropped from 11 to 5. Complaint from dancer in class. Lost a few dancers from one or two of my other classes. Someone also complained a few months ago about my not giving feedback.	A popular Afro-Haitian instructor just started a class at the same time as mine. (Q1) Classes fluctuate a lot, and sometimes dwindle and get canceled. No one gets fired for it. (Q2) Two of my classes are actually growing; the 6 p.m. on Tuesday had 23 dancers last week. (Q3) Jill said I put together some lovely sequences, and several dancers standing around agreed. I'm good at choreographing teaching exercises. (Q4) Most likely the class will stabilize at this number. At the worst I'll lose one of seven classes. (Q5) Only one person has actually been fired, and that was for encouraging movements that risk injury. I doubt I'll be fired for a class with low attendance. (Q6) The odds of being fired are less than 1 in 500. (Q8) I can individually ask other dancers about their reactions to the class. Also, I can focus on giving feedback to dancers in the back row, whom I often miss. (Q10)	One class has dwindled, and I'm not great at giving feedback. But fluctuations are normal. 95% No one gets fired except for putting students at risk of injury. 85% Many dancers like my class, and I have a plan for improving feedback. 90%	depressed 50 anxious 25

Notice that Holly had two strong feelings: depression and anxiety. That's because thoughts such as "I'm a fraud" and "I'm no good at this" tended to make her feel bad about herself and depressed. On the other hand, a thought such as "I'll lose my job" was scary and provoked anxiety. Under "Automatic thoughts," Holly really had two hot thoughts: "I'm a fraud" and "I'll lose my job." Both were rated 85, so they were major contributors to her feelings. Holly decided to work on "I'll lose my job" in this session with her journal because she was more anxious than depressed. Later, Holly went back and repeated the process for the hot thought "I'm a fraud."

Notice that under "Evidence for," Holly focused on facts. She included as evidence only what had actually happened or been said. She didn't include any feelings, opinions, or assumptions as evidence— only the facts.

In the "Evidence against" column, Holly used the ten key questions to uncover evidence contrary to her hot thought. A few of the questions weren't relevant, but many of them helped her remember past and present experiences that made losing her job seem unlikely.

Because Holly's "Evidence against" column was so substantial, she went through it carefully and underlined the items that seemed most convincing. To write her balanced thoughts, Holly acknowledged the truth of several problems in the "Evidence for" column but counterweighted them with strong evidence against. When Holly reevaluated her feelings, her anxiety was down substantially—from 80 to 25. However, her depression had improved only slightly. That's why she elected to work with her Thought and Evidence Journal again, using "I'm a fraud" as her hot thought.

Holly put a description of the situation and the hot thought "I'll lose my job" on one side of an index card. On the other side she wrote her balanced thoughts. Then she began by visualizing the problem situation while focusing on her hot thought. When she felt the first tinglings of anxiety, she turned the card over and visualized the problem situation in conjunction with her new, balanced thoughts. This exercise showed Holly that she could change her feelings by shifting from her hot thought to balanced thoughts.

Based on material in the "Evidence against" column, Holly came up with a two-part plan: asking for feedback from certain dancers she knew in class, and giving more attention to the dancers in the back row. Holly decided to implement her plan with three specific steps:

1. *Ask Maria, Eleanor, Michelle, and Farrin about my class in general and, specifically, find out what they've observed about the feedback I give dancers.*

2. *Bring the back row to the front halfway through every class.*

3. *Try to find something to praise about each dancer.*

SPECIAL CONSIDERATIONS

The Thought and Evidence Journal is a powerful tool against automatic thoughts, but you need to proceed systematically through all the steps. Here are a few tips to help you overcome some common obstacles to success:

- If you have more than one strong hot thought, do a separate Thought and Evidence Journal for each.

- If you have difficulty developing alternative interpretations to the hot thought (question 1), imagine how a friend or an objective observer might look at the situation.

- If you have difficulty identifying exceptions to generalizations made by your hot thought (question 3), think of times you've been in the situation without anything negative happening. Perhaps you even experienced something positive: Was there a time when you handled the situation particularly well? Were you ever praised in the situation?

- If you have difficulty remembering objective facts to counteract items in the "Evidence for" column (question 7), you might ask a friend or family member to help you.

- If you have difficulty assessing the odds of a feared outcome (question 8), make an estimate of all the times in the last year someone in the United States has been in this same situation and how many times the feared catastrophe has occurred.

- If you have difficulty making an action plan (question 10), imagine how a very competent friend or acquaintance would handle the same situation. What would he or she do, say, or try that might create a different outcome?

CHAPTER 5

Relaxation

Relaxation training differs from what we normally think of as relaxing. It's more than watching a movie to take your mind off things or going for a long, quiet walk to unwind. When psychologists talk about learning to relax, they are referring to regularly practicing one or more of a group of specific relaxation exercises. These exercises often involve a combination of deep breathing, muscle relaxation, and visualization techniques that have been proven to release the muscular tension that the body stores during times of stress.

During your relaxation training sessions, you will discover that racing thoughts start to slow and feelings of fear and anxiety ease considerably. In fact, when your body is completely relaxed, it's impossible to feel fear or anxiety. In 1975, cardiologist Herbert Benson studied how the body changes when a person is deeply relaxed. During the state that Benson termed the relaxation response, he observed that heart rate, breath rate, blood pressure, skeletal muscle tension, metabolic rate, oxygen consumption, and skin electrical conductivity all decreased. On the other hand, alpha brain-wave frequency, which is associated with a state of calm well-being, increased. Every one of these physical conditions is exactly opposite to reactions that anxiety and fear produce in the body. Deep relaxation and anxiety are physiological opposites.

SYMPTOM EFFECTIVENESS

When practiced regularly, relaxation training is effective in reducing general, interpersonal, and performance anxiety. The relaxation training outlined here is a key component in the treatment of phobias, chronic anger, worry, mild avoidance, and bad habits. Relaxation training is also recommended for treating chronic muscular tension, neck and back pain, insomnia, muscle spasms, and high blood pressure.

TIME TO MASTERY

In general, you can experience the benefits of deep relaxation within a session or two using any of the methods described below. Often, two or more methods can be combined to deepen your sense of relaxation; for instance, you could visualize a peaceful scene while practicing deep breathing.

Abdominal breathing, progressive muscle relaxation, relaxation without tension, and cue-controlled relaxation should be learned in sequence. You cannot do cue-controlled relaxation (the quickest and easiest of all the methods) until you've mastered the first three. The whole sequence will take two to four weeks to learn, depending on length and frequency of practice sessions.

INSTRUCTIONS

This chapter focuses on highly effective techniques that, when practiced regularly, can bring about deep states of relaxation.

Initially, you'll want to do your relaxation training in a quiet room where you won't be disturbed. Wear loose, nonbinding clothing. At the start of each exercise, assume a comfortable position, either lying down or sitting, in which your body feels well supported. If you wish, you can use white noise, such as a white noise machine or the humming of a fan, to cover up sounds that you have no control over.

Later, when you're more familiar with the exercises, you can try them in more distracting settings and public places.

Abdominal Breathing

One group of muscles that commonly tenses in response to stress are those located in the wall of your abdomen. When your abdominal muscles are tight, they push against your diaphragm as it extends downward to initiate each breath. This pushing action restricts the amount of air you take in and forces the air you do inhale to remain in the top part of your lungs.

If your breathing is high and shallow, you'll probably feel as though you aren't getting enough oxygen. This is stressful and sets off mental alarms that you are in danger. To make up for the lack of air, instead of relaxing your abdominal muscles and taking deeper breaths, you may take quick, shallow breaths. This shallow, rapid breathing can lead you to hyperventilate—one of the prime causes of panic.

Abdominal breathing reverses this process by relaxing the muscles that press against your diaphragm and slowing your breath rate. Three or four deep abdominal breaths can be an almost instant relaxer.

Abdominal breathing is usually easy to learn. Practice the following exercise for about ten minutes to acquire this simple but extremely effective skill:

1. Lie down and close your eyes. Take a moment to notice the sensations in your body, particularly where your body is holding any tension. Take several breaths and see what you notice about the quality of your breathing. Where is your breath centered? Are your lungs expanding fully? Does your chest move in and out when you breathe? Does your abdomen? Do both?

2. Place one hand on your chest and the other on your abdomen, right below your waist. As you breathe in, imagine that you're sending your breath as far down into your body as it will go. Feel your lungs expand as they fill up with air. As you do this, the hand on your chest should remain fairly still, and the hand on your abdomen should rise and fall with each breath. If you have difficulty getting the hand on your abdomen to move, or if both hands are moving, try gently pressing down with the hand on your abdomen. As you breathe, direct the air so it pushes up against the pressure of your hand, forcing it to rise.

3. Continue to gently breathe in and out. Let your breath find its own pace. If your breathing feels unnatural or forced in any way, just maintain your awareness of that sensation as you breathe in and out. Eventually any straining or unnaturalness should ease up by itself.

4. After breathing deeply for several breaths, begin to count each time you exhale. After ten exhalations, start the count over with one. When thoughts intrude and you lose track of the number you are on, simply return your attention to the exercise and start counting again from one. Continue counting your breaths for ten minutes, with some awareness devoted to ensuring that the hand on your abdomen continues to rise with each breath.

Progressive Muscle Relaxation

Progressive muscle relaxation (PMR) is a relaxation technique that involves tensing and relaxing all the various muscle groups in your body in a specific sequence. The technique was developed by physician and psychiatrist Edmund Jacobson in 1929. He realized that the body responded to anxious and fearful thoughts by storing tension in the muscles and found that this tension could be released by consciously tightening the muscles beyond their normal tension point and then suddenly relaxing them. He discovered that repeating this procedure with every muscle group in the body could induce a deep state of relaxation.

Jacobson's original instructions for PMR comprised a complex routine involving more than two hundred different muscle relaxation exercises. Since then, researchers have discovered that a much simpler regimen of exercises can be equally effective. These exercises divide the body into four major muscle groups: the arms, head, midsection, and legs.

If you practice PMR as outlined below, you'll experience the physical benefits that Herbert Benson defined as the relaxation response. More importantly, if you continue to regularly practice PMR for several months, the amount of anxiety, anger, or other painful emotions that habitually come up in your life will significantly diminish.

Practice the following exercise for about twenty or thirty minutes daily, whether you feel like it or not. You are developing a skill: the ability to relax. In the beginning, you may find that it takes you a long time to relax even a little bit. However, as you continue to practice, you'll learn to relax more deeply and more rapidly

As you go through the exercise, do two cycles of tensing and relaxing for each muscle group. Tighten each group for seven seconds, then relax for twenty seconds, then repeat. Each time you tense a muscle group, tighten the muscles as much as you can without straining. When it's time to release the tension, let go of it suddenly and completely and notice the feeling of relaxation. Do your muscles feel heavy, warm, or tingly? Learning to recognize the physical signs of relaxation is a key part of the process.

The progression from one muscle group to the next follows a logical sequence, from arms to head to midsection to legs. Most people find that after practicing PMR a few times they can easily remember the sequence. If you have trouble remembering the order, you may want to make an audio recording of the instructions or purchase a recording.

ARMS

1. Clench both hands tightly, making them into fists. Hold the tightness for seven seconds. Pay attention to the sensations in the muscles as they contract. Then, all at once, let go of the tension and notice the difference. Stay focused on the sensations you feel. After twenty seconds of allowing the muscles to relax, clench your fists again. Hold the tension for seven seconds, then relax for twenty seconds.

2. Next, bend both elbows and flex your biceps. Hold this pose for seven seconds, then let go of the tension. Pay attention to the physical sensations of relaxation. Flex a second time, then relax.

3. Tense your triceps—the muscles on the back of your upper arms—by locking your elbows and stretching your arms down by your sides as hard as you can. Let go of the tension and notice the sensations of relaxation. Flex and release a second time.

HEAD

1. Raise your eyebrows up as high as you can and feel the tension in your forehead. Hold for seven seconds, then suddenly let your brow drop and become smooth for twenty seconds. Repeat.

2. Squinch up your entire face as though you were trying to make every part of it meet on the tip of your nose. Hold for seven seconds and feel where the strain is. Then release the tension and notice the feeling of relaxation. Repeat.

3. Close your eyes tightly and stretch your mouth open as wide as you can, then relax. Repeat.

4. Clench your jaw and push your tongue up to the roof of your mouth, then release. Notice how the sensations change. Repeat.

5. Open your mouth into a big, wide O, then release so that your jaw goes back into a normal position. Feel the relaxation and notice the difference. Repeat.

6. Tilt your head back as far as you can until it presses against the back of your neck, then relax. Repeat.

7. Stretch your head to one side so it rests near your shoulder, then relax. Repeat. Roll your head over to the other side, so it rests near your other shoulder, then relax. Repeat, and then lift your head to its natural resting position and feel the tension drain away. Let your mouth fall open slightly.

8. Stretch your head forward until your chin is resting on your chest. Feel the release of tension as you return your head to its natural resting position. Repeat.

MIDSECTION

1. Bring your shoulders up as high as you can, as though you're trying to bring them up to your ears. Hold for seven seconds, then let them fall back down and relax for twenty seconds. Feel the heaviness in the muscles as they relax. Repeat.

2. Stretch your shoulders back, as though you were trying to touch your shoulder blades together, then let your shoulders relax. Repeat.

3. Bring your arms straight out in front of you at chest level and, while keeping them straight, cross them as high up on your arms as you can and feel the stretch in your upper back. Then let your arms drop down to your sides and notice the sensation of letting go. Repeat.

4. Take a deep breath. Before you exhale, contract all the muscles in your stomach and abdomen, then exhale and release the contraction. Repeat.

5. Gently arch your back, then relax. Repeat.

LEGS

1. Tighten your buttocks and thighs. Increase the tension by straightening your legs and pushing down hard through your heels and hold this position for seven seconds. Let go for twenty seconds and notice the feeling of relaxation. Repeat.

2. Tense your inner thigh muscles by pressing your legs together as hard as you can. Release and feel the sense of ease spread throughout your legs. Repeat.

3. Tighten your leg muscles while pointing your toes, then release as you return your toes to a neutral position. Repeat.

4. Flex your toes, drawing them up toward your head as you tighten your shin and calf muscles, then release and let your feet hang loosely. Repeat.

Shorthand Muscle Relaxation

Although the basic PMR procedure is an excellent way to relax, it takes so long to go through all the different muscle groups sequentially that it isn't a practical tool for on-the-spot relaxation. To relax your body quickly, you need to learn the following shorthand PMR method.

The key to shorthand PMR is learning to simultaneously relax the muscles in each of the four body areas. You will tense and hold each group for seven seconds, then allow that entire group of muscles to relax for twenty seconds. As you become more adept, you may need less time for both tensing and relaxing. Here are the steps for shorthand PMR:

1. Make tight fists while flexing your biceps and forearms. Hold the tension for seven seconds, then relax for twenty seconds.

2. Press your head back as far as you can. Roll it clockwise once, in a complete circle, then roll it counterclockwise once. As you do this, wrinkle up your face as though you were trying to make every part of it meet at your nose. Relax. Next, tense your jaw and throat muscles and hunch your shoulders up, then relax.

3. Gently arch your back as you take a deep breath. Hold this position, then relax. Take another deep breath, and this time push your abdomen out as you inhale, then relax.

4. Point your toes up toward your face while tightening your calf and shin muscles, then relax. Next, curl your toes while tightening your calf, thigh, and buttock muscles, then relax.

Relaxation without Tension

Within seven to fourteen PMR practice sessions, you should be adept at recognizing and releasing tension in your muscles. After that, you may not need to deliberately contract each muscle group before you relax it. Instead, scan your body for tension by running your attention through the four areas of the body in sequence. If you find any tightness, simply let go of it, just as you did after each contraction in the PMR exercises. Stay focused and really feel each sensation. Work with each muscle group until the muscles seem completely relaxed. If you come to an area that feels tight and won't let go, tighten that one muscle or muscle group and then release the tension. This method is even faster than the PMR shorthand procedure. It's also a good way to relax sore muscles that you don't want to aggravate by overtensing.

Cue-Controlled Relaxation

In cue-controlled relaxation, you learn to relax your muscles whenever you want by combining a verbal suggestion with abdominal breathing. First, get in a comfortable position, and then release as much tension as you can using the technique for relaxing without tension described just above. Focus on your belly as it moves in and out with each breath, and make your breaths slow and rhythmic. With each breath, let yourself become more and more relaxed.

Then, on every inhalation, say the words "breathe in" to yourself, and as you exhale, say the word "relax." Just keep saying to yourself, "breathe in…relax…breathe in…relax," while letting go of tension throughout your body. Continue this practice for five minutes, repeating the cue words with each breath.

The cue-controlled method teaches your body to associate the word "relax" with the feeling of relaxation. After you have practiced this technique for a while and the association is strong, you'll be able to relax your muscles anytime, anywhere, just by mentally repeating, "breathe in… relax," and releasing any feelings of tightness throughout your body. Cue-controlled relaxation can give you stress relief in less than a minute and is a major component of the treatment plans for anxiety and anger management.

Visualizing a Peaceful Scene

Another way to relax is by mentally constructing a peaceful scene that you can enter whenever you feel stressed. Your peaceful scene should be a setting that you find interesting and appealing. It will be a place that will make you feel safe and secure when you imagine it—where you will be able to let your guard down and completely relax.

FINDING YOUR PEACEFUL SCENE

Find a comfortable position, either sitting or lying down, and take a few minutes to practice cue-controlled relaxation. Visualization is most effective when you are completely relaxed, so be sure to take enough time to relax thoroughly.

Now simply ask your unconscious to show you your peaceful scene. A picture may start to form in your imagination. Or, instead of an image, you may mentally hear a word, phrase, or sound that will start to stir an image to life. However it happens, if an image starts to show itself, don't question it. Accept this as a setting that has a restful resonance for you.

If a scene doesn't start to appear to you, choose a place or an activity that appeals to you. Where would you like to be right now? In the country, the woods, or a meadow? On a boat? In a cabin? At the house where you grew up? In a penthouse overlooking Central Park?

Once your imagination has settled on a scene, notice what objects you have around you in the scene. See their colors and shapes. What sounds do you hear? What scents are in the air? What are you doing? What physical sensations are you feeling? Try to notice everything about the scene. You may find that parts of your scene remain unclear or hazy, no matter how hard you try to bring them into focus. This is perfectly normal. Don't be disappointed. With practice, you'll be able to draw out the details and make your scene more vivid.

VISUALIZATION SKILLS

Visualization is a skill. Like many skills, such as drawing, cabinet making, or sewing, some people are initially more adept at it than others. You may be a person who can sit down and re-create a scene so clearly that you feel like you're actually there. Or you might find it difficult to see anything at all.

Even if you aren't a natural at visualization, you can develop this skill with practice. The following guidelines will help you bring your visualizations to life:

- Once an image appears, if there are any gaps in the scene—if one part seems hazy or void of any image at all—put all of your concentration on that area and ask, "What is it?" Hold your attention on that area and see if it starts to clear. Even if the image is fuzzy or blank, watch whatever appears in your imagination as intently as you can.

- It's important to make your imagined scene as real as possible. One way to accomplish this is by adding as much detail as you can gather from at least three of your five senses. Visually, you can bring out the shapes in your scene by running your attention over the outlines of the images as though you were tracing them with a pencil. Notice the colors in your scene. Are they vivid or faded? Locate the light source. How does the light falling on an object affect its color? What areas are in shadow? Try to notice everything you could actually see if you were there.

- Pay attention to the information you would gather through your other senses. What sounds would you hear if you were actually there? What would the environment smell like? What can you feel through your sense of touch? Are there areas that are hot or cold? Is a breeze blowing? Imagine running your hand over various objects and notice their texture and the sensations this action creates in your body.

- Pay attention to the perspective from which you're viewing the scene. Are you viewing it as though you're an outsider looking in? The clue to the "outside looking in" perspective is when you actually see an imagined "you" in your scene. If you do, you need to shift perspective so that your view is what you'd see if you were actually in the scene. For example, if your peaceful scene involves lying underneath some trees, instead of seeing yourself reclining on the ground, shift your perspective so you see the branches of the trees against a clear blue sky. By seeing things from a perspective inside the scene, you'll draw yourself completely into the image and are more likely to feel that you're living the scene rather than just viewing it.

- When unrelated thoughts intrude, notice their content and then return your attention to the scene you're creating.

EXAMPLES OF PEACEFUL SCENES

Here are a few examples that may give you an idea of how to put your scenes together. Adopt the details that appeal to you and add others of your own that you find particularly relaxing.

The beach. You have just descended a long flight of wooden stairs and now find yourself standing on a stretch of the most pristine beach you have ever seen. It is wide and stretches as far as you can see in either direction. You sit down on the sand and find that it's white, smooth, warm, and heavy. You let the sand sift through your fingers, and it seems almost liquid. You lie on your stomach and find that the warm sand instantly conforms to the shape of your body. A breeze touches your face. The soft sand holds you. The surf rumbles as it rises into long white crests that gently break toward you and then dissolve into the sand a few yards away from you. The air smells of salt and sea life, and you breathe it in deeply. You feel calm and safe.

The forest. You are in a forest, lying down in a circle of very tall trees. Underneath you is a cushion of soft, dry moss. The air is strongly scented with laurel and pine, and the atmosphere feels deep, still, and serene. You drink in the warmth of the sun as it streams through the branches, dappling the carpet of moss. A warm breeze rises. The tall trees around you sway, and the leaves rustle rhythmically with each waft of wind. Each time the breeze swells, every muscle in your body becomes more relaxed. Two songbirds warble in the distance. A chipmunk chatters above. A sense of ease, peace, and joy spreads from head to toe.

The train. You are riding in a private car at the very end of a long train. The entire ceiling of the car is a dome of tinted glass and the walls of the car are glass, creating the illusion that you are out in the open, flying through the vast countryside. A plush couch sits at the far end, with two overstuffed chairs opposite and a coffee table in the middle, complete with your favorite magazines. You sink deeply into one of the chairs, push off your shoes, and put your feet on the table. Outside there's an ever-receding panorama: mountains, trees, snowcapped peaks, a lake shimmering in the distance. The sun has almost set and the sky is awash in purples and reds, with towering red-orange clouds. As you gaze at these scenes, you ease into the rhythm of the clacking wheels and feel the lull of the rocking motion of the train.

CHAPTER 6

Worry Control

Everybody worries from time to time. It's a natural response to anticipated future problems. But when worry gets out of hand, it can become an almost full-time preoccupation. You have a serious problem with worry if you regularly experience any of the following:

- Chronic anxiety about future dangers or threats

- Consistently making negative predictions about the future

- Often overestimating the probability or seriousness of bad things happening

- Inability to stop repeating the same worries over and over

- Escaping worry by distracting yourself or avoiding certain situations

- Having difficulty using worry constructively to produce solutions to problems

People who tell you to just stop worrying don't realize how the human mind works. It's like a famous psychological conundrum. Imagine that we offered you a thousand dollars to not think of a white bear for a full minute. You might go for months or years without thinking about a white bear, but as soon as you decide to *not* think about it, you can't get that damned bear out of your mind. Just try it.

This chapter will teach you to control worry in four ways. First, it will direct you to regularly practice the relaxation techniques you learned in chapter 5. Second, it will teach you to conduct accurate risk assessments to counter any tendency to overestimate future danger. Third, it will teach you worry exposure. In simplest terms, worry exposure means scheduling a thirty-minute period each day for full-scale, concentrated, organized worrying. You'll do all of your worrying then. If you're tempted to worry at any other time, you'll postpone it until your next scheduled worry exposure session. Worry exposure makes worrying less distressing and more productive.

Finally, this chapter also teaches worry behavior prevention, a technique for controlling ineffective strategies you may be using to reduce your worries somewhat in the short term that actually perpetuate them in the long term. For example, you'll discover ways to get places on time without obsessively checking your watch or circling the block because you're too early, or how to stop excessively calling to check up on loved ones about whom you worry too much.

SYMPTOM EFFECTIVENESS

Relaxation, risk assessment, and worry exposure have been proven effective in reducing the excessive worry that is the chief feature of generalized anxiety disorder (O'Leary, Brown, and Barlow 1992). Worry behavior prevention has also been found to be helpful in curbing ritualistic, preventive, and corrective behaviors that tend to perpetuate worry. It also helps treat perfectionism and obsessional thinking.

Considering the superiority of cognitive behavioral techniques in the treatment of panic attacks, you would expect success in treating worry with similar techniques. However, studies to date indicate that cognitive behavioral techniques work only about as well as other interventions to control or diminish worry (Brown, Hertz, and Barlow 1992). This may be because clinicians haven't hit upon just the right combination of techniques, because of unclear diagnostic categories and treatment protocols in some of the early studies, or because we simply don't understand what makes worry so persistent.

TIME TO MASTERY

It will take you one or two weeks to learn to relax using deep breathing, cue-controlled relaxation, and visualization. During this time, you can also begin the process of assessing risks. Then you can begin to conduct worry exposure. You should notice improvements by your second or third exposure session.

Worry prevention takes only an hour or two to put into practice, and its benefits can be felt immediately. All told, you can expect to see progress in about a month.

INSTRUCTIONS

Worry isn't just a mental process. When you worry, you enter into a cyclical pattern that involves your thoughts, body, and behavior, as shown in the diagram of the worry system below.

Worry System

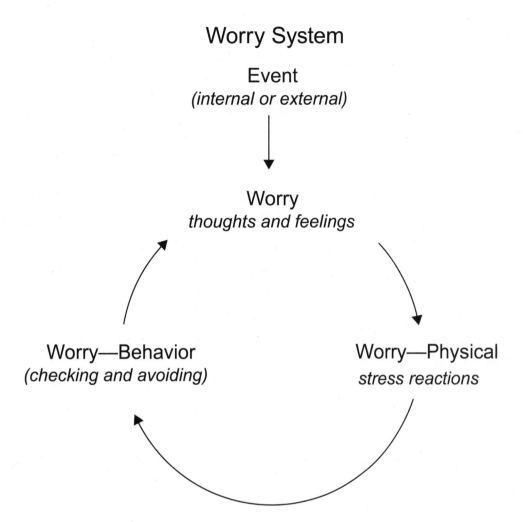

An event—for example, the sight of an ambulance or the thought of a loved one getting hurt—starts worry thoughts going, and you start feeling anxious.

On the physical level, your heart starts beating faster, your breathing quickens, your skin gets sweaty, your muscles tense, and you may have other physical symptoms associated with the fight-or-flight response.

On the behavioral level, you may take action to avoid the upsetting situation or place. Or you may begin checking behavior, such as calling to see if a loved one is all right or proofreading a report for the fifth time.

To control worry, you need to approach it on all these levels. First, you will deal with physical stress reactions by practicing relaxation exercises. To address the cognitive features of worry, you'll practice risk assessment and worry exposure. Then you'll get behavioral problems under control with worry behavior prevention.

Relaxation

If you haven't learned the relaxation skills in the previous chapter, work through that chapter first, and master progressive muscle relaxation and cue-controlled relaxation. Chronic worry creates chronic muscular tension. By practicing relaxation daily, you can provide yourself with crucial breaks in the cycle of fight-or-flight reactions that worry causes.

Take the time once a day to perform the full progressive muscle-relaxation procedure. Set aside a dedicated time each day when, no matter what else is going on, you will do this exercise. It's important that you practice daily and not skip or shorten your sessions. Reaching a profound level of deep relaxation once a day is an important part of worry control that cannot be postponed. You can't catch up on it tomorrow if you skip it today.

Five times a day, at more or less regular intervals, do a quick cue-controlled relaxation. This only takes a moment, and you can do it anywhere. Frequent relaxing moments will keep your overall level of physical stress under control.

Risk Assessment

If worry is a problem for you, you probably haven't learned the skill and art of risk assessment. No one can escape risk in life. The trick is to know which risks you can avoid, which you should prepare for, and which you simply don't have to worry about. There are two main aspects of risk assessment: estimating probability and predicting outcomes. Once you understand them, you'll be ready to use the Risk Assessment Worksheet we've provided.

ESTIMATING PROBABILITY

People who worry a lot consistently overestimate risk. Some think that there's a high chance of a traffic accident every time they start the car. Others worry excessively about making a mistake at work, even though they perform their job well and have seldom or never made a big mistake. Overestimation happens because of some combination of experience and belief: how much weight you give to your personal experience, and what beliefs you hold about the function of worry.

Experience. There are two ways that your personal history can influence your worrying. One way is if nothing too bad has ever happened to you, but you ignore this historical evidence. It doesn't stop you from worrying about forgetting something important or losing an important relationship. If you think this way, it seems that every day that passes without disaster increases the odds of bad things happening. The other way personal history influences worrying is if something bad did happen to you once and you give this historical evidence too much weight. You figure that anything that happened once is likely to happen again—that lightning not only strikes twice, but actually likes to strike the same spot over and over.

Belief. There are two ways that deeply held, unexamined beliefs can make worry worse. First, you might believe in the predictive power of worry. A woman who worried about her husband leaving her believed that the fact that she thought about it a lot indicated that he was indeed likely to leave. The second way belief can trap you is if you believe in the preventive power of worry. In this case, you unconsciously assume that bad things haven't happened to you because your worry about them has kept trouble at bay. You feel like a sentry on guard, ever vigilant.

The problem with these errors in estimating risk is that they subtly increase your worry until it becomes a bigger problem than the dangers you worry about. The way out of this trap is to learn accurate risk assessment.

PREDICTING OUTCOMES

Even if what you worry about comes to pass, will the outcome be as catastrophic as you fear? Most people who worry a lot consistently predict unreasonably catastrophic outcomes. This is catastrophizing. For example, a man who worried about losing his job actually did lose his job. But instead of ending up homeless and poor, he got another job. It paid a little less, but he liked the work more. The catastrophic outcome he predicted didn't occur.

When you worry, your anxiety makes you forget that people routinely cope with even the most serious disasters. You forget that you and your family and friends will probably find a way to cope with whatever happens.

USING THE RISK ASSESSMENT WORKSHEET

You can use the following Risk Assessment Worksheet to make accurate risk assessments by estimating accurate probabilities and making reasonable predictions about outcomes. This will help lower your anxiety. On the first line, record one of your worries in the form of a feared event. Write down the worst possible version of your worry you can think of. For example, if you worry about your teenager going out at night, imagine the worst: a head-on collision of drunk teens and a big truck, and everybody dead on impact or dying in the emergency room after suffering horribly.

Next, write the automatic thoughts that typically come up: "She'll die… I'll die… Blood and pain… Things will never be the same… Awful… Can't stand it…" Jot down whatever comes to mind, even if it's just an image or a fleeting word.

Next, rate your anxiety when considering this worst-case scenario, using a scale of 0 to 100 where 0 is no anxiety and 100 is the worst fear you've ever experienced. Then rate the probability of this worst-case scenario coming to pass, from 0 percent for no likelihood at all to 100 percent for absolute inevitability.

The next section deals with catastrophic thinking. Assuming that the worst did happen, predict the consequences you most fear. Then spend some time figuring out what you would tell yourself and what you would do in order to cope with the catastrophe. When you have a clear picture of possible coping strategies, make a revised prediction of the likely consequences if what you fear does come to pass. Then rate your anxiety again and see if it has diminished.

The next section addresses the issue of overestimation. List the evidence against the very worst outcome happening. Figure the odds as realistically as you can. Then list all of the alternative outcomes you can think of. Finally, once again rate your anxiety and the probability of the event. You should find that both your anxiety and your probability ratings have declined as the result of your doing this full and objective risk assessment.

Make copies of the blank form and fill one out whenever you're confronted by a significant worry or return to a worry more than once. It's important to do this exercise consistently. Each risk assessment helps you change old habits of catastrophic thinking. If you'd like to see an example, after the blank form we've provided one filled out by Sally, who was afraid of failure in general, and specifically worried about her oral exam for her marriage, family, and child counselor license.

When you've completed a risk assessment, keep the form. You may wish to refer to it again when confronting a similar worry.

Risk Assessment Worksheet

Feared event: _____

_____

Automatic thoughts: _____

_____

Rate your anxiety from 0 to 100: _____

Rate the probability of the event from 0 to 100 percent: _____

Assuming the worst happens

    Predict the worst possible consequences: _____

    _____

    Possible coping thoughts: _____

    _____

    Possible coping actions: _____

    _____

    Revised prediction of consequences: _____

    _____

Rate your anxiety from 0 to 100 once again: _____

Evidence against the worst possible outcome: _____

_____

Alternative outcomes: _____

_____

_____

Rate your anxiety from 0 to 100 once again: _____

Rate the probability of the event from 0 to 100 percent once again: _____

Sally's Risk Assessment Worksheet

Feared event: _Flunking my orals_

Automatic thoughts: _I can't do it. I'll choke up and sound stupid._

Rate your anxiety from 0 to 100:   _95_

Rate the probability of the event from 0 to 100 percent: _90_

Assuming the worst happens

   Predict the worst possible consequences: _I'll be a failure. All my schooling will be wasted._

   Possible coping thoughts: _Many people don't pass on the first try. I can take the test again._

   Possible coping actions: _Study some. Hire an orals exam coach to practice with. Try again._

   Revised prediction of consequences: _I won't fail permanently. It will just take me a little longer._

Rate your anxiety from 0 to 100 once again: _60_

Evidence against the worst possible outcome: _I've studied hard, and I got good grades on my course work._

Alternative outcomes: _I might do well and pass easily. I might stammer and choke but squeak by and pass anyway. I might fail and have to take the orals over and then pass. It might even take me three tries._

Rate your anxiety from 0 to 100 once again: _40_

Rate the probability of the event from 0 to 100 percent once again: _30_

Worry Exposure

When practicing worry exposure, you expose yourself to minor worries first, experiencing them for thirty minutes at a time. When minor worries no longer cause you painful anxiety, you move on to more distressing worries. Gradually, you learn to take on your major worries with little or no anxiety.

Worry exposure is a form of prolonged imagery exposure, a technique that floods your imagination with fearful images until you grow tired of them. Given enough time and focused attention, even the most upsetting material becomes overly familiar and boring, making it less upsetting the next time you encounter it. This effect doesn't happen when you simply worry on your own, because you don't spend enough time dwelling on only the worst possible outcome. When you do "free-form" worrying, without a structure, you try to distract yourself, argue with yourself, escape into another topic, perform ritual checking or avoiding behaviors, and so on, and therefore gain none of the benefits of structured worry exposure.

Worry exposure also works well because it concentrates your worrying time. When you know that you'll be worrying intensely during your daily exposure session, it's easier to clear your mind of worry during the rest of the day. Worry exposure consists of eight simple steps:

1. List your worries.

2. Rank your worries.

3. Relax.

4. Visualize a worry.

5. Rate your peak anxiety from 0 to 100.

6. Imagine alternative outcomes.

7. Rate your anxiety from 0 to 100 again.

8. Repeat steps 4 through 7.

STEP 1: LIST YOUR WORRIES

Write a list of the things you typically worry about. Include worries about success and failure, holding relationships together, performance at school or work, physical danger, health, making mistakes, rejection, shame over past events, and so on.

STEP 2: RANK YOUR WORRIES

Pick the least anxiety-provoking item on your list of worries and write it at the top of a new list. Then put down the next least distressing worry. Continue until you have reordered all of your worries, ranking them into a hierarchy that runs from the least to the most anxiety provoking. Here's an example of a hierarchy composed by Rachel.

Rachel's Hierarchy of Worries	
1	Forgetting to send my sister a birthday card
2	Driving on the school field trip and losing my way
3	Forgetting to pick up Cathy after school
4	Missing a doctor's appointment
5	Missing the property tax deadline
6	Making a mistake on taxes at work and getting audited
7	Screwing up the payroll so that people don't get their paychecks

STEP 3: RELAX

You are ready to work with the first worry on your list. Get into a comfortable position, breathe deeply, and do cue-controlled relaxation. Let any tension drain out of your body.

STEP 4: VISUALIZE A WORRY

Vividly imagine the first (easiest) item from your hierarchy of worries. See this situation occurring over and over again. Stick with the worst possible outcome of that situation and focus on the sights, sounds, tastes, scents, and sensations as if the event were really happening to you. Using all five senses makes your scene much more vivid. Don't just see the scene from an outside vantage point, as if you were watching a movie. Rather, imagine that you are an active participant, in the middle of the action. (See "Special Considerations" in chapter 16, "Changing Core Beliefs with Visualization," for more help with creating vivid imagery.)

Try not to imagine any alternative scenarios. Stick with the worst possible outcome. Don't allow your mind to wander and escape into distraction. Do this for twenty-five minutes. Set a kitchen timer to keep track of the time. Don't stop early, even if your anxiety is high, or even if you're bored.

Rachel imagined getting a phone call from her sister Mary. She heard Mary's ring tone and saw her hand reach into her purse for her cell phone. She felt the cool, slick plastic of the phone as she turned it on and held it to her ear. She heard her sister's voice say, "Well hi, stranger," just as she realized with horror that Mary's birthday was last week and she hadn't sent a card, bought a present, or even called her. She focused on the shame and embarrassment and imagined Mary sarcastically saying, "So, you've been busy, or you just don't love me anymore?" Rachel continued imagining this outcome for the full twenty-five minutes, going over the scene again and again and adding enriching details. She resisted any engaging with alternative scenarios until the twenty-five minutes were up.

If you try this approach and find that your anxiety is low, nowhere near the level you feel during a "real" worry session, you may be having trouble creating sufficiently vivid images. Try switching to different senses. Most people imagine with visual images, but some do better with sounds, textures, or scents. For example, John couldn't feel really anxious using visual images of being in a car wreck. Then he switched to other senses and imagined the sounds of screeching tires, metal smashing, glass breaking, and sirens. He imagined the texture of asphalt and broken glass, and the smell of leaking gasoline, blood, and smoke. These sensory images worked so well that he rated his anxiety at 95 out of a 100.

STEP 5: RATE YOUR PEAK ANXIETY FROM 0 TO 100

While you're visualizing, rate your highest anxiety level. You can jot down numbers on a piece of scrap paper without even opening your eyes. Use a rating of 0 for no anxiety and a rating of 100 for the worst anxiety you've ever experienced. Rachel gave her scene a 70 after the first five minutes. But later in the scene, she really frightened herself and raised the rating to a 90.

STEP 6: IMAGINE ALTERNATIVE OUTCOMES

After a full twenty-five minutes of visualizing the worst possible outcome, allow yourself to visualize alternative, less stressful outcomes. Don't start early, and once you do start, spend just five minutes imagining an outcome that isn't as bad as your worst-case scenario. For example, after a full twenty-five minutes of shame and horror, Rachel imagined that she had initiated the call, and that she called just one day after her sister's birthday. She imagined apologizing and saying that a belated gift was in the mail.

STEP 7: RATE YOUR ANXIETY FROM 0 TO 100 AGAIN

After five minutes of imagining alternative outcomes, rate your anxiety again. It will probably be notably lower than your previous rating. Rachel rated her final scene at 30.

STEP 8: REPEAT STEPS 4 THROUGH 7

Continue working with the same worry, repeating steps 4 through 7 until your peak anxiety when imagining the worst possible outcome is 25 or less. Then do these same steps for the next worry on your hierarchy. Do at least one session each day. If you have time and can tolerate it, you can do several sessions a day. By the time you've worked through your hierarchy, you should find that your worry is significantly reduced.

It took Rachel four weeks to work through her hierarchy, averaging one-and-a-half sessions a day. During that period, she worried a lot less. Whenever she started to worry, she told herself that she could postpone the worry until her next scheduled session. Even after she stopped doing regular worry exposure, Rachel found that her fear of making mistakes and forgetting things was significantly reduced. She would start to worry, remember her exposure sessions, and think, "I've worried this into the ground already." She was usually able to stop worrying soon, or at least switch to a more balanced assessment of alternative outcomes.

Worry Behavior Prevention

You may habitually perform or avoid certain behaviors to keep bad things from happening. For example, Pete never read the obituaries or drove past the cemetery, feeling that his avoidance would somehow keep loved ones from dying. His mother always knocked on wood whenever she made a positive prediction.

However, such ritual or preventive behaviors actually perpetuate worry and have no power to prevent bad things from happening. For Pete, active avoidance of the obituaries and the cemetery just made him worry about death more often, and he knew intellectually that such avoidance couldn't actually keep people from dying.

The good news is, stopping these behaviors is a relatively straightforward process that involves five simple steps:

1. Record your worry behavior.

2. Pick the easiest behavior to stop and predict the consequences of stopping it.

3. Stop the easiest behavior or replace it with a new behavior.

4. Assess your anxiety before and after.

5. Repeat steps 2 through 4 with the next-easiest behavior.

STEP 1: RECORD YOUR WORRY BEHAVIOR

Write down the things you do or avoid doing to prevent the disasters you worry about from happening:

_____

_____

_____

_____

_____

_____

Here's an example from Carly, who was very worried about social disapproval. She couldn't stand the thought that others might think she was impolite, a bad hostess, or not doing her fair share. She identified three worry behaviors:

- *Getting to appointments and parties too early, and then driving around the block for twenty minutes until it's time to go in.*

- *Taking a main dish, a salad, and a dessert to potlucks, instead of just one dish, as expected.*

- *Making way too much food for parties at my house.*

STEP 2: PICK THE EASIEST BEHAVIOR TO STOP AND PREDICT THE CONSEQUENCES OF STOPPING IT

Pick the worry behavior that would be easiest to stop and write it here. Then write down the predicted consequences.

Behavior: _____

_____

Consequences: _____

_____

Carly picked making too much food for her parties. She predicted simply: "We'd run out of food halfway through the party."

STEP 3: STOP THE EASIEST BEHAVIOR OR REPLACE IT WITH A NEW BEHAVIOR

This is the hard part. In order to find out if your prediction will come true, you have to be a good scientist and actually run the experiment. Resolve to refrain from the behavior the next time you start worrying. For example, Carly firmly decided that she would not make too much food for her husband's birthday party. Unfortunately, she couldn't just stop the worry behavior entirely—she had to make *some* food. First she considered just making half the amount of food she would normally make. But this was hard to judge. Finally, she carefully figured out how much food the average party guest ate at her house and how many guests were really likely to come, and then prepared just enough food based on those calculations. Every time she felt the temptation to add a fudge factor, she stifled it.

If your worry behavior is a form of avoidance, such as not driving past the cemetery or never reading the obituaries, you need to take a different approach: You have to start doing what you've been avoiding. Resolve to drive past the cemetery every morning on the way to work or to read the obituaries with your morning coffee.

Sometimes even the seemingly easiest behavior to stop isn't so easy. In that case, you need to create a hierarchy of replacement behaviors that allows you to taper off from your worry behavior. For example, Peggy was a perfectionistic legal secretary who worried about making mistakes on the senior partner's contracts and briefs. She would take an important brief home on her laptop and spend hours of her own time proofing and reproofing it, agonizing over possible typos, and changing type sizes and fonts far into the night. Every time she made the slightest alteration, she would run the entire document through the spell-checker again.

The thought of spell-checking and proofing just once and declaring a brief done was too alarming for Peggy to even consider. So she made up this hierarchy and resolved to start with the first (easiest) item on her list that day.

Peggy's Hierarchy of Replacement Behaviors	
1	Take brief home and do three extra passes through it.
2	Take brief home and do two extra passes.
3	Take brief home and do one extra pass.
4	Stay up to one hour late and leave brief at work. No extra pass.
5	Leave brief at work and go home on time. No extra pass.
6	Deliberately leave one punctuation error in brief.
7	Deliberately leave one grammatical error.
8	Deliberately leave one spelling error.

Peggy worked her way through each step of her hierarchy. For each, she predicted dire consequences and experienced high anxiety. At each step, however, those consequences failed to occur, so she gained confidence for the next step. You'll notice that the last three steps involve making deliberate mistakes. This is a good strategy to extinguish checking behaviors designed to prevent mistakes. In Peggy's case, she found that making small mistakes didn't cause the firm to lose cases, and also didn't get her fired. Nobody even noticed the errors. She was eventually able to eliminate other checking behaviors and reduce her perfectionism to what she called "high but not inflexible standards."

STEP 4: ASSESS YOUR ANXIETY BEFORE AND AFTER

When you felt like performing your old behavior and knew you weren't going to do it, how anxious were you? Rate your anxiety on a scale of 0 to 100, where 0 means no anxiety. Then assess how anxious you felt after performing your new behavior or cutting out your old behavior, using the same scale. Did your anxiety diminish?

Carly, the woman who habitually prepared too much food for guests, rated her anxiety a full 100 just before her husband's birthday party. She was gratified to find it had reduced to just 25 by the end of the party, when there was still a little food left and the party had been a success.

Also be sure to observe the actual consequences. What actually happened as a result of your behavioral change? Did your dire predictions come true? In Carly's case, her prediction didn't come true; she didn't run out of food halfway through the party. She felt an improved sense of confidence about her ability to enter into a social engagement without excessive worry and preventive behavior.

STEP 5: REPEAT STEPS 2 THROUGH 4 WITH THE NEXT-EASIEST BEHAVIOR

From your initial list, pick the worry behavior that is the next-easiest to stop and repeat the steps: Predict the consequences of stopping the behavior. Then stop it and replace it with a new behavior if appropriate. Finally, assess your anxiety level before and after the experiment.

Example

Rhonda's experience with worry control shows how all four steps fit together. She was chronically worried about being rejected by her boyfriend, her boss, her parents, and complete strangers. She avoided meeting new people for fear that they would reject her. She kept checking with her boyfriend, Josh, to make sure he still loved her. She would say, "I love you," to him in such a way that he had to respond, "I love you too." Some evenings she'd do this five or six times, until it started to annoy Josh, who complained about her neediness.

Rhonda learned progressive muscle relaxation and did it every evening after dinner or just before she went to bed. She also mastered cue-controlled relaxation and set her watch alarm to go off every three hours so she would remember to stop, take a few deep breaths, and relax several times a day. This helped her reduce her ongoing arousal level so the chronic worries in the back of her mind didn't build as much throughout the day.

Rhonda worked on her Risk Assessment Worksheet while she was learning relaxation skills. When she assessed the risk of Josh dumping her, she realized two things: first, that the odds were greatly against him dumping her; and second, if he did dump her, she could survive the rejection and cope with the loneliness. She found it very interesting and instructive to see how persistent overestimation and catastrophizing had been feeding her worry.

Next, Rhonda made a hierarchy of rejection experiences to use in worry exposure. She started with the mild rejection experience of being asked by a bus driver to step to the rear of the bus. After only two sessions, that scene elicited only minor anxiety, so she went on to extinguish her reaction to scenes involving her boss asking her to redo some sloppy work, her mom rejecting her ideas for the family reunion, and, finally, Josh saying that he thought they should break up.

She concluded her worry control treatment with two kinds of worry behavior prevention. She prevented her avoidance of strangers by forcing herself to say something to whoever sat next to her on the bus each morning. She learned that some people responded and some didn't—and that she survived both types of responses. To change her checking behavior with Josh, she resolved to say, "I love you," only twice a day. Then she cut it down to once a day. Then she said it every other day. Interestingly, she noticed that the less she said, "I love you," to Josh, the more he said it to her without prompting.

CHAPTER 7

Coping with Panic

P anic disorder has been likened to standing on a trapdoor many stories in the air and never knowing when or if it will open. When panic strikes, there's an overwhelming feeling of terror that you could die or completely lose control. The body reacts with a host of stress symptoms, which may include a racing heart, shortness of breath, weakness, dizziness, or feeling flushed or faint, as well as feelings of detachment, spaciness, unreality, or depersonalization. For many people struggling with panic disorder, feelings of unreality and depersonalization are the most frightening symptoms because they are interpreted as signs of insanity.

Panic often arises unpredictably, and as a result, panic-prone individuals are burdened with anticipatory dread. They try to avoid any situation where they feel at all vulnerable to panic. This explains why untreated panic disorder often evolves into agoraphobia: the fear of leaving a safe place, such as one's home. Fortunately, several research teams (Barlow and Craske 1989; Clark 1989) have developed excellent treatment programs for coping with panic.

SYMPTOM EFFECTIVENESS

The techniques taught in this chapter are effective in relieving panic symptoms associated with agoraphobia or other mood disorders characterized by a fight-or-flight stress reaction. Researchers have found that a variation on the treatment program described in this chapter freed 87 percent of panic disorder subjects from symptoms of panic (Barlow and Craske 1989). This treatment response was maintained at a two-year follow-up. Many other researchers have reported 80 to 90 percent effectiveness with similar protocols. Another study, in which participants used self-help manuals during a four-week study, showed that panic disorder treatments can be effective with minimal therapist contact (Hackmann et al. 1992).

TIME TO MASTERY

Some people can use the program in this chapter to master panic symptoms in as little as six to eight weeks. However, if you are struggling with significant problems of avoidance or agoraphobia, effective treatment will require additional steps to expose you to situations where you fear having a panic attack. See chapter 13, "Brief Exposure," and chapter 14, "Prolonged Exposure."

INSTRUCTIONS

The treatment program for controlling panic has four main components:

- Understanding panic: what causes it and how it can be controlled

- Breath control training: a simple technique to simultaneously relax your diaphragm and slow your breath rate

- Cognitive restructuring: learning to reinterpret frightening physical symptoms while controlling catastrophic thinking

- Interoceptive desensitization: a technique that exposes you to your most feared physical sensations in a safe, controlled way so they will no longer be associated with panic

Understanding Panic

Panic disorder differs from most forms of anxiety in that the primary focus is not external dangers and events. Rather, it centers on events going on inside your body: physical sensations that scare you and make you afraid of losing control.

If you're prone to panic, you may be hyperalert to physical symptoms that you associate with anxiety and vigilant for the first sign of a racing heart, shortness of breath, or feelings of detachment and unreality. You may monitor your body for sensations of weakness, dizziness, or light-headedness. This vigilance has one purpose: to brace you for a rush of panic. By watching and worrying about bodily sensations, you are trying to prepare for that awful moment when the panic swells, screaming that you are going to die or go insane.

THE PANIC SEQUENCE

Ironically, it is this vigilance and fear of the body's symptoms that actually causes a panic attack. The diagram below shows how it works.

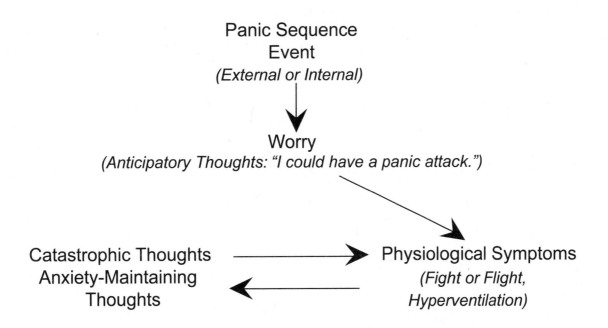

Panic starts with an event that can be internal or external. External events include upcoming stresses and challenges, or situations where you've experienced panic before. Internal events are the physical symptoms you've begun to recognize as the precursors of panic.

The event triggers worry. Here are some typical worry thoughts:

- *Oh no, the meeting room is crowded and stuffy! I could start feeling weird. I might lose control.*

- *I hope the plane doesn't sit too long on the runway. I'll feel trapped and freak out.*

- *I hope I can sell the marketing plan to our new account. All eyes will be on me. I could get all spacey and panic in front of everybody.*

- *My heart's going kind of fast. What's that about? And I'm getting hot—am I losing it?*

- *I feel dizzy, funny, unreal, out of it… I'm not myself… Stop it! Oh no, it's happening again.*

Worry thoughts anticipate danger. They interpret external stressors and key bodily sensations as signals to get ready for catastrophe. This step in the panic sequence can be lightning fast. Worry thoughts often appear in a shorthand that's so compressed that you may not even notice them. Nevertheless, they set the panic cycle into motion.

The next phase in the panic sequence is an intensification of physiological symptoms called the fight-or-flight response. Your body starts to get ready to confront danger. Heart rate increases to provide blood to the large muscles needed to run or do battle. As blood accumulates in your legs, they may feel weak and shaky, despite the fact that the extra blood makes them stronger. Your breathing rate increases to provide more oxygen for sudden, strenuous movement. A common, harmless side effect of this is the feeling that you can't get enough air, accompanied by pain or tightness in the chest.

The blood supply to your brain decreases, producing feelings of dizziness, confusion, and unreality. Blood flow also diminishes to the skin, fingers, and toes to reduce bleeding if you are injured. This makes your extremities cold, though you may simultaneously feel flushed.

The fight-or-flight response triggers sweating, making your skin slippery and hard for a predator to grasp. It also slows digestion, often causing cramping, nausea, and so on.

While fight-or-flight symptoms are harmless, they are quite noticeable and sometimes even dramatic, bringing you to the next phase of the panic sequence: having catastrophic thoughts about your fight-or-flight sensations. Here are some examples:

- *I'm going to have a heart attack.*

- *I'll stop breathing. I'm going to suffocate.*

- *I'll pass out while I'm driving or on the street.*

- *I'll get too weak to walk. I'll fall down and humiliate myself.*

- *I'm going to lose my balance. I can't stand up.*

- *I'm too spacey to think or work.*

These catastrophic thoughts cause the release of adrenaline, signaling your body to intensify its preparations for danger. All of the fight-or-flight symptoms start cranking up. Your heart rate and respiration increase further, you may start to hyperventilate, your legs feel shakier and weaker, and you find yourself feeling even dizzier, hotter, and more depersonalized. Observing these symptoms, your catastrophic thinking becomes more dire:

- *I'm going to die.*

- *I'm losing control. I'm going to run and jump and scream and go crazy.*

- *I'll never recover from this.*

From here, the cycle gathers momentum: catastrophic thoughts trigger the release of more adrenaline and lead to more fight-or-flight symptoms, which generate more catastrophic thoughts, a vicious cycle that continues until you pass the panic threshold. At this point, anxiety-maintaining thoughts can keep the fight-or-flight reaction going for hours. Here's a typical sequence of anxiety-maintaining thoughts, to help illustrate how this works:

I'm falling apart.

⇩

This will continue until I can't function.

⇩

I won't be able to work.

⇩

I'll lose my house and end up on the street.

⇩

I won't be able to take care of my kids.

⇩

My kids will be put in a foster home.

⇩

My life is over.

BREAKING THE CYCLE

Fortunately, the cycle need not continue in this way. How long panic lasts is within your control. When you find yourself caught up in the cycle, here's the most important fact to remember about panic: If you stop scaring yourself with anxious thoughts, panic can't last more than five minutes. It's a medical reality. Because adrenaline from the fight-or-flight reaction is metabolized in five minutes or less, panic will end if new anxious thoughts don't cause the release of more adrenaline. The key is to stop focusing on and buying into catastrophic thoughts and other thoughts that maintain anxiety.

One important strategy for doing so is to change how you interpret and react to normal stress symptoms. Learning to recognize the dizziness, shortness of breath, and spacey, depersonalized feelings as harmless symptoms of the fight-or-flight response is a crucial step toward controlling panic. The interoceptive desensitization techniques later in this chapter will help you do just that. In the meanwhile, study the following table, which provides medical explanations for the symptoms of panic. Put an asterisk by the symptoms that most disturb you. Then write the medical explanation for each symptom you marked on an index card and carry it with you. Whenever you experience symptoms of panic, refer to the card to remind yourself of the medical reality.

Symptom Explanation Chart

Physical symptoms	Catastrophic thought	Medical reality
Increased heart rate or palpitations	"I'll have a heart attack."	According to panic specialist Dr. Claire Weekes (1997), a healthy heart can pump 200 beats per minute for days, even weeks, without damage. Your heart was made to handle stress. An hour of panic is nothing compared to what the heart was designed to deal with.

Feeling faint and light-headed	"I'll pass out while driving or walking."	The light-headed feeling is caused by reduced blood and oxygen supply to the brain, but it almost never results in fainting. Panic triggers higher blood pressure—quite the opposite of low blood pressure problems associated with fainting.
Feeling you can't get your breath, or pain or pressure in your chest	"I'll stop breathing. Here comes a heart attack."	The fight-or-flight reaction causes chest and abdominal muscles to tighten. This can create pressure and muscular pain in your chest, as well as reduced lung capacity. To compensate, you may start to hyperventilate, which just makes the feeling worse. No one has ever stopped breathing due to panic. No matter how uncomfortable the feeling, you will always get enough air.
Feeling dizzy	"I'll fall if I stand up."	The dizzy feeling is caused by hyperventilation and reduced blood and oxygen flow to the brain—a brief and harmless reaction. It's very rare, even during the worst panic, for people to lose their balance.
A weak, shaky feeling in the legs	"I'm too weak to walk; I'll fall down."	The fight-or-flight reaction causes temporary dilation of the blood vessels in your legs, allowing blood to accumulate in the large muscles. Your legs are as strong and able to carry you as ever.
Feeling hot and flushed	"Here comes the panic."	Sensations of being hot and flushed come from increased oxygen and brief changes in your circulatory system. They're harmless and will not cause panic unless you interpret the symptom as a cause for alarm.
Feeling spacey, unreal, or depersonalized	"I'm going crazy. I'm losing hold of myself and won't make it back this time."	Spaciness, feeling unreal, and other mental effects are harmless aspects of the fight-or-flight reaction associated with hyperventilation and reduced blood and oxygen flow to the brain. They are temporary and never result in insanity or losing control of your actions. There are no reported incidents of schizophrenia, paralysis, or running amok following a panic attack.

Breath Control Training

This exercise, which has been adapted from Nick Masi's audio recording *Breath of Life* (1993), is designed specifically for individuals with panic disorder. When most people feel panic, they have a tendency to gasp, take in a breath, and hold on to it. Then they take short, shallow breaths that fail to empty their lungs. This creates a sensation of fullness in the chest or lungs and a feeling that you can't get enough air, but this is an illusion, a simple consequence of not emptying your lungs. Even though you are, in fact, getting plenty of air, your breath comes faster and faster. Eventually, you may cross the threshold into hyperventilation, which is likely to trigger a panic attack. Here are the five simple steps of breath control training.

Step 1: Exhale first. At the first sign of nervousness or panic or the first worry thought about a physical symptom, completely empty your lungs. It's important that you exhale first so you feel like there's plenty of room to take a full, deep breath.

Step 2: Inhale and exhale through your nose. Inhaling through your nose will automatically slow down your breathing and prevent hyperventilation.

Step 3: Breathe deeply into your abdomen. Put one hand on your stomach and the other on your chest. Breathe so that the hand on your stomach moves and the one on your chest remains nearly still. By directing the breath deep into your abdomen, you stretch your diaphragm and relax tight muscles that make it seem hard to breathe.

Step 4: Count while you breathe. Exhale first, then breathe in through your nose, counting, "One… two…three." Pause for one second, then breathe out through your mouth, counting, "One…two… three…four." The counting protects you from the rapid breathing characteristic of panic. Your exhalation should always be one count longer than your inhalation. This will ensure that you empty your lungs between breaths.

Step 5: Slow your breathing by one beat. Breathe in and count, "One…two…three…four." Pause for one second, then breathe out, counting, "One…two…three…four…five." As before, exhale for one count longer than you inhale.

Breath control training is an extraordinarily effective way to slow your breathing and prevent the hyperventilation so often associated with panic. If you can slow your breathing at the first sign of anxiety, you can often protect yourself from the worst of the fight-or-flight symptoms.

The key is practice. Your first efforts at breath control training should occur only in safe and relaxing environments where you won't be disturbed. In the beginning, don't try to use this technique when you're panicked or even anxious. Get comfortable and competent at slowing your breath in nonthreatening environments. After several weeks of daily practice the technique will become "overlearned." When you can easily initiate deep breaths while counting, start using breath control in situations where you feel mildly nervous. Then try breath control as you approach situations where you are worried about panic or when you first notice disturbing physical symptoms.

Don't try breath control training during full-blown panic yet. Wait until you've mastered interoceptive desensitization, which you'll learn later in this chapter. That will give you the experience you need so you can slow your breathing even during the most disturbing anxiety symptoms.

If you have difficulty counting during breath control exercises, you can make a recording to help you learn the proper pacing. Here are instructions for making a twelve-breaths-per-minute recording:

1. Say the word "in" for two seconds.

2. Say the word "out" for two seconds.

3. Pause for one second.

4. Continue repeating "in" for two seconds, then "out" for two seconds followed by a one-second pause for about five minutes.

To further slow your breath, make an eight-breaths-per-minute recording, saying "in" and "out" for three seconds each, and still pausing for one second after saying "out."

Cognitive Restructuring

Human beings are constantly trying to make sense of their experience. People try to label events and predict what those events will mean for the future. When you're anxious and on guard against the possibility of a panic attack, you tend to make two crucial errors of thinking. The first is overestimation: exaggerating the odds that a negative event is likely to occur. The second is catastrophizing: assuming that outcomes will be far more painful and unmanageable than you can endure.

Overestimation and catastrophizing probably contribute to your anxiety. However, there's a way to overcome these patterns of thinking and diminish your anxiety in the process. It involves exploring hard evidence about your fears and identifying alternative coping strategies. This technique makes use of a special kind of thought record called the Probability Form. A blank Probability Form appears below. Make numerous copies of the blank form and use it to respond to catastrophic or maintaining thoughts whenever they occur.

Here's how to use the Probability Form. In the first column, write down the event that's triggering anxiety. Remember, it can be external (meeting friends at a theater) or internal (feeling dizzy and spacey). Under "Automatic thoughts," write your interpretations and beliefs about the event. Try to include your worst and most catastrophic thoughts.

As you focus on your automatic thoughts, use the next two columns to rate the percent probability that what you fear will come true and the intensity of your anxiety. A probability rating of 100 percent means the catastrophe will assuredly happen. Note that many probabilities are less than 1 percent (less than 1 chance in 100 of occurring); these can be expressed as a decimal (1 in 200 would be 0.5 percent; 1 in 1,000 would be 0.1 percent; 1 in 100,000 would be 0.001 percent, and so on). Rate your anxiety on a scale of 0 to 100, where 100 is the worst anxiety you've ever experienced.

These ratings of probability and anxiety are very important, because you can track them and note how they change. After you fill in the "Evidence" and "Coping alternatives" columns, you may see significant reductions in your scores.

The next two columns will help you examine your automatic thoughts. Under "Evidence," write down any facts or experiences that either support or contradict your automatic thoughts. Ask yourself these key questions:

- Out of all the times I've done or felt this in the past, how many times did the catastrophe occur?

- What has usually happened in similar circumstances in the past?

- Is there anything in my past that leads me expect a better outcome than I fear?

- What are the objective facts? (Be sure to include the relevant medical realities you've read about in this chapter.)

- How long is this experience likely to last? Can I cope with it for that long?

After you've listed all the evidence you can think of, move on to the "Coping alternatives" column. Here, describe your action plan if the worst should occur, how you'd cope with the crisis. Even though coming up with a coping strategy is uncomfortable, it's helpful to face what you fear most. You can get through nearly every outcome, no matter how difficult, if you have a plan to cope. Include the following in your plan:

- Any relaxation or breathing skills that might be helpful

- Any resources you have for coping (support from friends or family, financial resources, problem-solving skills)

- Successful coping strategies you've used in the past

- Strategies others might use in this situation

Take your time with the "Coping alternatives" column. Brainstorm until you've developed at least three believable coping strategies. If an alternative doesn't seem realistic for you, leave it out. But if there's a chance it might work, include it and evaluate the potential outcome later.

The last step in completing the Probability Form is to once again rate percent probability and anxiety. Typically, people discover that the probability of catastrophe seems lower after weighing the evidence and developing coping alternatives, as does intensity of anxiety.

Use the Probability Form whenever you feel anxious. Try to fill it out as soon after the event as possible, and no later than the evening of that same day. Be sure to use the form even for events that are only physical sensations. This makes sense when you consider that catastrophic interpretations of bodily sensations are the prime cause of panic. If you use the form consistently over the course of three to four weeks, you'll develop new confidence in your ability to handle fear.

If you need a little help getting started, after the blank form you'll find an example from Sandra, a thirty-two-year-old single mother who had been experiencing panic attacks for about three months. She was terrified of the physical symptoms but also worried about losing her ability to function as a mother and investment analyst. The example covers just her first day of record keeping.

Probability Form

Event *External or internal*	Automatic thoughts	Probability (0-100%)	Anxiety (0-100)	Evidence	Coping alternatives	Probability (0-100%)	Anxiety (0-100)

Sandra's Probability Form

Event External or internal	Automatic thoughts	Probability (0-100%)	Anxiety (0-100)	Evidence	Coping alternatives	Probability (0-100%)	Anxiety (0-100)
Drank coffee, feel jittery	I'm going to slide into a panic.	80%	80	I've drunk coffee thousands of times and only on two occasions had a panic attack. The odds are pretty low, particularly if I start coping right away.	I can do my breath control and remember the medical reality rather than focusing on scary thoughts. It will be over in five minutes.	30%	35
Anxious feelings getting ready for work	I'm ruining my reputation at work. I may lose my job if I stay like this.	65%	70	I felt anxious a lot at work over the past few months, but I always get things done. My performance evaluation was good in spite of being anxious.	If I get negative feedback, I'll find out what I need to change in my behavior and make a plan. If I lose my job, I'll look for something part-time and less stressful. My dad would help me with money. I could also work at home and have more time for my son.	35%	15
"Jelly legs"	I'm going to fall and humiliate myself.	85%	90	I've felt this way at least fifty times, and I've never fallen. It's just blood pooling in my muscles due to the fight-or-flight response, not real weakness.	If I fell, I'd have someone help me to a place where I could sit until the feeling passed. It would be embarrassing, but I'd get over it.	20%	35

Event External or internal	Automatic thoughts	Probability (0–100%)	Anxiety (0–100)	Evidence	Coping alternatives	Probability (0–100%)	Anxiety (0–100)
Heart racing, anxious	I can't stand this. I think I might have a heart attack.	90%	100	I can stand this. My heart beats at least this hard when I exercise. The doctor says I have a healthy heart that can go 200 beats a minute for weeks. Mine's been at 140 for five minutes. My heart's built to handle this.	If I had a heart problem, I'd get treatment, change my diet, get more exercise, and try to really take care of myself. I'd cope because I had to.	45%	55
Spacey, unreal feeling while talking to my boss	I can't think; I'm not myself. This is a sign that I'm losing my mind and that I'll be spacey all the time.	80%	95	The spacey feeling usually passes after I relax. I've felt this way dozens of times. It always passes with no lasting effects. It's just the fight-or-flight reaction—a temporary reduction in blood flow to my head.	If I lost my ability to concentrate and felt out of it, I'd be very sad. But I'd try to get an undemanding job. Even if I was spacey, I'd still love my son and be a mom to him.	45%	60

Sandra's Probability Form (continued)

Need to call ex-husband regarding late child-support payment	I won't be able to deal with him. I'll be upset by his anger. I might feel panicky.	50%	60	Usually when I call to remind him, he's cold and cutting but not raging. I'm okay when he's cold. He's just his usual jerk self.	I'll remind myself that it's his problem and that nothing really bad is happening. He always pays even if he's late. I'll use controlled breathing and keep repeating my request.	5%	20
Mowed the lawn after dinner, feel hot	Oh no, I might panic. This is going to ruin my night.	90%	90	I'm hot from exercising, not anxiety. I've worked hard and I'm perspiring. From past experience, this feeling can be over very soon. I can still enjoy my evening.	I'll do controlled breathing, not focus on the fear thoughts, and wait it out for a few minutes.	15%	20

Interoceptive Desensitization

Interoceptive desensitization is among the most effective—and challenging—components of the treatment program for panic disorder. It involves re-creating, in a safe way, bodily sensations similar to those you associate with panic (*interoceptive* means "related to stimuli arising within the body"). This allows you to learn to experience these sensations as something uncomfortable but not frightening. Dizziness, rapid heart beat, and even feelings of unreality can become no more than annoying effects of the fight-or-flight response. When these feelings are no longer associated with panic, you'll find yourself less vigilant toward and less focused on these physical sensations.

STAGE 1: INITIAL INTEROCEPTIVE EXPOSURE

Desensitizing to frightening bodily sensations is accomplished in three stages. In the first stage you briefly expose yourself to ten specific sensations and then rate your reactions. Most of the following exposure exercises were developed and tested by Michelle Craske and David Barlow (2008). They induce feelings similar to those many people report prior to or during an episode of panic.

1. Shaking your head from side to side for 30 seconds

2. Repeatedly lowering your head between your legs and then lifting it for 30 seconds

3. Running in place for 60 seconds (check with your doctor first)

4. Running in place for 60 seconds while wearing a heavy jacket

5. Holding your breath for 30 seconds

6. Tensing major muscles, particularly in your abdomen, for 60 seconds or as long as you can

7. Spinning while you sit in a swivel chair (not while standing up) for 60 seconds

8. Breathing very rapidly for up to 60 seconds

9. Breathing through a narrow straw for 120 seconds

10. Staring at yourself in a mirror for 90 seconds

As you review this list, you can probably already tell that some of these sensations will be quite uncomfortable. But to recover from panic disorder, it is precisely the feelings you most fear that you must become desensitized to. If exposing yourself to these physical sensations feels too frightening to do alone, enlist a support person to be present throughout the exercise. Later you can forgo the support person as you get more comfortable with the sensations.

In the first stage of interoceptive exposure, you'll expose yourself to each of the ten sensations to identify which create the most anxiety and are most similar to your panic feelings. After you do each of the ten exercises, fill in your ratings of anxiety and similarity to panic sensations in the following Interoceptive Assessment Chart (you may wish to use a copy and keep the form in the book blank). Use the same scale of 0 to 100 for anxiety, in which 100 is the worst anxiety you've ever experienced. Use a percentage to rate how similar each sensation is to what you typically experience during panic, with 100 percent indicating absolutely identical feelings. (An example filled out by Sandra follows the blank form.)

Interoceptive Assessment Chart

Exercise	Anxiety (0-100)	Similarity to panic (0-100%)
Shaking your head from side to side		
Repeatedly lowering and lifting your head		
Running in place		
Running in place while wearing a heavy jacket		
Holding your breath		
Tensing major muscles, especially abdomen		
Spinning while sitting in a swivel chair		
Breathing very rapidly		
Breathing through a narrow straw		
Staring at yourself in a mirror		

Sandra's Interoceptive Assessment Chart

Exercise	Anxiety (0-100)	Similarity to panic (0-100%)
Shaking your head from side to side	10	20%
Repeatedly lowering and lifting your head	0	0%
Running in place	60	80%
Running in place while wearing a heavy jacket	70	90%
Holding your breath	45	50%
Tensing major muscles, especially abdomen	15	10%
Spinning while sitting in a swivel chair	25	30%
Breathing very rapidly	80	95%
Breathing through a narrow straw	50	60%
Staring at yourself in a mirror	40	45%

The assessment was scary for Sandra. To help her get through it, she asked her best friend to be present during the exercises. It took her two sessions to finish, but she found the results interesting. Exercises that created dizzy or light-headed sensations felt dissimilar to actual panic feelings and didn't bother her much. But exercises that made her heart race or overheated her evoked higher levels of anxiety and felt similar to her experiences of panic. Rapid breathing induced sensations almost exactly like her panic feelings, and were also the most frightening of all the sensations.

STAGE 2: CREATE AN INTEROCEPTIVE EXPOSURE HIERARCHY

Stage 2 of interoceptive desensitization involves making a hierarchy of frightening sensations from the Interoceptive Assessment Chart you filled out in stage 1. Start by checking off each exercise that you rated at 40 percent or greater in similarity to the panic sensations you experience. Then, using a copy of the blank Exposure Hierarchy and Anxiety Intensity Chart below, rank the exercises you checked off from least to greatest anxiety rating. Fill in the anxiety ratings from your first exposure under Trial 1. (An example filled out by Sandra follows the blank form.)

Exposure Hierarchy and Anxiety Intensity Chart

Exercise	Trial 1	Trial 2	Trial 3	Trial 4	Trial 5	Trial 6	Trial 7	Trial 8
1.								
2.								
3.								
4.								
5.								
6.								
7.								
8.								
9.								
10.								

Sandra's Exposure Hierarchy and Anxiety Intensity Chart

Exercise	Trial 1	Trial 2	Trial 3	Trial 4	Trial 5	Trial 6	Trial 7	Trial 8
1. *Staring in the mirror*	40							
2. *Holding breath*	45							
3. *Breathing through straw*	50							
4. *Running in place*	60							
5. *Running wearing jacket*	70							
6. *Breathing rapidly*	80							
7.								
8.								
9.								
10.								

Sandra was careful to include in her hierarchy only items rated 40 percent or greater in similarity to actual panic feelings, which she ranked from the exercise with the lowest anxiety intensity (staring in the mirror rated 40) to the highest (rapid breathing, rated 80).

STAGE 3: DESENSITIZE VIA INDUCED INTEROCEPTIVE EXPOSURE

Once you've developed your hierarchy, it's time to begin stage 3, the actual desensitization process. Start with the item on your hierarchy with the lowest anxiety rating. If you need to have a support person present during the first few trials, that's fine; however, you must begin to do the exposures on your own as soon as possible. Here are the steps for practicing induced interoceptive exposure to desensitize yourself to these physical sensations:

1. Begin the exercise and note the point where you first experience uncomfortable sensations. Stick with the exercise for at least thirty seconds after the onset of uncomfortable sensations. The longer you can stick with it, the better.

2. As soon as you stop, record your anxiety rating in the box for that exposure trial on your Exposure Hierarchy and Anxiety Intensity Chart.

3. Practice controlled breathing.

4. As you continue to practice controlled breathing, remind yourself of the medical realities relevant to the bodily sensations you're experiencing. For example, if you feel light-headed or dizzy after rapid breathing, remind yourself that this is a temporary and harmless sensation caused by

reduced oxygen to the brain. Or if you have a rapid heart rate after running in place, remind yourself that a healthy heart can beat two hundred times per minute for weeks without damage, so it's certainly capable of handling this little bit of exercise.

5. Continue doing trials for that exercise until your anxiety rating is no more than 25 when you do it without a support person present, indicating that you've become desensitized to that particular sensation.

6. Repeat steps 1 through 5 for each item on your hierarchy, working your way up step-by-step.

If you have difficulty desensitizing during interoceptive exposure, it may be because you have catastrophic thoughts that haven't been addressed. As you begin an exposure exercise, monitor your thoughts about the bodily sensations that come up. What are you telling yourself? What terrible thing do you fear might happen? What is the worst possible outcome? Once you've identified one or more catastrophic beliefs, complete a Probability Form. Then review the "Evidence" and "Coping alternatives" columns to identify realistic responses that you can use during exposure.

Sandra began the desensitization process with her best friend present. She started with the first exercise on her hierarchy: staring at herself in the mirror. It took fifty seconds to set off some of her familiar feelings of unreality, and she stuck with the exercise for another minute. After each trial, Sandra immediately initiated breath control. She reminded herself that feelings of unreality were harmless fight-or-flight reactions triggered by reduced oxygen to the brain.

By trial 3, Sandra's anxiety intensity was down to 20, so it was time for her to face the feeling alone. In her first trial alone, her anxiety jumped to 40 again, but in trial 5 it reduced to 20 once again, indicating she was ready to move on to the next exercise, holding her breath, which felt easier than she'd expected. After one trial with her friend present, she continued alone until her anxiety dipped below 25. Breath control helped her relax quickly after each trial, and also offered the helpful reminder that she could easily remedy the out-of-breath feeling by inhaling deeply.

Sandra's greatest challenge during interoceptive desensitization was rapid breathing. The spacey, unreal feelings it induced deeply frightened her. On the second trial her anxiety intensity was 90, even though her friend held her hand. It took eight trials with her friend present before it went down to 25, then she did the exercise alone for four more trials. She learned to remind herself during the exercise that her scary feelings were just brief effects from hyperventilation and the fight-or-flight response, and that with a few minutes of controlled breathing, they'd be over.

As Sandra developed more trust in her ability to calm herself after rapid breathing, the feelings became far less scary. Instead of fearing that she might lose control, she saw hyperventilation as something uncomfortable but manageable.

During all of the exercises, Sandra found that her greatest problem was a tendency to catastrophize. She was aware of saying to herself, "I can't stand this" and "This is too much." But working with the Probability Form had helped her learn to talk back to these thoughts. As she proceeded through her hierarchy, she was increasingly able to reassure herself with the thought "I can stand anything for a few minutes. It can't really harm me."

INTEROCEPTIVE DESENSITIZATION IN REAL-LIFE SETTINGS

After you've used induced interoceptive exposure to desensitize to physical symptoms of panic and none of the exercises triggers an anxiety rating greater than 25, you can practice desensitization in real-life settings. With medical clearance, you can begin practicing exposure to activities and experiences you've avoided because you feared a panic attack. Make a list of these activities and arrange them on an Exposure Hierarchy and Anxiety Intensity Chart, again ranking them from least anxiety-evoking to most. Then proceed as in stage 3 above.

To help illustrate the process, we'll continue with Sandra as an example. Her desensitization hierarchy for real-life settings appears below. When a coworker asked Sandra to lunch, she accepted and used the opportunity as her first exercise in desensitizing to her fear of going to restaurants, the easiest item on her hierarchy. While at lunch, she used both controlled breathing and helpful items from her Probability Form to cope. Since her main fear in the restaurant was feeling spacey and unreal, Sandra reminded herself that it was a harmless feeling and wouldn't be noticed by her companion. Using similar strategies, Sandra worked through all of the items on her hierarchy, doing however many trials were needed to bring the anxiety intensity for each down to 25 or below.

When Sandra reached the end of her hierarchy, she felt far less afraid of panic, in part because she'd gone several weeks without having a panic attack, but also because she no longer watched for and feared sensations she'd always associated with panic. Now her heart could beat fast without scaring her, and she could feel hot or spacey without the clutching anxiety that a panic attack was near.

Sandra's Exposure Hierarchy and Anxiety Intensity Chart

Exercise	Trial 1	Trial 2	Trial 3	Trial 4	Trial 5	Trial 6	Trial 7	Trial 8
1. Going to restaurants	35	30	20					
2. Drinking coffee	50	30	35	25				
3. Brisk one-mile walk on a cool day	55	40	15					
4. Brisk one-mile walk on a hot day while wearing a jacket	65	60	50	35	25			
5. Running uphill	80	55	25	30	20			

CHAPTER 8

Coping Imagery

Coping imagery (Freeman 1990) is a blend of brief exposure (chapter 13) and covert modeling (chapter 18). It combines the best features of both to enhance performance in problematic situations while simultaneously lowering anxiety. It involves identifying the detailed sequence of events that makes up a problematic situation—everything you do from beginning to end in the situation—and determining which elements of the sequence are the most anxiety evoking. Then you rehearse performing the entire sequence while using specific relaxation techniques and coping thoughts to lower anxiety at crucial junctures in the sequence. Finally, you apply your coping imagery to real-life situations. More specifically, coping imagery will help you do the following:

- See yourself successfully handling an anxiety-arousing situation, perhaps one you have avoided for a long time.

- Prepare relaxation and cognitive coping strategies specifically tailored for this situation.

- Rehearse and refine your coping strategies at crucial anxiety-arousing points as the situation unfolds. This builds your confidence that you can reduce your anxiety response in vivo (in real life).

- Prepare for each step in the sequence that you will perform in real life.

SYMPTOM EFFECTIVENESS

Coping imagery is most effective at reducing anxiety and avoidance symptoms associated with an existing problematic situation. It can be used to reduce avoidance behavior due to phobias and performance anxiety and to increase assertiveness. Coping imagery can also be helpful in reducing the procrastination, resentment, and depression that often result when you don't cope successfully with specific anxiety-provoking situations.

Coping imagery relies on your ability to conceive clear and detailed images. If it is difficult for you to achieve clear visual images, the alternative is to create a detailed image using auditory or physical impressions. If either approach enables you to clearly imagine the scene, you can successfully use this technique.

TIME TO MASTERY

You may get results after as few as six to eight fifteen-minute sessions.

INSTRUCTIONS

Coping imagery involves six simple steps that you can master with regular practice:

1. Learn relaxation skills.

2. Write a narrative describing a problematic situation.

3. Identify the stress points in the situation.

4. Plan coping strategies for each stress point.

5. Rehearse applying your coping strategies.

6. Use your coping strategies in real life.

Step 1: Learn Relaxation Skills

To use the approach in this chapter, you need to master cue-controlled relaxation, from chapter 5. Cue-controlled relaxation builds on other relaxation skills, so you must first learn and practice progressive muscle relaxation and relaxation without tension. Don't proceed past step 4 here until you have learned and practiced each of these skills. We suggest that you "overlearn" cue-controlled relaxation to the point where you can do it automatically. Eventually, you should be able to attain deep muscle relaxation in two minutes or less. The more you practice, the more quickly you'll be able to relax and the deeper your relaxation will be.

Step 2: Write a Narrative Describing a Problematic Situation

Even while learning relaxation skills, you can take additional steps to prepare for using coping imagery. Right now, choose a real-life situation that makes you anxious—something you want or need to do but also tend to avoid or struggle with. It can be anything from going to job interviews or visiting your critical in-laws to making a date or explaining your needs to an angry friend.

Ask yourself how and why this situation makes you anxious. What particular aspects of the situation are most difficult for you to deal with? What are your worst fears about what might happen? At which points do your emotions feel most out of control? The answers to these questions are not always clear, particularly if you're facing a complex situation. However, the more you understand the situation you're facing, the easier it will be to cope.

Begin by writing out the sequence of events that make up the problematic situation. Write it in the form of a narrative, using as much detail as possible. The sequence should start with your anticipation of the situation, then move on to describe the opening of the scene, and continue until the situation is resolved. We recommend that you include two possible conclusions to the scenario, one negative and one positive. This will allow you to prepare for either possibility so you can minimize surprises. The most important details to include are those aspects of the situation that make you anxious. Also include how the anxiety affects you, and be specific: What are your physical and emotional responses? How and why are these responses intensified by the scene? (We've included two example narratives, one in the next section and the other near the end of the chapter.)

Step 3: Identify the Stress Points in the Situation

Next, use your narrative to identify the particular parts of the sequence that are most stressful to you. An effective way to do this is through visualization. Record yourself reading the narrative slowly. Include both of your alternative conclusions. Then play it back while sitting in a relaxed state, eyes closed, with all of your attention focused on creating the scene in your mind. Alternatively, you could have a friend slowly read the sequence to you while you visualize the scene.

The object is to experience the scene as vividly and in as much detail as possible. Where are you? Who is present there? Is it warm or cool? What sounds can you hear in the distance? What scents surround you? Engage as many senses as you can to create the scene in your mind. Using all five senses makes your scene much more vivid. (See "Special Considerations" in chapter 16, "Changing Core Beliefs with Visualization," for more help with creating vivid imagery.) Continue through the sequence, paying close attention to the physical and emotional reactions you experience. Common symptoms of anxiety include tense muscles, increased heart rate, and quickened respiration.

When you come to a segment of the sequence where you experience elevated anxiety, make a mental note of it. After you've imagined the entire scenario, mark each of these points in your narrative with an asterisk. These are stress points. Later, when you visualize the sequence, these will be points where you pause to do special relaxation and coping exercises.

Here's a narrative written by Dave, a lawyer specializing in nonprofit governance who had to give a presentation at a workshop for board members of various charities in his region. A senior partner in his firm usually gave this kind of talk, and Dave felt a lot of pressure when asked to speak in the partner's place. Though Dave felt confident in his interactions with individuals, the thought of standing before a group was frightening. To prepare for the presentation, Dave wrote out the sequence of events as he imagined it would go, including two possible conclusions, one negative and one positive. After recording this narrative, he listened to it and visualized the situation from beginning to end. Afterward, he marked all of the stress points with an asterisk.

I'm on my way to the presentation, hoping it goes well but imagining making embarrassing mistakes.* In my mind, I'm picturing people whispering in the audience during my presentation. I arrive in the parking lot and experience another wave of worry as I see the building where I'll give the presentation.* I go through the front door and greet the receptionist. As I wait for the elevator, I check my briefcase to see if all of my papers are in order. I have another wave of anxiety as I look at the file folder containing the outline of my presentation.* I ride the elevator up to the third floor and then walk toward the room. I recognize several people in the hall and try not to appear nervous as I greet them. I stand outside the meeting room, saying hello as people arrive. I set up the mike and adjust the tabletop podium. Most of the people have arrived now, and they're looking at me expectantly.* I glance down at my outline and have a wave of concern about the coherence and usefulness of the material.*

I clear my throat, which quiets the room substantially, and greet the audience: "Glad you could make it."* I'm aware of the sound of my voice as everyone becomes silent. All eyes are on me.* I begin with my introduction, trying to stay focused on what I'm saying. At one point during the presentation, I lose my place in the outline and have to stop for a moment to reorient myself. The silence is heavy in the room, and I imagine that people are doubting my competence.* My face feels flushed, and I worry that my nervousness is apparent. I continue my presentation, aware of people shifting in their chairs and mumbling in the back of the room. As I continue, I begin to feel anxious about the question-and-answer period that grows closer as I near the end of my presentation.* I wrap it up as best I can and invite everyone's feedback.

Possible Conclusion 1: I open the floor for comments or questions, but people seem hesitant to respond.* There's a long silence during which I feel at a loss for what to say next. Someone finally offers feedback by questioning the usefulness of the information. I feel embarrassed and hurt but struggle not to respond defensively.* The next question is about something only mildly related to the subject matter, and I am unable to answer it. There is another long silence before I finally thank the group and begin to put my papers away. I am eager to get back to my car and hope that I can put the whole experience behind me.

Possible Conclusion 2: People seem pleased with the presentation, and several people offer feedback. Their questions are pertinent, allowing me to explain aspects that needed clarification. I feel very relieved that it's over and that I made it through successfully. I congratulate myself for managing my fear and anxiety.

Step 4: Plan Coping Strategies for Each Stress Point

Most anxiety-provoking situations are made up of several combined stresses. In Dave's case, the stresses that contributed to his anxiety included the pressure of an audience, his own doubts about the content of his presentation, and his discomfort with appearing uneasy and scared.

One of the main goals in writing out a narrative and identifying the stress points is to demystify the sources of anxiety. If you can see the situation as a combination of smaller stresses, your anxiety will be much easier to understand and manage.

Anxiety reactions have two basic components: a physiological stress response and thoughts that interpret a situation as dangerous. Therefore, coping imagery must include a method of physical relaxation as well as a set of statements that are calming and reassuring to you.

RELAXATION

As you visualize the sequence, use cue-controlled relaxation with deep breathing at each stress point.

COGNITIVE COPING STATEMENTS

You also need to develop cognitive coping statements for each stress point in your sequence. Effective coping statements remind you that you have the ability to handle the situation and may offer specific strategies to deal with problems. Here are some examples of effective statements: "There's no need to panic; I can get through this," "It doesn't need to be perfect; my best is good enough," "It will be over in a few minutes," "I have a plan if there's a problem," and "I know how to do this." You'll find that each stress point carries its own set of worries. Try to find statements for each that really address and relieve the worry in that moment.

Here are some important functions that cognitive coping statements can serve:

- Emphasizing that you have a plan to cope and specifying what the plan is in that situation

- Reassuring you that there's no need to panic, that you have the skills to cope with the situation

- Helping you remind yourself just to relax away stress

- Asserting that a catastrophic fear isn't true and providing a more realistic assessment of the worst that could happen

- Lowering unreasonably high expectations

- Instructing yourself to stop focusing on catastrophic thoughts and instead get down to meeting the challenge.

Here are a few examples of coping statements that Dave developed for the stress points in his narrative:

- *Imagining making embarrassing mistakes.*

  "Relax, breathe deeply. It's okay to make some mistakes. I will be satisfied with my best effort."

- *Another wave of worry as I see the building where I'll give the presentation.*

  "I can do this. It's okay to feel scared. Just keep breathing."

- *The silence is heavy in the room, and I imagine that people are doubting my competence.*

  "Take a deep breath, relax. I know my stuff. I'll just pick up where I left off."

- *I begin to feel anxious about the question-and-answer period.*

  "Relax. The hard part is over. I made it this far, just hang in there until the end."

- *I feel embarrassed and hurt but struggle not to respond defensively.*

  "My best is good enough. I can accept criticism. I know I'm okay."

See chapter 13, "Brief Exposure," for more examples of coping statements and how to develop them. Record your narrative once again, this time including instructions for cue-controlled relaxation and specific coping thoughts at each stress point. As you make the recording, give yourself time at the stress points to relax and let your coping thoughts sink in.

Step 5: Rehearse Applying Your Coping Strategies

Now it's time to listen to your recorded narrative while using your coping strategies. The goal of this step is to keep practicing the sequence until your anxiety is below 4 on a scale of 0 to 10, where 0 means no anxiety at all and 10 is the highest level of anxiety you've ever experienced. It's not necessary to bring your anxiety level down to 0, but you should reduce it. Keep in mind that some stress points in your narrative may be more difficult to cope with than others. The key word here is "practice." As you hone your coping skills and get more familiar with the procedure, your coping strategies will become increasingly effective.

If after a few repetitions you don't feel any reduction in anxiety, you may need to revise your coping strategy. Here are a couple of recommendations for doing so:

- **Devote more practice to your relaxation skills.** Relaxation is critical to the effectiveness of your coping efforts. Make sure that the cue-controlled relaxation is, in fact, helping you to relax. If not, you may need to focus on practicing it separately for a period of time.

- **Review your coping statements.** Sometimes it's hard to pinpoint what the real source of anxiety is at each stress point. It's possible that some of your coping statements aren't addressing the main elements that are making you anxious. Practicing the sequence will help you identify which statements you need to rewrite and what you need to add to make them more effective.

Step 6: Use Your Coping Strategies in Real Life

The final step in mastering coping imagery is applying it to real-life situations. When you can visualize the entire sequence while successfully reducing your level of anxiety at each stress point, you're ready to approach the situation in vivo. Of course, you'll have less control over your environment in real situations than you had during your visualizations, but you need not feel out of control. One of the most important skills you've learned from this technique is how to stay in control of your emotional and physical reactions. Feelings and tension that used to trigger fear can now be seen as cues to relax and encourage yourself.

If possible, use your new coping strategies with a mildly to moderately stressful situation at first. Because real-life situations are usually more difficult to cope with than visualizations, one of your priorities should be avoiding feeling overwhelmed. Allow yourself time for practice, and expect a few setbacks before your coping strategies feel totally comfortable and effective in real life.

As with each of the prior steps in this technique, practice is the key to success. As you become more adept at using coping imagery in actual situations, it may become a significant resource for you in dealing with many different sources of stress.

Example

For as long as Susan could remember, she dreaded dentist visits. The fear that she experienced every time she was due for an appointment often caused her to avoid needed dental work for months. The longer she avoided seeing the dentist, the more she dreaded it and the harder it became to face the inevitable. In an attempt to break that downward spiral, she set out to overcome some of her fear about visiting the dentist. While she was learning cue-controlled relaxation, she wrote a narrative describing what she expected would happen when she finally went to the dentist, then recorded herself reading it slowly. Later, when she had plenty of time and no distractions, she used the recording to visualize the entire sequence and mentally noted each part of the narrative that elevated her anxiety, then marked each with an asterisk. Here is her narrative:

I'm in my car, on the way to the dentist. My teeth are freshly brushed and flossed. My tongue feels around for the swollen parts of my gums that were bleeding slightly when I brushed this morning. I think about the weeks I neglected to floss and imagine the dentist will know immediately how irresponsible I've been.* I know that whatever dental problems I have are worse now that I'm two months late for an appointment. I scold myself for being the kind of person who cannot handle basic adult responsibilities. As I near the office building, I become irritable with the traffic around me* and feel my stress level start to increase.

As I park the car and approach the building,* I am already rehearsing excuses for the dentist as to why I waited so long to come in. I decide not to take the crowded elevator because I'm afraid the waiting will make me more anxious and irritable. The empty staircase gives me a moment to myself. I listen to my footsteps echo in the staircase, trying to disconnect myself from what I'm doing. The *receptionist recognizes me as I enter the office and instructs me to sit down. I am acutely aware of the smell of disinfectant and nitrous oxide,* which gives me a slight feeling of nausea. I attempt to read a magazine, but it isn't enough to draw my attention from the sound of the drill coming from down the hall. The longer I sit waiting, the more anxious I become. In my mind I can hear the dentist's voice as he peers into my mouth: "Oh no! we've got some problems."**

I can see the receptionist joking around with another woman behind the desk. I'm irritated with her lack of empathy, and I feel more isolated in my fear and anxiety. The assistant calls my name* in a happy, singsong voice. I try not to look resentful as she leads me to a room. I lie back in the chair. The sound of the chair moving is cold and electric.* I hope that I lessen the impact by describing the condition of my mouth before she looks at it.

Now I am in the chair, head back and mouth open, feeling robbed of all my power and dignity. I can feel the assistant's pointed instrument moving across my teeth and gums. I know when she's getting close to a sore spot,* and I tighten my whole body in anticipation of the pain. When she hits it, I jump.* I imagine that makes her angry. After scribbling some notes, she explains to me regretfully that I have a lot of plaque that should have been removed sooner. Some of my pockets are deeper, and there's been some bone loss.* Now she's getting ready to clean my teeth. Out of the corner of my eye, I can see the metal tray containing the instruments. My whole body is tense, and my jaw is starting to ache from holding it open.* I can feel her latex gloves and hear the scraping of the metal instrument on my teeth.

Possible Conclusion 1. She finishes and calls in the dentist. I listen as she describes everything she found wrong with my teeth and gums. He nods and glances at me occasionally. My mouth is inspected again.* He too expresses his regret that I didn't come in sooner. They both explain the importance of flossing.* I feel humiliated, as though I'm being treated like a child. I can't wait to get out of there so I can be a real person again. The assistant hands me some free floss and a toothbrush and leads me to the receptionist to set a time for my next appointment. I leave with a sense of relief that it's over.

Possible Conclusion 2. She finishes and calls in the dentist. He reviews the notes the assistant made and carefully checks my mouth for himself. He explains that with daily flossing and brushing correctly, I can reverse a lot of the damage. He gives me some special mouthwash that will help get things under control again. He tells me to have a nice day, and I walk out to the receptionist to make an appointment. I feel relieved upon leaving, and I'm filled with hope that next time may not be as bad.

Next, Susan wrote out a set of coping statements that addressed the particular fears and worries that intensified her anxiety at each stress point. Here are some examples of her statements:

- *I…imagine the dentist will know immediately how irresponsible I've been.*

  "I forgive myself. I do the best I can. He will be a good source of information."

- *I am acutely aware of the smell of disinfectant and nitrous oxide.*

  "I made it all the way here. I can get through this. I'll relax my stomach."

- *I tighten my whole body in anticipation of the pain.*

  "Breathe deeply. Relax. It's almost over. It's worth a little pain to get my teeth really clean."

- *I feel humiliated, as though I'm being treated like a child.*

  "I forgive myself. They say the same thing to everyone. I made it through. I'm glad it's finally over."

With her coping statements completed, Susan was ready to rehearse her sequence. She recorded her narrative again, this time including a reminder to use cue-controlled relaxation and specific coping thoughts at each stress point. After four repetitions, Susan had successfully reduced her anxiety at most stress points to about 5 on the 0 to 10 scale. However, two of the stress points remained at about 9. The next time she visualized the sequence, she paid extra attention to the feelings she was experiencing at those two stress points. She experimented with different coping statements and found alternatives that were more effective in reducing her anxiety. After ten days of practice, her anxiety ratings never exceeded 4 and she felt confident enough to call the dentist and schedule an appointment.

CHAPTER 9

Mindfulness

Mindfulness is the practice of observing your experience in a nonjudgmental, compassionate, and accepting manner. It begins with simple awareness, paying attention to your experience from moment to moment. You can be mindful of your inner world—your thoughts, emotions, and physical sensations—as well as the external world.

As you practice mindfulness, you realize that all of your sensations, thoughts, and emotions, both painful and pleasant, are transitory. They come and go, independent of a part of you that is not your sensations, thoughts, and emotions. When you step back and notice this process from the perspective of a friendly, impartial observer, you become aware of your own biases and gain a fresher, clearer picture of each unfolding moment. Rather than automatically responding to negative thoughts and floundering in a sea of negative emotions, you can calmly observe the distortions and fallacies of your thinking and their impact on your feelings. This often naturally leads to making wiser choices.

Mindfulness was developed centuries ago by Buddhists in Asia as a central technique in several types of meditation. In the West, mindfulness has been studied by medical researcher and author Jon Kabat-Zinn, who founded the Stress Reduction Program at the University of Massachusetts and developed mindfulness-based stress reduction (MBSR; Kabat-Zinn 1990). Mindfulness is also a core skill in acceptance and commitment therapy, mindfulness-based cognitive therapy, and dialectical behavior therapy.

SYMPTOM EFFECTIVENESS

In clinical studies, mindfulness has been shown to significantly reduce anxiety and panic (Kabat-Zinn et al. 1992), depression, and anger, as well as confusion among cancer patients (Speca et al. 2000), and chronic pain (Kabat-Zinn et al. 1986). Mindfulness has also been helpful in reducing symptoms of stress (Astin 1997), psoriasis (Kabat-Zinn et al. 1998), binge eating (Kristeller 1999), and fibromyalgia (Kaplan, Goldenberg, and Galvin-Nadeau 1993). Mindfulness is also used as part of the treatment program for worry, phobias, and interpersonal conflict.

TIME TO MASTERY

You can begin practicing mindfulness and enjoying its benefits immediately. The more you practice, the more skill you'll gain and the more you'll get out of it. Since the ultimate goal of mindfulness is to be fully aware in every moment of your waking life, you can never really master mindfulness. However, since the chief benefit of the practice comes from refocusing your mind on the here and now after your attention has wandered, you can experience benefits from mindfulness for the rest of your life.

INSTRUCTIONS

There are two main paths to developing mindfulness: observing your body and observing your thoughts. This chapter offers many techniques for each approach. Begin by practicing mindfulness of the breath. Breathing is the foundation of any form of meditation and serves as an excellent point of focus as you train your mind to observe one thing at a time. Once you've worked with mindful breathing for a while, move on to the other practices, working through them sequentially. Try each several times and assess which are the best fit for you, then focus on those practices. Because developing mindfulness is a lifelong endeavor, you may want to revisit this chapter from time to time and try working with alternative practices.

Observing Your Body

The shortest path to mindfulness is observing your body. By consciously paying attention to processes that are normally unconscious, like breathing, you become mindful of your physical existence in the moment. Breathing deeply, counting or labeling your breaths, or just noticing sensations that you usually ignore can offer simple but profound rewards. After you've worked with mindfulness of the breath for a while, you can begin to shift your awareness to other physical sensations with Body Scanning. Then move on to the Inner-Outer Shuttle, a practice that will help you fine-tune your ability to tell the difference between your internal bodily sensations and external sensory experience.

MINDFUL BREATHING

Breathing mindfully is the best way to begin practicing mindfulness. To start, lie down on your back and close your eyes. Place one hand on your chest and the other on your belly. Take slow breaths and breathe deeply into the bottom of your lungs, so that your belly rises and your chest stays relatively still.

If you have trouble keeping your breath low, gently push down on your belly with your hand. Apply light pressure and try to push your hand away with each breath. (This is essentially the same as Abdominal Breathing, in chapter 5.)

When your breathing settles into a regular rhythm, observe as much detail about your breath as you can. Notice the coolness of the air as it flows into your nostrils, down the back of your throat, and into your lungs. Be aware of how your diaphragm feels as it sinks with each inhalation. Feel how much warmer the exhaled air is as it carries a fraction of your body heat with it. Focus on every detail you can tease out of the simple act of deep breathing.

Finally, add a repeated thought, or mantra. For example, as you breathe in, you might say, "Live this moment," to yourself, and as you breathe out, you might say, "Accept this moment." Use any word or short phrase that is meaningful to you. As you practice breathing mindfully day after day, you can change your mantra to reflect current concerns or what you want from a particular session.

Understand that your mind will wander; that's natural. Random thoughts are bound to intrude. When it happens, just start over, establishing a smooth rhythm, paying attention to the sensory details, and mentally repeating your mantra.

Practice breathing mindfully twice a day for about a week, and notice how it changes your mood and thoughts.

BREATH COUNTING

Initially, practice counting your breaths while lying or sitting quietly. Later, you'll be able to do this technique almost anytime or anywhere—while walking, working, riding the bus, and so on. At the beginning of the first inhalation, mentally label it "In one." As soon as you start to exhale, label that as "Out one." As you start to breathe in again, mentally say, "In two," and as you start to exhale, mentally say, "Out two." Continue until you get to four. Then start over at one.

Four complete breaths are about as many as most beginners can keep track of with good concentration. You may find that you're easily distracted and lose track of where you are. You may even think, "This is stupid. Why am I wasting my time?" If that happens, just refocus your mind and start over at one.

Because this exercise is simple and unobtrusive, you can practice it in busy, noisy environments when you want to calm yourself by becoming more mindful.

BREATH LABELING

Some people don't like counting their breaths or get so relaxed that they lose count easily. Others just like to make a sound while doing breathing exercises. In all of these cases, labeling the breath out loud is a good alternative.

You can practice this technique with your eyes open or closed. Get comfortable and breathe in. As you inhale, whisper to yourself, "Innnnnnn," drawing the word out as long as the inhalation. If you like to pause between inhale and exhale, do so and say, "Hold," to yourself. Then exhale and whisper, "Ooooouuuut," drawing the word out as long as the exhalation lasts. Pause and say, "Hold," if you like and continue in this way: "Innnnn… Hold… Ouuuut… Hold… Innnn… Hold… Ouuuut… Hold…" and so on.

For this exercise, don't try to regulate your breathing rate or keep a steady rhythm. Just let your breath come naturally. Practice for two or three minutes at a time, noticing how your breathing slows down and speeds up and how the words tend to lose their meaning if you repeat them long enough. You can also do this exercise when other people are around by just barely moving your lips and not making any sound. Try it for just one or two cycles of breath for a quick relaxer.

BODY SCANNING

Once you've practiced breathing mindfully for a while, you can begin to extend your mindful awareness throughout your body.

Lie on your back and close your eyes. Take a few deep, slow breaths and let your attention drift down to your toes. Wiggle them around and just notice how they feel. Are they warm or cool? Are your shoes tight, or are your feet bare? Rotate your ankles and flex your feet back and forth. Notice how the complex bones, tendons, and muscles in your feet feel.

Scan upward to your calves and shins and knees. Notice how they feel: the texture of your clothing against your skin, the ambient temperature, the pressure where the backs of your calves rest on the surface you're lying on. Do you have any aches and pains? Itches or tingling sensations? You can scratch or shift or just lie there and notice the sensations.

Move your attention up to your pelvis and lower back. Is there any stiffness or discomfort? Tilt your pelvis back and forth a little and notice how that feels. How much is your back arched? How does your bottom settle into the surface it's resting on?

Now scan your chest and belly as you breathe in and out. Place one hand on your chest and the other on your belly. Notice how they move in relation to each other. Notice how your torso feels as your diaphragm moves downward and upward and your lungs fill with air and then expel it. Does your chest feel loose and open or tight and constricted? Are there any sensations of warmth or pressure?

Shift your attention to your fingers. Wiggle them around. Rub your fingertips together. Are they smooth or rough? Make a fist and bend your wrists back and forth, then around in a circle. How do your fingers and hands feel? Put your hands by your sides and feel the texture of the surface you're lying on.

Move your attention up your arms to your shoulders. Bend your elbows a little and shrug. Notice any pain or tension that you carry in your arms or shoulders. Then become aware of your neck. Roll your head in slow motion from side to side and notice all the subtle sensations in your neck as your spine and tendons and muscles interact. Can you hear faint clicks and liquid sounds as your neck twists?

Stop rolling your head and let it come to rest. Feel its weight and how it meets the surface you're lying on. Notice the overall sensation of temperature. Does your head feel warm or cool or neutral? Notice if you have any trace of headache or sinus pressure.

Now observe your face. Is your brow frowning or is it smooth and soft? Are your eyelids resting lightly over your eyes, or does it take a bit of effort to keep your eyes shut? Are you breathing through your nose or mouth? How does your nose or mouth feel as your breathing moves air in and out? Are your teeth touching or apart? How does your tongue lie in your mouth? You can spend a lot of time observing what is going on in your face.

As you scan your body, random thoughts will intrude. They may pertain to your body, the exercise, or something entirely different. They may be negative, positive, or just plain irrelevant:

- *God, I'm so fat.*

- *I should get more exercise.*

- *My thighs are still good.*

- *This is boring.*

- *I'm getting old.*

- *Don't forget to buy bread.*

- *My skin is so dry.*

- *I'm pretty good at this.*

- *Scrawny, no muscles.*

- *I'm too fidgety for this.*

- *I wish Randy would call.*

- *This isn't working.*

- *I'll never get this right.*

Whenever thoughts intrude, and whatever those thoughts may be, just notice that you've been distracted by a thought and refocus on the exercise. Later, these thoughts themselves will become the object of mindfulness.

INNER-OUTER SHUTTLE

Inner-Outer Shuttle is a valuable variation on Body Scanning in which you focus on distinguishing between internal bodily sensations and outside sensory experiences. This will help you become more mindful of your environment and how your body reacts to it.

Sit quietly in a chair and close your eyes. Start as before by scanning your body and noticing one aspect of how you feel inside: how full your stomach feels, for instance. Then shift your awareness to a sensation coming from outside your body, such as the texture of the arm of the chair. Switch back to an interior sensation, like a tight muscle in your calf. Then go outside and notice a sensation such as the heat of the sun on your hand. Switch to interior awareness and realize that you're a little thirsty. Then look outward and hear the sound of the neighbor's dog barking. Keep shuttling back and forth for three minutes: inner, outer, inner, outer.

By shuttling rapidly from interior to exterior sensation, you sharpen your awareness in general. You notice that some sensations are subtle and ambiguous. Is a piece of food stuck in your teeth an internal or external sensation? What about a lingering taste in your mouth or stinging cheeks upon entering a heated room on a frigid winter day?

More important, doing this exercise makes you notice the noticer: the "you" that is separate from your sensations. Unpleasant sensations like a headache or loud noises are not you. They don't define you. They are just sensations that will pass and be replaced by other sensations.

Observing Your Thoughts

White Room is a powerful exercise to help you identify and detach from judgmental thoughts. Inner Shuttling helps you refine your awareness of internal sensations, emotions, and thoughts. Building on the awareness you develop in these exercises, Conveyor Belt and Wise Mind Diagram train you to step back from, observe, and objectively label the entirety of your experience in the here and now.

WHITE ROOM

White Room is a practice in which you observe your mind at work, imagining that your mind is a white room through which your thoughts pass. You can do the exercise in any quiet place, sitting or lying down. Close your eyes and begin by taking several slow, deep breaths. Keep your breathing slow and steady throughout the exercise.

Imagine that you are in a white room of medium size with two doors. Thoughts enter by the front door and leave by the back door. As each thought enters, pay close attention to it and label it as either "judging" or "nonjudging."

Watch each thought attentively, curiously, and compassionately until it leaves. Don't try to analyze it beyond noticing whether it is judgmental or not. Don't argue with it or believe it or disbelieve it. Just acknowledge that it is a thought, a brief moment in your mental life, a passing visitor to the white room.

Beware of the thoughts you label as "judging." They will try to hook you, to make you buy into the judgment. The whole point of this exercise is to notice how sticky judgmental thoughts are—how they can get stuck in your mind and be hard to shake off. You'll know that you're entertaining a troublesome, judgmental thought if it stays in the white room for a long time or you start feeling emotional about it.

As best you can, stay aware of your breathing and keep it steady, continue to visualize the white room and the doors, and keep watching and labeling your thoughts. Remember that a thought is just a thought. You are so much more than your thoughts. You are the being who is creating the white room through which the thoughts are allowed to pass. You've had a million thoughts that are now gone, and you are still here. A thought doesn't require you to do anything. A thought doesn't mean you believe it. A thought isn't you.

Just observe your thoughts as they pass through the white room. Allow them to have their brief life and tell yourself that your thoughts are okay as they are, even the judgmental ones. Just acknowledge them, let them leave when they're ready, and be prepared to greet the next thought—and the next, and the next.

Keep observing and labeling until you genuinely feel detached from your thoughts. Persist until even the judgmental thoughts flow through the room without lingering.

INNER SHUTTLING

Inner Shuttling is similar to Inner-Outer Shuttle, but in this case you shuttle between physical sensations and emotions, and then between thoughts and emotions.

Start by sitting quietly and breathing deeply and slowly. Close your eyes and scan your body for the first physical sensation that comes up. Perhaps your feet are hot and tired. Then scan your inner landscape for an emotional feeling. Perhaps you're feeling a little sad. Now switch back to a physical feeling, then an emotional one, and so on for two or three minutes.

Some people like to do this exercise with their eyes open, jotting notes on a piece of paper to keep track of what they detect as they shuttle from the physical to the emotional.

Physical Sensation	Emotion
Feet hurt	Sad
Tingling earlobes	Depressed
Upset stomach	Irritable
Tight shoulders	Still irritable, grouchy

After a couple of minutes, vary the practice by shuttling between thoughts and emotions.

Thought	Emotion
Dinner is late.	Angry
She doesn't care.	Pissed off
I must have disappointed her.	Guilty
Maybe I'm overreacting.	Confused

Try to maintain a compassionate, nonjudging attitude during this exercise. When you shuttle from physical sensations to emotions, or from thoughts to emotions, you train yourself in noticing two things: first, that unpleasant thoughts tend to precede unpleasant emotions, and second, that your observing self can remain somewhat detached from painful experiences, thoughts, and emotions.

CONVEYOR BELT

In this exercise, you practice noticing and labeling whatever passes through your mind, as if your mind were a conveyor belt moving from the present into the past. Close your eyes and breathe slowly and deeply. Imagine that you're looking down on a slow conveyor belt that is passing from right to left.

Take a moment to visualize the rubber surface of the belt, noticing what color it is and how wide it is. Imagine hearing the low hum of an electric motor. Keep this image in the back of your mind.

Now open your mind to whatever comes up first. Whatever occurs to you, give it a descriptive label: Here are some suggestions:

Thought	Memory	Feeling
Urge	Desire	Regret
Yearning	Image	Impulse
Feeling	Wish	Plan
Idea		

Use your own labels if these don't seem accurate. As soon as you've decided on a label, imagine it is printed on a small block of wood. Place the block on the conveyor belt and allow it to be carried away into the past. Then let the next thought or feeling or whatever come up, label it on a block, and let the conveyor belt carry it to the past.

Doing this exercise helps you observe your mind and categorize its ramblings without getting caught up in the content or falling into habitual mental patterns.

WISE MIND DIAGRAM

Sometimes painful memories, thoughts, feelings, and impulses are so tightly packed together in your mind that you cannot easily separate them in eyes-closed exercises like shuttling or the conveyor belt. For example, Josh was tormented by the memory of his breakup with his girlfriend, Haley. He had stopped by her apartment to check whether he'd left his iPod there and saw a strange car in the driveway. He walked in on Haley and a big, handsome stranger making out on the couch. Josh smashed a lamp and ran out of the apartment, slamming the door so hard he wrenched his shoulder. He broke up with Haley in a tearful and shouting phone call later that day.

Over the next few days, when Josh tried to do mindfulness exercises, images of that day flashed across his mind, interspersed with pain in his shoulder, explosions of orange fire, and a sound like an earthquake. It was like an experimental movie—very impressionistic but hard to separate into components that could be labeled. So Josh decided to sort out his traumatic memories by drawing a Wise Mind Diagram—a simple but effective technique for teasing apart thoughts, feelings, and actions.

Wise Mind Diagram

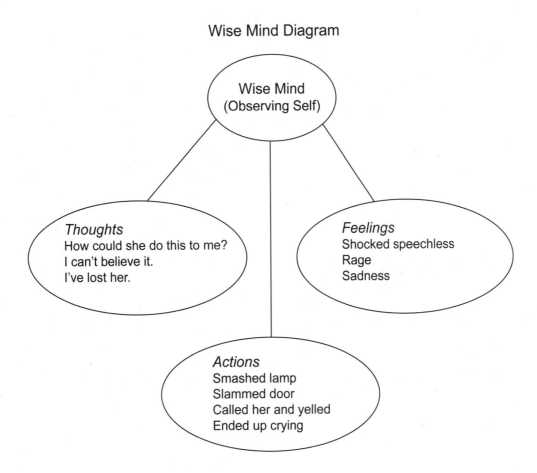

In an early version of his diagram, Josh had an oval labeled "Impulses" in which he wrote, "Kill Haley. Kill myself." He felt guilty and ashamed of these impulses, but because he never acted on them, he decided they didn't count and erased them. Everybody has impulses that never become actions. It's the actions you actually take that count. Laying out his reaction in this way helped Josh separate himself from his thoughts, feelings, and actions enough to gain some perspective on one of the worst days of his life.

If you tried the eyes-closed exercises and had trouble labeling your thoughts, emotions, memories, urges, and so on, try creating a Wise Mind Diagram (using the blank version on the next page) to help separate out the different aspects of your experience. The most important space is the "Wise Mind" space. It reminds you that you are an observing self who is separate from your thoughts, separate from your feelings, and even separate from your actions.

Wise Mind Diagram

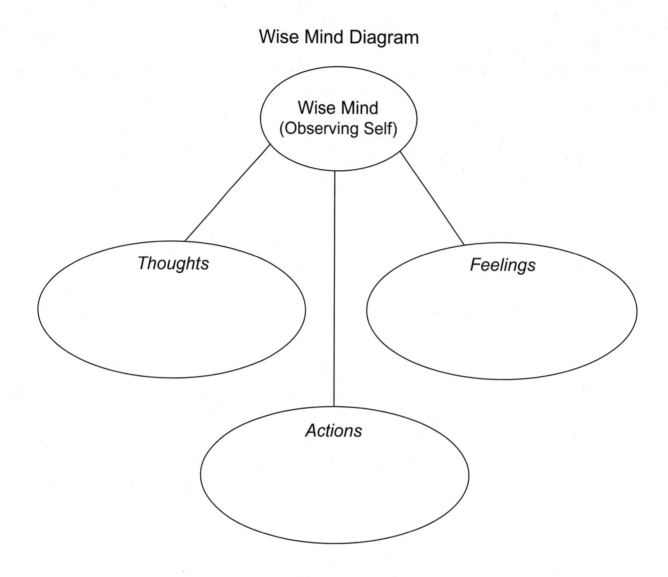

Example

Maria, a divorced mother of two school-age children, felt fat, old, depressed, stressed-out, and isolated. She envied her two older sisters and thought they were more attractive and successful. Her job at a medical center was dull and leading her nowhere. She hadn't had a date for nine months and didn't have the energy for dating anyway. Her kids were barely scraping through second and fourth grade, and Maria didn't have any energy for helping them with their problems.

Maria was seeing a counselor and started doing mindfulness exercises because they sounded like they required the least work of all her therapist's suggestions. At first she just appreciated how restful the exercises were. But soon she noticed that she felt refreshed after a few minutes of deep breathing and labeling her thoughts. The idea that she was separate from the momentary contents of her mind was very reassuring.

For Maria, the most beneficial result of mindfulness was subtle. Although parts of her life still seemed dissatisfactory, she became more interested in and enlivened by other parts of her life, like cooking, talking nonsense with her seven-year-old, or browsing through her gardening and needlework catalogs. She came to realize that she didn't have to fix every part of her life before she could have a life. She could acknowledge the depressing, negative thoughts that drifted through her mind while simultaneously doing things that were important to her, like planning an herb garden, taking her kids to the zoo, or knitting her mom a new scarf.

CHAPTER 10

Defusion

"Defusion" is a term coined by Steven Hayes, one of the developers of acceptance and commitment therapy (Hayes, Strosahl, and Wilson 1999). It refers to the Buddhist practice of observing and distancing from your mind and thereby changing your relationship to your mind and your thoughts. Instead of "fusing" with painful cognitions and getting caught in long chains of fearful or depressing thoughts, you can use defusion to help you watch and let go of even the most disturbing mental chatter.

By observing your mind, then labeling and releasing thoughts, you can detach from your thoughts and take them less seriously. Instead of *being* your thoughts ("I *am* ugly" or "I *am* in danger"), with defusion you learn to simply *have* them ("I am *having a thought* that I'm fat" or "I am *having a thought* that I'm in danger"). Being a thought makes it seems absolutely true or defining and leaves you stuck with that thought, whereas having a thought helps you recognize that it is just a thought, one of about sixty thousand you'll have on any given day. You can let it pass through and drift away. And because it's just a product of your mind, it doesn't necessarily reflect truth or reality.

Your mind helps you survive by anticipating danger, separating the world into things that are beneficial or damaging, and explaining why things happen so you can predict or change them. Often, this is a good thing. But as it turns out, these exact same tendencies are also the mind's downside. Your mind can scare you by constantly predicting danger, depress you by judging what you do as bad, and explain things in such a way that you feel wrong and responsible for every painful event that happens, or feel enraged that someone else is responsible for painful events. The techniques you'll learn in this chapter will help you stop buying into negative thoughts and jumping down the rabbit hole of angry, scary, or depressing cognitions.

It should be noted that although defusion is aimed at cognitions, it's entirely different from the cognitive restructuring techniques in chapters 3 and 4. In cognitive restructuring, the focus is on confronting, disputing, and ultimately changing your thoughts. Defusion changes your relationship to your thoughts rather than their content.

SYMPTOM EFFECTIVENESS

While relatively little research has been done on defusion alone, this technique is one of the core skills in acceptance and commitment therapy, and numerous studies have found acceptance and commitment therapy to be effective against anxiety (Eifert and Forsythe 2005), depressive disorders (Zettle 2007), anger (Saavedra 2007), and rumination (Ovchinikov 2010), along with a host of other psychological and health problems, including obsessive thinking and shame. The research on rumination is particularly important because defusion (as an element of acceptance and commitment therapy) appears to enhance cognitive flexibility and get people unstuck from obsessive mental processes.

TIME TO MASTERY

It will take less than a week to learn and begin to practice some of the basic defusion techniques. We encourage you to try all of them so you can determine which ones work best for you and are easiest for you to use. Once you've settled on the defusion techniques that feel like the best fit for you, it will take two to four weeks for your negative thoughts to begin feeling less urgent, less powerful, and easier to let go of.

INSTRUCTIONS

In this chapter we present a number of exercises that will help you develop your capacity for defusion. We begin with practices to help you learn to watch your thoughts. Next we provide practices for labeling thoughts and letting go of thoughts, and then offer some advice on combining these techniques. The final section of exercises will help you develop more distance from your thoughts.

Watching Your Thoughts

The starting point for defusion is learning how to watch your mind. There are two good ways to get comfortable doing this: the White Room Meditation and Mindful Focusing.

WHITE ROOM MEDITATION

Imagine that you are in a white room completely empty of furniture or any adornments. You can position yourself anywhere in the room—at the ceiling, on the floor, in one of the corners. But wherever you put yourself, visualize an open doorway on your left and a second open doorway on your right. The doors open onto darkness; you can't see anything beyond.

Imagine that your thoughts are entering from the doorway on your left, passing across your field of vision, and exiting through the doorway on your right. As your thoughts cross the room, you can attach them to a visual image (a bird flying, an animal running, a hulking mafioso, a balloon, a cloud, or anything else). Or you can simply say the word "thought" to yourself. Don't analyze or explore your thoughts. Allow each to have a brief moment in your awareness and then exit through the doorway to your right.

Some thoughts may feel urgent or compelling. Some may want to stick around longer than others. Just let each one move on out the door to make room for the next thought. As new thoughts show up, make sure you've relinquished the old ones, but don't worry if they show up again. Lots of thoughts tend to repeat themselves, and the visitors to your white room may be no exception.

Do this meditation for five minutes. When you're finished, take some time to reflect on the experience. Did your thoughts speed up, slow down, or continue at about the same rate? How easy or hard was it to let go of each thought and make room for new ones? Did your thoughts feel more urgent and engaging, less engaging, or about the same? Finally, did you feel calmer, more tense, or about the same?

For many people, the mere act of observing thoughts slows them down and makes them feel less urgent. Some people experience greater calmness because they are watching instead of getting fully caught up in their thinking.

MINDFUL FOCUSING

Whatever your reaction to the White Room Meditation, we encourage you to observe your thoughts with a second exercise: Mindful Focusing. In this exercise, you don't start by looking at your thoughts. Instead you begin with your breath, noticing the feeling of the cool air washing over the back of your throat and into your lungs, your ribs expanding and contracting, and your diaphragm tensing and then releasing as you let go of a breath. Keep observing your breathing and noticing each part of the physical experience.

As you focus on anything, your breath included, it's inevitable that you'll have thoughts. Use the experience of observing your breath as an opportunity to be aware of what your mind is doing. As each thought comes up, acknowledge it ("There's a thought") and then return your attention to your breath. So the sequence is breathe, notice a thought arising, acknowledge that thought, and then return to awareness of breathing.

Watching how thoughts intrude into your consciousness even as you are focusing on something else is a good way to recognize the power of the mind. No matter how you try to stay with the breath, thoughts keep showing up. This is normal and inevitable, but as you practice Mindful Focusing, you can learn to acknowledge your mind while staying with your physical experience.

Practice Mindful Focusing for about five minutes. Then reflect on how this practice changes your relationship to your thoughts. Is there any shift in terms of frequency, intensity, believability, or intrusiveness?

Labeling

After you've learned to watch your thoughts, it's time to label them. Describing what your mind is doing creates distance from your thoughts, reducing how believable or compelling they are. Here are two techniques that work well.

"I'M HAVING THE THOUGHT THAT…"

One way to label thoughts is to use the phrase "I'm having the thought that…": "I'm having the thought that I'm selfish." "I'm having the thought that I will never get a promotion." "I'm having a thought that the pain in my stomach is a tumor." Notice how the mere act of labeling puts you farther away from the cognition, often making it feel less urgent and believable.

"NOW MY MIND IS HAVING A _____ THOUGHT"

Another labeling technique uses the phrase "Now my mind is having a _____ thought." Specific labels you can use for this exercise might include "fear thoughts," "judgmental thoughts," "not-good-enough thoughts," "mistake thoughts," "should thoughts," and so on. Make up your own labels for your most common categories of thinking. As you observe a sequence of cognitions, the labeling might go like this: "Now my mind is having a self-critical thought… Now my mind is having a fear-of-the-future thought… Now my mind is having an angry thought… Now my mind is having another fear-of-the-future thought.…" and so on.

Letting Go of Thoughts

A third set of defusion techniques involves letting go of thoughts. Among the wide variety of such exercises, here are a few that we recommend. All are easy to learn and use.

LEAVES ON A STREAM

Imagine each thought as an autumn leaf detaching from a tree and falling into a swiftly moving stream. As the leaf hits the water, it gets caught in the current and is swept rapidly downstream, around a bend, and out of sight. As each new thought shows up in your mind, visualize it as a newly falling leaf, landing on the stream to be swept downstream and out of sight.

BILLBOARDS

Imagine yourself driving down a long stretch of highway, with billboards occasionally showing up on either side of the road. Visualize each thought as a message on one of the billboards. Notice it briefly, then imagine your car sweeping past. As your thought goes out of sight, the next new thought appears on another billboard and is briefly noted until your car roars by.

BALLOONS

Imagine a clown holding the strings to a dozen red balloons. As each new thought arrives, attach it to a balloon, then let the balloon detach from the group and float up into the sky and out of sight. If the image moves slowly and it takes too long for the balloons to drift out of sight, imagine a stiff wind blowing each one away.

COMPUTER POP-UPS

Imagine each thought as a pop-up advertisement or reminder on your computer screen. Briefly note the thought, then close the pop-up or simply let it disappear, and allow the screen to remain blank until the next pop-up appears.

TRAINS AND BOATS

Imagine yourself at a railroad crossing, watching a slow freight train passing by in front of you. Each boxcar is a new thought, slowly rolling past. Or imagine yourself on a bridge, watching fishing boats pass slowly beneath you on their way out to sea. Each boat represents a thought moving slowly out of slight.

PHYSICALLY LETTING GO

Whereas all of the previous letting-go exercises are based solely in imagery, this one is more physical. As each thought enters your mind, imagine that you're holding it in your hand, palm up. Actually hold your hand out, palm up. Then slowly rotate your hand until your palm is facing down and imagine the thought dropping out of your hand and out of sight. Then return your hand to the palm-up position to receive the next new thought. When the next thought arrives, again turn your hand and visualize the thought dropping away. Making the letting-go process physical helps it feel more powerful and real.

Combining Watching, Labeling, and Letting Go

When defusing from your thoughts, it's helpful to establish a sequence of responses to use with each cognition. The simplest way to do this is to choose a method of labeling and combine it with one of the letting-go visualizations or the physical letting-go technique.

Mark, who ruminates about scary future possibilities, chose to respond to these thoughts by labeling each with "I'm having a thought that…" and then visualizing the image of leaves floating on a stream. After trying this for a while, he realized that it was hard to call up the image of leaves floating on a stream when he was in social situations. So he replaced it with a physical letting-go. Rather than turning his palm, he subtly spread his fingers to represent letting go of the thought. Mark found that when he used this combination of labeling and letting go, his old what-if cognitions felt less believable and upsetting.

Distancing

Certain defusion exercises are especially helpful for gaining distance from thoughts and taking them less seriously. When you distance yourself from thoughts, they have less power to make you sad or mad or scared. Distancing exercises have one thing in common: They embrace a painful thought while letting it shrink and diminish in importance. You'll come to understand that paradox as you explore the following practices.

THANK YOUR MIND

As mentioned earlier, your mind offers many thoughts, even problematic thoughts, in an effort to protect you. It's trying to predict dangerous possibilities, judge what's good or bad for you, or figure out why things happen. So your mind is working hard to help you survive and overcome problems. However, your mind can run amok and obsessively focus on thoughts that only make you miserable.

One way to deal with these thoughts is to thank your mind for its efforts to protect you. As each negative thought shows up, simply say, "Thank you, Mind, for that thought." You don't have to get involved with the thought. You don't have to understand or explore it. You can just appreciate that your mind gave you that thought in an effort to protect you. "Thank you, Mind" is a mantra that acknowledges your mind's goodwill while distancing you from the painful thoughts it throws at you: "Thank you, Mind, for that scary thought… Thank you, Mind, for that I'm-no-good thought… Thank you, Mind, for predicting failure… Thank you, Mind, for the thought that my relationship will collapse."

When you thank your mind, you're also creating distance from each thought as it arises. You're appreciating your mind's efforts while recognizing that it may have gone astray.

NEGATIVE LABEL REPETITION

Edward Titchener (1916) discovered that if you keep repeating a word fifty or more times, it begins to lose its meaning. It becomes just a sound rather than a concept. Take, for example, the word "milk." When you hear the word just once, you can imagine the color and smell of milk and feel of the cool liquid flowing down your throat. But consider what happens if you say the word "milk" out loud over and over again. Go ahead and actually do that right now: Keep saying "milk" as fast as you can while still pronouncing it clearly for at least sixty seconds.

What happened to the meaning of the word? Did it still evoke those same sense impressions and associations, or did it feel odd or empty? Did it become more a sound than a word?

The fact that repetition changes and diminishes meaning is very useful for defusion. You can repeat negative self-judgments or feared future outcomes until they lose their sting and ability to disturb you. Try it right now. Choose a negative label you often apply to yourself. Repeat it for a minute or two, as quickly as you can while still pronouncing it clearly, and notice what happens to the thoughts associated with that label.

OBJECTIFYING THOUGHTS

A classic way to make thoughts less important and disturbing is to objectify them, by which we mean imagining them as objects. For example, assign a color to a sticky thought that keeps bothering you. You can also give the thought a shape, texture, or size—or all of the above. It's easier to distance yourself from a thought when you imagine that it is green and as big as a basketball and has the texture of cheesecake and the shape of a starfish.

CARD CARRYING

Some thoughts keep showing up, sort of like unwelcome relatives who keep coming for another visit. One way to create distance from these thoughts is to write them on an index card and carry the card with you. Whenever one of those thoughts reoccurs, you can remind yourself, "I have it on the card."

WEARING SIGNS

Sometimes it's helpful to openly acknowledge the most painful thoughts your mind can create. Write the thought on a sticky note or name tag and wear it for a few hours. (You'll probably want do this only in the privacy of your home or when you're with close friends.) You'll find that it doesn't take long for the power and sting of the thought to diminish once you've begun to wear it. Many people find this especially helpful for judgmental thoughts, such as "I'm stupid," "I'm a bad parent," or "I'm lonely and empty." Acknowledging a thought seems to have the magical effect of making it seem farther away and less important.

THE DISTANCING DRILL

For thoughts that are particularly sticky and painful, or that show up frequently, we suggest you use the following four-step process whenever the thought shows up.

Step 1: Ask yourself how old the thought is. Did it start when you lost your job three years ago, does it go back to when your first wife asked for a divorce, or do you remember having the thought in childhood? If you're not sure when it started, make a rough guess of how long it's been around—five years, ten, twenty?

Step 2: Examine the function of the thought. What is this thought in the service of? Most negative thoughts have a single function: trying to help you prevent pain by avoiding a particular action or situation. Ask yourself what behavior the thought drives you to do or not do. What is it trying to protect you from feeling?

Step 3: Examine the workability of the thought. Is it helping you avoid pain, or is it just paralyzing you and making it hard to do the things that matter? For example, if you realize that a thought is trying to protect you from fear, you might examine whether listening to that thought makes you more or less fearful. You might also ask whether the thought is helping you do the things you want to do or getting in your way. In the end, the answer to workability is pretty straightforward. Either the thought is helping or it isn't.

Step 4: Ask yourself whether you'd be willing to have this thought while still doing whatever it's trying to scare you away from. For example, if the thought is telling you to ignore an attractive person at a party because he or she might reject you, would you be willing to have the thought and talk to that person anyway? Ultimately, it comes down to whether you are going to let your scary and discouraging thoughts control your behavior or are going to do the things that really matter in your life despite what your mind may say.

This four-step process will help even the most painful and persistent thoughts seem less important and diminish their influence. It will give you some distance from paralyzing thoughts so you don't let them discourage you from doing the things you care about.

Example

Walker, a twenty-eight-year-old draftsman, struggled for years with anxious and self-denigrating thoughts. He had judgmental thoughts about his competence at work and his ability to socialize and make interesting conversation. He also had fearful thoughts about being rejected and judged, and others about losing his job, his apartment, and his independence. He wanted to go back to school to pursue a degree in mechanical engineering, but thoughts about failure and potential financial disaster with school loans were keeping him from moving forward.

After learning about defusion, Walker chose a simple process to observe and let go of difficult thoughts. As each cognition showed up, he said to himself, "Now my mind's having a judgment thought" or "Now my mind's having a fear thought." Then he turned his hand over, palm down, and imagined the thought falling through the floor and out of sight.

As Walker became more skilled at labeling and letting go of thoughts, he noticed a shift in how he related to his mind. Instead of feeling that each judgmental or fearful thought was terribly important, he began to regard them as just thoughts and part of his endless mental chatter.

Despite these positive changes, some of his fearful thoughts were still very sticky and powerful. Chief among these was the thought that he would fail if he returned to school. Walker first tried Titchener's repetition and the card carrying strategy to distance himself from these thoughts. Finally, he committed to using the Distancing Drill to give himself some breathing room with these cognitions.

Each time one of the fearful thoughts about going back to school came to mind, Walker asked how old it was. He realized that these thoughts had begun around the time he first entered college, eleven years ago. The function of the thoughts was always the same: to protect himself from failure and anxiety about failure by avoiding difficult challenges.

When Walker turned to the workability question, he recognized that these thoughts had never been helpful. During his first years in college they drove him to avoid the hard engineering courses, and ultimately they caused him to drop out. He also remembered that, rather than protecting him from anxiety, these thoughts made his college years a nervous nightmare. And now, every time he thought about going to school, his heart raced and he felt a surge of anxiety. Instead of protecting him from anxiety and failure, his thoughts were filling him with fear and guaranteeing failure.

Finally, Walker asked himself the most important question: Would he be willing to have these thoughts and still fill out college applications? He decided to go for it, regardless of how much failure and disaster his mind predicted.

SPECIAL CONSIDERATIONS

Defusion isn't about arguing with or disputing your thoughts. The two chapters on cognitive restructuring in this book (chapter 3, "Changing Patterns of Limited Thinking," and chapter 4, "Changing Hot Thoughts") are about trying to alter your thinking and replace negative thoughts with more positive or accurate cognitions. With defusion, on the other hand, you seek to accept your thoughts, whatever form they may take. Whether your thoughts are positive or negative, or accurate or distorted, defusion encourages you to let your thoughts be what they are.

If you're trying to argue with your thoughts, you aren't distancing from them, and therefore you aren't doing defusion. Remember, defusion aims not at the management or restructuring of thoughts, but rather at changing your relationship to your mind. Instead of disputing what you think, see it as one of many thoughts, without any special truth or accuracy. Each thought is simply what your mind is telling you right now: a string of words you can observe, label, and let go of.

Sometimes your mind will resist the defusion process. It will insist that a particular thought is important and predict dire consequences if you ignore it. This is just another thought, one in a long string, and no more true or important than any other. Observe the thought, label it, and let it go. If the thought tenaciously returns again and again, use the Distancing Drill to explore its history, function, and workability. When it's clear that the thought hasn't helped you, just let it go.

CHAPTER 11

Getting Mobilized

One of the effects of depression is feeling immobilized. It's hard to push yourself to do normal self-care activities, and pleasure seems all but absent from your life. Feeling immobilized is not only a symptom of depression; it is also a cause. The less you do, the more depressed you feel, and the more depressed you feel, the less you do. It's a downward spiral that maintains withdrawal from life and prolongs depression.

The solution is to push yourself to higher levels of activity even though you don't feel like it. A technique known as activity scheduling, developed and refined by cognitive behavioral psychologists, can reenergize you and offer significant help in overcoming depression (Beck et al. 1979; Freeman et al. 2004; Greenberger and Padesky 1995). In this technique, you focus on adding two different types of activities to your schedule: activities that are pleasurable, and activities that give you a sense of mastery. These categories aren't mutually exclusive; some activities may give you a sense of both pleasure and mastery. This chapter explains activity scheduling in detail and will help you implement the technique.

SYMPTOM EFFECTIVENESS

Several studies by the National Institute of Mental Health have demonstrated the effectiveness of activity scheduling as a component in the cognitive behavioral treatment protocol for depression (see Cuijpers, van Straten, and Warmerdam 2007). Numerous studies have shown that simply increasing your activity level, without any other intervention, can significantly reduce depression.

Marsha Linehan (1993), creator of dialectical behavior therapy, has found that self-soothing in the form of scheduling pleasurable activities is an effective intervention for all types of emotion dysregulation, not just depression.

TIME TO MASTERY

The first step in this process is monitoring and recording your activities for one week. After that, you will take four to eight weeks to schedule and gradually increase specific types of activities. You may begin to see some benefits as soon as you start engaging in newly scheduled activities.

INSTRUCTIONS

As mentioned, you'll begin by monitoring and recording your daily activities; you'll also rate how pleasurable they are or the degree of mastery you feel when engaging in them. Then you'll identify activities you can add to your schedule and start engaging in them. Here's an overview of the process:

1. Record and rate your activities for one week.

2. Identify times to schedule new activities.

3. Select new pleasure and mastery activities and schedule them.

4. Predict your level of pleasure or mastery for new activities.

5. Compare actual levels of pleasurable or mastery to predictions.

Step 1: Record and Rate Your Activities for One Week

Make at least eight photocopies of the blank Weekly Activity Schedule below. Over the next week, record your main activity or activities during each hour. If you don't have time to record your activities during the day, be sure to record them no later than that evening.

You'll use the information you gather in a few different ways: to assess which of your current activities give you a sense of pleasure or mastery; to find times when you can schedule additional pleasure or mastery activities; and to establish an activity baseline so you can recognize your progress in the weeks ahead as you implement your plan to both mobilize yourself and help yourself feel less depressed.

When monitoring and recording your activities during this first week, pay attention to two aspects of your experience: pleasure and mastery. If an activity has provided you any pleasure at all, write the letter P in that box and rate how pleasurable the activity was on a scale from 1 (minimal pleasure) to 10 (extreme pleasure).

Also identify mastery activities, in which you take care of yourself or others. Tasks you may have been avoiding, like answering a letter, weeding your garden, preparing a healthful meal, or running an errand, are particularly good choices for mastery items. (A list of typical mastery activities appears in step 3.) If an activity gave you a sense of mastery, write the letter M in that box and rate your sense of mastery, *given how tired or depressed you may have felt at the time*. Again, use a scale from 1 (minimal sense of mastery) to 10 (extreme sense of mastery). Don't rate how much you objectively achieved or what you think you would have achieved before you were depressed. Rather, assess your sense of mastery taking into account how hard this activity was in light of how you were feeling.

If you need some help getting started, after the blank form you'll find an example from Alicia, a depressed college student who works as a retail phone clerk and often feels like she's stuck in a dead-end job. Notice that every box is filled in, even if she was only sleeping. Also notice which activities she labels as pleasure or mastery.

Identifying and rating pleasure and mastery activities is a crucial aspect of this first step. It may help you recognize how your life has gotten out of balance, that many things you formerly enjoyed are no longer part of your week, or that your current activities provide very little emotional nourishment. Pleasure ratings also give you information about the activities you still enjoy and which ones offer the best boost to your mood. Noticing and rating your mastery activities may help you recognize that, despite everything, you're still trying hard. You're still doing things to cope. And even though you may not be as efficient or effective as you were before you became depressed, the things you do are real achievements, given how you feel.

Weekly Activity Schedule

	Mon.	Tues.	Wed.	Thurs.	Fri.	Sat.	Sun.
6 a.m.							
7 a.m.							
8 a.m.							
9 a.m.							
10 a.m.							
11 a.m.							
12 noon							
1 p.m.							
2 p.m.							
3 p.m.							
4 p.m.							
5 p.m.							
6 p.m.							
7 p.m.							
8 p.m.							
9 p.m.							
10 p.m.							
11 p.m.							
12-6 a.m.							

Alicia's Weekly Activity Schedule

	Mon.	Tues.	Wed.	Thurs.	Fri.	Sat.	Sun.
6 a.m.	Sleep	Sleep	Sleep	Coffee, read paper **P3**	Sleep	Sleep	Sleep
7 a.m.	Sleep	Sleep	Sleep	Shower, dress **M2**	Sleep	Sleep	Sleep
8 a.m.	Shower, dress **M2**	Dress, no makeup	Dress, worry	Dress, no makeup	Shower, dress **M2**	Sleep	Sleep
9 a.m.	Class **M1**	Sit around house thinking	Class **M1**	Sit around, crossword puzzles	Class **M3**	Lie in bed	Sleep
10 a.m.	Class **M1**	Sit around house thinking	Class **M1**	Sit around, crossword puzzles	Class **M3**	Lie in bed	Lie in bed
11 a.m.	Class **M2**	Call Bill **P2**	Class **M1**	Reading	Class **M3**	Make breakfast **M2**	Read novel in bed
12 noon	Lunch, ice cream **P1**	Sandwich at home	Buy school supplies **M3**	Sandwich at home	Sleep in car	Sit around house thinking	Eat out **P1**
1 p.m.	Taking orders **M3**	Taking orders **M2**	Taking orders **M3**	Taking orders M3	Taking orders **M2**	Sit around house thinking	TV
2 p.m.	Taking orders **M3**	Taking orders **M3**	Taking orders **M3**	Taking orders **M3**	Taking orders **M2**	Bill comes back, talk **P2**	TV
3 p.m.	Taking orders **M3**	Writing new phone script **P3 M7**	Taking orders **M3**	Taking orders **M3**	Research project at work **M6**	Make love **P5**	TV
4 p.m.	Talking to Rita at work **P3**	Ice cream with Rita	Taking orders **M2**	Talking to Rita **P3**	Research project at work **M6**	TV	TV
5 p.m.	Work until 5:45, drive home	Sit in car reading	Sit around at home	Study **M3**	Clean desk **M3**	TV	Nap
6 p.m.	Make and eat dinner **M3**	Eat out **P3**	Make and eat dinner **M2**	Make and eat dinner **M2**	No food in house, order pizza	Dinner out, fight with Bill	Study, can't focus **M1**

7 p.m.	TV **P1**	Study, can't focus **M2**	TV	Brother calls **P3**	Kissing, talking to Bill **P5**	TV	TV while eating
8 p.m.	TV	Give up, watch TV	TV	TV	Movie **P4**	TV	TV
9 p.m.	TV	TV	Call Susan, Lori **P4**	TV	Movie **P4**	TV **P2**	TV
10 p.m.	TV, good program	TV	TV **P1**	TV **P1**	Talking with Bill **P4**	TV	TV
11 p.m.	Make love with Bill (rushed) **P3**	Worry about school	Reading **P2**	Study **M3**	Reading **P2**	TV	Lying in bed thinking
12-6 a.m.	Reading until 2:30, can't sleep **P1**	Sleep	Sleep	Watch TV until 2:30, can't sleep	Reading until 1:00 **P2**	Sleep	Reading, TV until 2, can't sleep **P1**

When Alicia reviewed her activity schedule at the end of the week, she made some interesting discoveries. First of all, she was watching a lot of TV without enjoying it. Most of her pleasure came from interacting with people and sometimes from reading. She also noticed that sitting around the house or lying in bed late in the morning seemed to be associated with increased depression.

Alicia had higher mastery ratings at school when she had studied the night before. And while she usually had at least a small sense of mastery at work, her mastery ratings were higher when doing a special project. She also felt more mastery when she made her own dinner and devoted some attention to her appearance before going out.

Step 2: Identify Times to Schedule New Activities

Once you've filled out your Weekly Activity Schedule for the first week, use it to look for times when you can schedule additional pleasure and mastery activities during your week. Identify at least ten hours when you're engaged in an optional activity that provides neither pleasure nor a sense of mastery. See if you can find one or two hours each day when you can schedule new pleasure or mastery activities to replace old, unprofitable activities.

Step 3: Select New Pleasure and Mastery Activities and Schedule Them

Analyzing your pleasure and mastery ratings for the first week may give you some direction in scheduling new pleasure and mastery activities. However, you'll probably need to branch out beyond what you've been doing and identify new activities to try, or start engaging in former activities once again. If you've been depressed for a while, you may have a hard time coming up with ideas, so we've provided lists of common pleasure and mastery activities for inspiration. You may also get some ideas by consulting with friends or family members.

Pleasure Activities

- Visiting friends or family
- Talking to friends or family on the phone
- Going to movies or plays
- Watching videos or TV
- Exercising
- Doing sports
- Playing games
- Doing computer activities
- Surfing the Internet
- Chatting on the Internet
- Listening to music
- Going away for a weekend
- Planning a vacation
- Pursuing a hobby
- Collecting
- Doing crafts
- Enjoying the sun
- Relaxing with a hot drink
- Listening to audio books or guided relaxation recordings

- Walking or hiking
- Shopping
- Taking a hot bath
- Reading
- Gardening
- Writing
- Going out to eat
- Eating a favorite treat
- Being held or touched
- Getting a massage
- Engaging in sexual activities
- Going for a drive
- Going on a picnic
- Going to a favorite place
- Sitting in a peaceful place
- Writing letters
- Engaging in artistic pursuits
- Watching or reading the news

This list includes just a few of the many possibilities for activities that might bring you pleasure. In the space below, write some of your ideas about activities that would be pleasurable for you. Think back over the years to the things you've enjoyed. Try to remember everything you've ever done that was fun. Review the list above and try to identify specific activities within those generic categories that might be pleasurable for you. For instance, in terms of playing games, you might enjoy pool or cards. For crafts, you might enjoy needlepoint or building model airplanes. Artistic pursuits could mean going to galleries or writing haiku. When it comes to calling or visiting friends, there may be certain people you'd enjoy spending more time with. Take some time right now to fill in all of the blanks below with specific activities that you have enjoyed or can imagine enjoying in the future.

Some of my pleasure activities

_____

_____

_____

_____

_____

_____

_____

_____

_____

_____

_____

_____

_____

_____

_____

_____

_____

Don't be surprised if you currently have a hard time imagining enjoying or even being interested in many of the things you've enjoyed in the past. They may even seem like a hassle or a burden. This is due to depression. When you begin to include more pleasurable activities in your week you'll feel better, even if those activities seem uninteresting now. Right now, select five to seven pleasure activities from your list to schedule for the next week.

You also need to add new mastery activities. Often these are self-care activities that you may have neglected. You may need to shop for groceries, run errands, clean or straighten up around the house, write letters, or make important calls. When you're depressed and immobilized, even these normal daily tasks can seem impossibly hard. Here's a list of some typical mastery activities you might schedule into your week.

Mastery Activities

- Shopping
- Going to the bank
- Helping your children with homework
- Supervising your children's bedtime activities
- Bathing
- Preparing a hot meal
- Paying bills
- Getting up before 9:00 a.m.
- Walking the dog
- Fixing something
- Cleaning something
- Doing dishes
- Exercising or stretching
- Resolving a conflict
- Doing laundry or going to the cleaner's
- Gardening
- Running an errand
- Going to work
- Tackling challenging tasks at work
- Folding and putting away clothes
- Solving a problem
- Straightening up or putting things in order
- Improving your home environment or decorating
- Doing car maintenance
- Making a business call
- Returning telephone calls
- Writing in a journal
- Doing self-help exercises
- Engaging in spiritual or religious activities
- Grooming
- Getting a haircut
- Dressing up
- Writing letters
- Arranging activities for your children
- Engaging in artistic pursuits
- Driving your children to activities

As with pleasure activities, these are just a few of the many possibilities for mastery activities, and most are fairly generic. After reviewing the list, make your own list of specific activities that might give you a sense of mastery or accomplishment. Take some time right now to fill in all of the blanks below with mastery activities that you might schedule into your week.

Some of my mastery activities

_____

_____

_____

_____

_____

_____

_____

_____

_____

_____

_____

_____

_____

_____

_____

_____

Right now, select five to seven mastery activities to sprinkle throughout the coming week, with a particular focus on tasks you may have been avoiding. If you've been putting off doing the recycling, make an appointment with yourself on your Weekly Activity Schedule to get it done. If you've been putting off renewing your driver's license, write in a definite time when you'll accomplish this task.

However, don't try to do more than one extra mastery activity each day; that may be pushing too hard and leave you feeling overwhelmed.

In your Weekly Activity Schedule from the first week, look for times when you've been unproductive and had neither pleasure nor a sense of mastery. These are ideal times to substitute a mastery activity that can give you a sense of achievement.

Note that some mastery activities may be too involved to accomplish in an hour or too overwhelming when tackled all at once. In such cases, it may help to break the activity into smaller steps that you can accomplish in fifteen minutes or less. For example, a plan to improve the appearance of your living room might involve many steps, starting with a decision to buy and hang a new poster. Some mastery activities may stretch over two or more weeks as you work through each step in the process.

On the next page, you'll find the Weekly Activity Schedule Alicia filled out, showing the new activities she scheduled for the second week of her program to get mobilized. Alicia typically struggled to do any studying at all. Because her first week of recording her activities revealed that she had a greater sense of mastery in class when she studied the day before, she scheduled two hours of study time before each day of classes, often with an hour of relaxation in between.

Alicia's mastery list included items such as ordering new checks, doing her laundry, and food shopping. She integrated these items into her week during times when she would otherwise have been watching television or brooding. For new pleasure activities, she selected items such as listening to new music, reading in the tub, playing backboard tennis, hiking, and going for a walk. These were all activities she had enjoyed in the past and felt willing to try in the coming week.

When Alicia wrote an item on her Weekly Activity Schedule, she considered it a commitment to herself. She tried to think of it as an appointment she was making with someone she respected and didn't want to disappoint. We encourage you to do the same, and to make your commitment to pleasure activities as important as your commitment to mastery activities. Increasing the number of enjoyable experiences in your week is an essential step to overcoming depression and getting your life back in balance.

Step 4: Predict Your Level of Pleasure or Mastery for New Activities

An important part of planning new activities is trying to anticipate how they will make you feel. Now that you've filled out a new Weekly Activity Schedule for the coming week, take some time right now to predict how much of a sense of pleasure or mastery you'll get from each activity. Use the same scale of P1 to P10 for pleasure activities and M1 to M10 for mastery activities, where 10 indicates extreme pleasure or mastery, and then circle your ratings. Here's Alicia's Weekly Activity Schedule for the second week, which includes her ratings. Her P1 prediction for playing some backboard tennis indicates that she expected very little enjoyment from this activity. Her P3 prediction for going out for dinner and a movie suggests that she expected to have a modestly good time.

Alicia's Weekly Activity Schedule—Week 2

	Mon.	Tues.	Wed.	Thurs.	Fri.	Sat.	Sun.
6 a.m.							
7 a.m.							
8 a.m.							
9 a.m.		Call to order new checks **M2**		Backboard tennis **P1**			
10 a.m.						Grocery shopping **M1**	Study **M2**
11 a.m.							Study **M2**
12 noon						Hike in Muir Woods **P2**	
1 p.m.							Walk at Lake Mercel **P3**
2 p.m.							
3 p.m.							
4 p.m.							
5 p.m.	Shop for some new music **P2**						
6 p.m.					Dinner at Solerno's **P3**		
7 p.m.	Listen to new music **P3**	Study **M2**	Laundry I've put off **M1**	Study **M2**	Dinner at Solerno's **P3**		
8 p.m.		Listen to music **P2**	Call Sandi or Gail **P2**	Read novel in tub **P3**	Movie **P3**		
9 p.m.		Study **M2**		Study **M2**	Movie **P3**		
10 p.m.			Fold clothes **M1**	Watch video **P2**			
11 p.m.				Watch video **P2**			
12-6 a.m.							

Most depressed people make very conservative predictions about the amount of pleasure or achievement they'll feel during a planned activity. It's okay to not feel hopeful. You may anticipate very little in the way of good feelings from your planned activities. But do them anyway and evaluate what happens.

Step 5: Compare Actual Levels of Pleasure or Mastery to Predictions

During the week, write your actual pleasure or mastery rating for each new activity next to your circled prediction. You're likely to find that your actual ratings are higher than your predictions. As noted earlier, depression tends to make you pessimistic. Comparing your prediction to the actual level of pleasure or mastery you experience may help you recognize how depression distorts your view of things. The fact that your new activities are more enjoyable and fulfilling than you anticipated could help you resist the discouraging inner voice that tells you, "Don't bother with anything new; it's a lot of work, and you'll still feel lousy." Here's Alicia's Weekly Activity Schedule after the second week, with her ratings for actual pleasure or sense of mastery during newly scheduled activities.

Alicia's Weekly Activity Schedule—Week 2

	Mon.	Tues.	Wed.	Thurs.	Fri.	Sat.	Sun.
6 a.m.							
7 a.m.							
8 a.m.							
9 a.m.		*Call to order new checks* (M2) M3		*Backboard tennis* (P1) P4			
10 a.m.						*Grocery shopping* (M1) M4	*Study* (M2) M3
11 a.m.							*Study* (M2) M3
12 noon						*Hike in Muir Woods* (P2) *Didn't go*	
1 p.m.							*Walk at Lake Merced* (P3) P4
2 p.m.							
3 p.m.							
4 p.m.							
5 p.m.	*Shop for some new music* (P2) P4						
6 p.m.					*Dinner at Solerno's* (P3) P6		
7 p.m.	*Listen to new music* (P3) P5	*Study* (M2) M3	*Laundry I've put off* (M1) M4	*Study* (M2) M4	*Dinner at Solerno's* (P3) P5		
8 p.m.		*Listen to music* (P2) P4	*Call Sandi or Gail* (P2) P5	*Read novel in tub* (P3) P5	*Movie* (P3) P4		

9 p.m.		*Study* (M2) M3		*Study* (M2) M4	*Movie* (P3) P4	
10 p.m.			*Fold clothes* (M1) M3	*Watch video* (P2) P4		
11 p.m.				*Watch video* (P2) P4		
12-6 a.m.						

Alicia was surprised to learn that she usually enjoyed things more than she had thought she would. In particular, Alicia felt significantly more achievement and pleasure than she'd predicted in her new evening activities. She realized that television was numbing and had been adding to her depression. The new activities were a way to get her off the couch and doing something that offered a chance of feeling better.

After the second week, set a goal that you will add a combination of seven mastery and pleasure items to each new Weekly Activity Schedule. Try to continue with the previously added items if they were pleasurable or gave you a sense of mastery and are practical to repeat. But don't hesitate to drop anything that simply didn't work.

In Alicia's case, during week 3 she began to focus on replacing some of her TV time on the weekend. She chose additional items from her lists and used successes from the previous week (listening to music, calling friends, reading in the tub, and tennis) to replace the endless hours of weekend TV. While this was an effort, Alicia found that she felt much better when her weekend was dotted with scheduled activities. It kept her moving, and although she sometimes longed for the couch, she found she was less depressed as she did more.

SPECIAL CONSIDERATIONS

Some people feel they don't have time in their week for anything new. Because the weekly activity schedule is a crucial intervention for overcoming depression, you may need to limit or suspend some of your usual activities so you can work in more pleasure and mastery experiences. Go through your first Weekly Activity Schedule and cross out any box where the activity isn't absolutely essential. These are the hours when you can substitute new pleasure and mastery activities.

After four or five weeks of adding new activities, you're likely to find that your days are becoming rather full. At this point a certain amount of pruning may be in order to eliminate some of the new activities that offer little nourishment. At this stage, you can also cut down on the number of new activities you add each week. However, you should still continue to make plans on your Weekly Activity Schedule. Writing activities down increases the chance that you'll do them. Keep filling in planned mastery and pleasure activities in your weekly schedule until you feel a significant improvement in your level of depression.

CHAPTER 12

Putting Values into Action

Values-based behavior activation, a core approach in acceptance and commitment therapy (Hayes, Strosahl, and Wilson 1999), can be a major step in overcoming depression. Values-based action comes down to one key question: Given that your time on this planet is finite, how do you choose to spend it?

Your values reflect what you want your life to be about. They are not needs or preferences, such as water, a sunny day in winter, or Zumba dancing. They are generally articulated as intrinsic, abstract principles. The values you choose to live by are like the arrow on a compass, pointing the way for you to go. They are the path, the direction you want your life to take; for example, being honest in important relationships, or being a good parent. Goals, or intentions, are specific stepping-stones along that path that move you in the direction of your values, such as telling the truth about specific feelings, or helping your child with homework.

Identifying your values and specific associated intentions can get you mobilized. It can get your life moving when you've been stuck in depression and motivate you to do things you've been avoiding. Depression is often associated with shutting down and disconnecting from relationships, and values work can be immensely helpful in reversing this maintaining factor in depression.

SYMPTOM EFFECTIVENESS

Committing to values-based behavior improves your motivation and willingness to increase your activity level and overcome experiential avoidance—one of the key maintaining factors in depression and other emotional disorders (Hayes and Smith 2007). Acceptance and commitment therapy, in which values work is a core approach, has been shown to be highly effective in the treatment of depression (Zettle 2007).

TIME TO MASTERY

It will only take you a few hours to identify your values and commit to working on some concrete values-based intentions. Turning your values into specific committed actions (intentions) and becoming more mobilized is a process that can extend over several months.

INSTRUCTIONS

The exercises in this chapter will help you identify your key values—the things you care most about in life—and begin working toward living your life more in accordance with those values. The process we'll guide you through has five steps:

1. Clarify your values.

2. Compare how you're currently living with your key values.

3. Create intentions to increase values-based living.

4. Visualize accomplishing your intentions.

5. Commit to values-based action.

Step 1: Clarify Your Values

The first step in this process is identifying the aspects of your life that are important to you and what you value most in relation to each of these valued aspects. People tend to have strong values in most or all of the following ten general areas of life (Hayes and Smith 2005). Some of these general areas, or domains, will be more important to you than others. Read through the following descriptions of the ten domains, then complete the Important Life Domains and Key Values form that follows.

1. **Intimate relationships.** This refers to your partner, lover, boyfriend or girlfriend, or spouse. What kind of partner do you want to be to your significant other? If you aren't currently in a relationship, think in terms of your ideal intimate relationship. The values you associate with intimate relationships might include love, faithfulness, honesty, or openness.

2. **Parenting.** What is most important to you about the parenting role? For example, do you value nurturing, educating, mentoring, protecting, or loving?

3. **Education and learning.** Think about the areas of your life in which you are learning something new. Values associated with learning include understanding, skill, wisdom, and truth.

4. **Friends and social life.** Reflect on what qualities you most value in your friendships or would look for in your ideal friendship. These might include support, honesty, trust, loyalty, or love.

5. **Physical self-care and health.** Are you reaping the rewards of taking care of your body, or do you need to attend to this area or take some preventive measures? Values associated with physical self-care and health include vitality, strength, endurance, feeling good, mobility, and longevity.

6. **Family of origin.** What is most important about your relationships with your parents and siblings? These values might include acceptance, love, support, or respect.

7. **Spirituality.** Are you connected to something greater than yourself that transcends what you know with your five senses? Spirituality takes many forms: appreciating a beautiful sunset, participating in organized religion, and practicing meditation, to name a few. People value their relationship with God, their higher power, nature, or a universal life force.

8. **Community life and citizenship.** What do you do to contribute to the welfare of your community? Do you give to charity, volunteer, or participate politically? Typical values in this area include responsibility, justice, compassion, and charity.

9. **Recreation and leisure.** How do you like to spend your leisure time? How do you restore your energy and reconnect with friends and family? What values do your hobbies and interests reflect? Values associated with this area include life balance, fun, creativity, joy, and passion.

10. **Work and career.** Ideally, what do you want to accomplish through your work? What do you want to stand for? Typical values in regard to work include right livelihood, innovation, creativity, efficiency, conscientiousness, being productive, excellence, stewardship, and mentorship.

The following worksheet will help you clarify your key values and determine which life domains are most important to you. Because your priorities and values may change with time, make a copy and leave the version in the book blank for future use. To use the worksheet, start by filling in the right-hand column, writing a few words or phrases that summarize your key values for each domain. Use the blank rows to add any domains that are important to you that aren't on the list. Then rate the domains in terms of importance to you using a scale from 0 to 2, where 0 is not at all important, 1 is moderately important, and 2 is very important. (An example from Jose, a semiretired engineer, follows the blank worksheet.)

Important Life Domains and Key Values

Importance	Domain	Key values
	Intimate relationships	
	Parenting	
	Education and learning	
	Friends and social life	
	Physical self-care and health	
	Family of origin	
	Spirituality	
	Community and citizenship	
	Recreation and leisure	
	Work and career	

Jose's Important Life Domains and Key Values

Importance	Domain	Key values
2	Intimate relationships	*Mutual honesty, open communication, love, respect, and support*
2	Parenting	*Nurturing and mentoring my children without overprotecting them*
1	Education and learning	*Learning and developing critical thinking skills*
2	Friends and social life	*Trust, loyalty, and common interests*
2	Physical self-care and health	*Feeling good and having the vitality to be able to do the other things I value*
1	Family of origin	*Being supportive, understanding, and connected*
0	Spirituality	*Contemplating the mystery of the universe and remembering that everything is sacred*
1	Community and citizenship	*Helping make my community and the world a better place*
1	Recreation and leisure	*Enjoying my passions, being creative, and having fun*
1	Work and career	*Working in a way that allows me to be creative, useful, and productive*

Step 2: Compare How You're Currently Living with Your Key Values

Now that you've started clarifying your values, you can compare how you're currently living your life with your key values. To begin, review your responses on the Important Life Domains and Key Values form. For each domain, think about the values you associate with it and consider whether you're satisfied with what you're currently doing in your life in that domain. Do your actions in that area reflect your values? If not, consider what you could do differently to bring your life more into alignment with your values. Take some time to write about this on a separate piece of paper.

Here's an excerpt from what Jose wrote when he compared how he was living his life with his key values in some of his more important domains.

Physical self-care and health. *I value feeling good and having the vitality to be able to do all the other things I value in my life, and yet I'm not doing anything to lose weight. I need to take better care of my health!*

Work and career. *Trying to fix my house and occasionally doing consulting work are currently satisfying my work-related values.*

Intimate relationships. *I have a loving relationship with my wife and our communication is honest and open, but we need to work on mutual respect and support when our opinions or interests differ.*

Parenting. *Now that my children are grown, I want to continue to be nurturing, but without overprotecting them. I want to mentor them, but they tell me I'm lecturing. I'm still treating my kids as children, and I need to work on listening to rather than solving their problems.*

Family of origin. *While I value mutual support, loyalty, and connection with my family of origin, I avoid family events and don't initiate interactions because I feel down and exhausted.*

Step 3: Create Intentions to Increase Values-Based Living

In step 3, you'll create intentions that will bring your life into closer alignment with your key values in each of the domains that's important to you—those that you rated as 2 or 1 in importance. While you may have thought of multiple intentions you could work on in every domain, focus first on the domains and values most important to you. These are the areas in which you will be most motivated to act on your intentions.

A key quality of a good intention is that it be concrete and achievable. The following worksheet will help you create such intentions. Make several copies of the Intentions and Interior Barriers form so you can continue to use it for future values work.

In the left-hand column, write the domains you rated as important (2 or 1), along with at least one of your key values for each.

Next, think of a specific intention you'd like to accomplish that reflects the key value you wrote for each domain. Keep in mind that an intention should be something you can actually accomplish, given the conditions you face. It should also be very specific: What exactly will you do or say? Who, if anyone, will you do this with? When and where will you do this? After giving it some thought, record your intentions in the middle column. For now, leave the right-hand column blank. (An example from Jose appears in step 4.)

Intentions and Interior Barriers

Most important domains and values	Intentions *What? Who? When? Where?*	Internal barriers *Thoughts, feelings, and sensations*

Step 4: Visualize Accomplishing Your Intentions

Now that you have some specific values-based intentions, you'll imagine yourself going through the steps to accomplish your intentions. To begin, choose one intention to work on. Close your eyes and mentally walk yourself through the steps you need to take to achieve your goal. Use all of your senses to experience each step as vividly as you can. Who are you with? What do you do or say? What are the circumstances? As you visualize the sequence of events in detail, note any negative thoughts, feelings, and sensations that might interfere with acting in accordance with your values and achieving your goal. Is there any internal resistance? (See "Special Considerations" in chapter 16, "Changing Core Beliefs with Visualization," for more help with creating vivid imagery.)

In the right-hand column of your Intentions and Interior Barriers form, list any thoughts, feelings, or sensations that come up that might interfere with accomplishing this intention in real life. Repeat this process for each of your intentions. Here's an example of how Jose filled out his worksheet.

Jose's Intentions and Interior Barriers

Most important domains and values	Intentions What? Who? When? Where?	Internal barriers Thoughts, feelings, and sensations
Family of origin: Being supportive and connected	Create a family event to bring people together	Anxiety, a sense of exhaustion, and feeling overwhelmed. Thinking that I'm too tired, that I can't deal with it, and that it's too much.
Health: Feeling good, vitality	Lose 50 pounds over 2 years by walking 1 hour, 5 days a week, eating smaller portions, and minimizing sugary foods.	Low energy and thoughts that a candy bar will pick me up. Thinking I'm too tired to do this. Thinking it won't work and I can't stand it. Feeling hungry, irritable, hopeless, and sad.
Parenting: Nurturing without overprotecting	One phone call each week with each child, listening without lecturing or fixing.	Feeling worried, impatient, irritated, and guilty. Thinking that they do the dumbest things and will blow it, and that I'm a bad parent.
Intimate relationships: Mutual support and respect	Make an agreement with my wife to practice supportive and respectful listening and expressing at mealtimes.	Feeling annoyed. Tense muscles and upset stomach. Thinking that she isn't taking me seriously or being supportive.

Step 5: Commit to Values-Based Action

Committing to values-based action means acting on your value-based intentions in real life and being willing to mindfully notice and accept difficult internal experiences that may arise in the process. Keep in mind the value underlying your intention as well as your intention itself. This will inspire you to follow through with your action plan, even as you notice difficult thoughts, feelings, and sensations floating in and out of your awareness.

Begin by making several copies of the Commitment to Value-Based Action Worksheet so you can use it for various intentions. Use what you've written in your Intentions and Internal Barriers Worksheet to complete the first page of the worksheet, and then commit to acting on your intention. Be sure to use the log on the second page of the worksheet to monitor your progress on following through. In the left-hand column, write a brief description of each step in your action plan. Then check off each day that you take action on that step. Once you've completed a step, check it off in the "Done" column and congratulate yourself! Keeping a log will remind you of your commitment to take action, allow you keep track of what you have and haven't done, and show you that persistence with this approach can pay off.

After one month, evaluate your success and decide whether you want to continue with your current approach, change your action plan, or move on to another intention. (An example from Jose follows the blank worksheet.)

Commitment to Value-Based Action Worksheet

Because I value (key value/domain) _____

_____

I am willing to experience (internal barriers) _____

_____

_____

_____

in order to accomplish (intention) _____

_____

The specific steps of my action plan are: _____

_____

_____

_____

_____

_____

_____

I will monitor my success in keeping my commitments by _____

_____

_____

Step	Mon.	Tue.	Wed.	Thurs.	Fri.	Sat.	Sun.	Done

Jose's Commitment to Value-Based Action Worksheet

Because I value (key value/domain)   *being supportive and strongly connected to my family*

I am willing to experience (internal barriers)   *feeling anxious and overwhelmed, with thoughts like "I'm too tired" and "It's too much"*

in order to accomplish (intention)   *bringing my family together.*

The specific steps of my action plan are: *Clean up the backyard. Buy a new grill. Call everyone to invite them and catch up with each of them. Get the house in order. Buy food. Accept feelings of being anxious and overwhelmed and get things done anyway.*

I will monitor my success in keeping my commitments by   *filling out the log every day.*

Step	Mon.	Tue.	Wed.	Thurs.	Fri.	Sat.	Sun.	Done
Clean up backyard	X			X	X			
Buy grill						X		X
Invite at least one person	X	X		X		X	X	
Spruce up house		X					X	
Buy food								
Accept my feelings and still get things done	X	X		X	X	X	X	

Keeping a log of your actions on each step of your action plan is critical for success. Unless you focus, each day, on doing specific actions you've committed to, values-based behavior activation can easily fade out of your life. Notice that Jose included an action step that involved accepting his feelings (exhaustion, anxiety, a sense of being overwhelmed) and still getting things done. This is the key to acting on your values to overcome depression. No matter how down you feel and despite negative thoughts that may plague you, find a way to take steps toward your goals—every day.

CHAPTER 13

Brief Exposure

Brief exposure as taught in this chapter is the offspring of two pioneering techniques that had a huge impact on the treatment of anxiety and phobia: systematic desensitization and stress inoculation.

Systematic desensitization was developed by behavior therapist Joseph Wolpe in 1958. Wolpe assisted anxious people in developing a hierarchy of stressful scenes related to their phobia. The hierarchy stretched from scenes that produced almost no anxiety to images that were terrifying. Then he provided training in progressive muscle relaxation and helped people desensitize to the frightening scenes by pairing them with deep relaxation, with a goal of reducing anxiety to zero. This goal was simultaneously the strength and the weakness of the technique. People felt a tremendous sense of accomplishment and freedom when they were relaxed in situations that formerly provoked anxiety. But what if anxiety began to creep back in?

To solve this problem, Donald Meichenbaum developed stress inoculation. In his book *Cognitive Behavior Modification* (1977), he argued that a fear response can be conceived of as an interaction of two main elements: heightened physiological arousal (increased heart and respiration rates, sweating, muscle tension, chills, a lump in the throat, and so on); and thoughts that interpret your situation as dangerous or threatening and attribute your physiological arousal to fear. The actual stressful situation has very little to do with your emotional response; your appraisal of the danger and how you interpret your body's response are the real forces that create your anxiety.

Like Wolpe's systematic desensitization, Meichenbaum's stress inoculation technique included a hierarchy of increasingly stressful scenes and training in deep relaxation. In addition, it involved developing a private arsenal of coping thoughts that could be used to counteract habitual thoughts about danger and physical sensations. When anxiety rose during an exposure scene, people were instructed to use coping thoughts along with relaxation skills and stay in the scene rather than cutting it short.

More recently, cognitive behavioral practitioners and researchers have found that it's best to use relaxation and coping statements before and after exposure, not during exposure. This heightens the desensitization or habituation effect and doesn't run the risk of relaxation and coping becoming forms of covert avoidance of the scene.

Brief exposure can be done using both imagery and in vivo (real-life) processes. The same basic instructions apply to both.

SYMPTOM EFFECTIVENESS

Stress inoculation and systematic desensitization have been proven effective with a wide variety of phobias in dozens of studies. However, their effectiveness depends on real-life exposure. In other words, you have to actually do the things you've avoided in order to successfully complete an anxiety treatment program.

Brief imagery exposure, usually followed by prolonged imagery exposure, is effective in desensitizing to memories of past trauma. But for current avoidance symptoms due to post-traumatic stress disorder, use brief and then prolonged real-life exposure.

Brief exposure is not the first choice for treatment of generalized anxiety or panic disorder without phobia. For generalized anxiety, the approaches in chapter 6, "Worry Control," are more helpful, and for panic, chapter 7, "Coping with Panic," is recommended. For treating symptoms associated with obsessive-compulsive disorder, a more effective approach is that in the following chapter, "Prolonged Exposure," which uses prolonged in vivo exposure for phobic fears, and prolonged imagery exposure for pure obsessions without avoidant behavior.

Brief exposure is also helpful in combating perfectionism.

TIME TO MASTERY

Learning the relaxation techniques necessary for brief exposure will take two to four weeks. You can construct your hierarchy during that time. Once you being practicing systematic visualization of scenes, you'll probably notice results in the first several days. However, the average phobia will take one to four weeks to treat effectively with imagined scenes and in vivo exposure.

To completely recover from a phobia, you must conduct real-life exposure to the situations you're imagining in imagery exposure. Only when you learn to enter real-life situations that you used to avoid will you be certain that you can desensitize to your fear.

INSTRUCTIONS

Learning brief exposure is a six-step process:

1. Learn relaxation skills.

2. Choose a fear to work on.

3. Build a hierarchy.

4. Develop coping thoughts.

5. Conduct brief imagery exposure.

6. Conduct brief real-life exposure.

Step 1: Learn Relaxation Skills

If you haven't learned the relaxation skills in chapter 5, begin working through that chapter now. Start with learning abdominal breathing. Once you can reliably create feelings of relaxation, move on to progressive muscle relaxation (PMR), which will teach you what it feels like when your muscles have released all tension.

When you've mastered PMR and can relax the major muscle groups in your body, practice relaxation without tension. This technique uses the same sequence of muscle groups as in PMR but doesn't require that you tighten your muscles before releasing. Instead, you will them to relax and let go.

The next technique you'll learn is cue-controlled relaxation. This will allow you to relax your entire body by taking a series of deep breaths and using a cue word or phrase to trigger relaxed and peaceful feelings.

The final technique to master is learning to visualize a peaceful scene, imagining visual, auditory, and physical aspects of the scene to create in your mind a place where you feel calm, safe, and deeply relaxed.

While you're learning these relaxation skills, you can move on to steps 2 and 3 of brief exposure, choosing a fear to work on and building a hierarchy. By the time you've completed your relaxation training, you'll be ready to begin visualizing and desensitizing to the stressful scenes in your hierarchy.

Step 2: Choose a Fear to Work On

Almost everyone has something he or she really fears, and many people have more than one significant phobia. If you have only one fear and are ready to work on it, skip this section. But if you have several phobias and are uncertain which to work on first, or whether to work on them at all, do the following simple assessment exercise for each of your fears. (You may want to make a copy and leave the version in the book blank so you can assess additional fears.)

Fear Assessment Worksheet

FEAR 1: _____

How distressing is your fear?

| 0 | 1 | 2 | 3 | 4 | 5 | 6 | 7 | 8 | 9 | 10 |
| Not at all | | | | | | | | | | Extremely |

How frequently do you encounter your fear?

| 0 | 1 | 2 | 3 | 4 | 5 | 6 | 7 | 8 | 9 | 10 |
| Never | | | | | | | | | | Constantly |

How much does your fear limit you?

| 0 | 1 | 2 | 3 | 4 | 5 | 6 | 7 | 8 | 9 | 10 |
| Not at all | | | | | | | | | | Extremely |

FEAR 2: _____

How distressing is your fear?

| 0 | 1 | 2 | 3 | 4 | 5 | 6 | 7 | 8 | 9 | 10 |
| Not at all | | | | | | | | | | Extremely |

How frequently do you encounter your fear?

| 0 | 1 | 2 | 3 | 4 | 5 | 6 | 7 | 8 | 9 | 10 |
| Never | | | | | | | | | | Constantly |

How much does your fear limit you?

| 0 | 1 | 2 | 3 | 4 | 5 | 6 | 7 | 8 | 9 | 10 |
| Not at all | | | | | | | | | | Extremely |

FEAR 3: _____

How distressing is your fear?

| 0 | 1 | 2 | 3 | 4 | 5 | 6 | 7 | 8 | 9 | 10 |
| Not at all | | | | | | | | | | Extremely |

How frequently do you encounter your fear?

| 0 | 1 | 2 | 3 | 4 | 5 | 6 | 7 | 8 | 9 | 10 |
| Never | | | | | | | | | | Constantly |

How much does your fear limit you?

| 0 | 1 | 2 | 3 | 4 | 5 | 6 | 7 | 8 | 9 | 10 |
| Not at all | | | | | | | | | | Extremely |

Now you have a brief profile of how each of these fears affects you. Add up your three ratings for each fear to determine which fear has the highest total score. You might want to work on this one first. However, you might decide that one of the three factors you rated is more important than the others, in which case you'd probably want to start by working on whichever fear has the highest score for that factor. For example, many people are less concerned about how distressing or frequent a phobia is than by how much it limits their lives. Choosing which fear to begin with is your decision. Once you've made it, move on to step 3.

Step 3: Build a Hierarchy

If you're working on one simple phobia or one traumatic memory, you might be able to dispense with creating a hierarchy of scenes. If you want to try brief exposure using just one scene, skip ahead to step 4, "Develop Coping Thoughts." Go on to exposing yourself to your scene for sixty seconds, and if you can stay in the scene for that amount of time, congratulations. If you feel overwhelmed or withdraw from the scene early, relax and try again two more times. If you still can't stay in the scene for sixty seconds, the single-scene approach is too intense and you should come back to this step and build a hierarchy.

An exposure hierarchy should comprise from six to twenty scenes. To come up with this many steps with a relatively smooth gradation from least to most threatening, you can manipulate four variables:

1. **Spatial proximity:** how physically close you are to the feared object or situation. If you're afraid of driving on snowy roads, for example, you'd probably feel more fearful as you got closer to the mountains on an annual ski trip. You could create hierarchy scenes in which you imagine your car reaching the first prolonged grade to the mountains, being at an elevation high enough to see the first drifts by the side of the road, and so on.

2. **Temporal proximity or duration:** how close you are in time to the feared object or situation, or how much time you spend exposed to it. For example, a hierarchy for a fear of subways might have scenes in which you're getting closer and closer in time to the subway ride, or it might list rides of progressively longer duration.

3. **Degree of threat:** how difficult and scary the scene is. With a fear of elevators, for example, you can manipulate the degree of threat by altering the number of floors you'll ascend or descend.

4. **Degree of support:** how close you are to a support person during a threatening scene. For a fear of driving on the freeway, for example, your support person could be in the passenger seat next to you, behind you, behind you and out of sight, driving one car length behind you, driving five car lengths behind you, or just on call in case you need help.

You can use all four of these variables when thinking of scenes for your hierarchy. The following three sample hierarchies, marked SP for spatial proximity, TP for temporal proximity, T for degree of threat, and S for degree of support, will help you see how this works. Examining how these hierarchies are built will give you a better idea of how to use the variables to create many different scenes.

		Hierarchy for *phobia about driving on freeways*		
Variable	**Rank**	**Scene**
TP	1	*Thinking about driving on the freeway the day before a practice session*
SP	2	*Sitting in parked car on a side street watching an on-ramp*
T	3	*Riding on a freeway with someone else driving*
S	4	*Driving one exit with a support person in the front seat—light traffic*
T	5	*Driving one exit with a support person in the front seat—heavier traffic*
S	6	*Driving one exit alone—light traffic*
T	7	*Driving one exit alone—heavier traffic*
T, S	8	*Driving two exits with a support person in the front seat—heavy traffic*
S	9	*Driving two exits with a support person in the back seat—heavy traffic*
S	10	*Driving two exits alone—heavy traffic*
T, S	11	*Driving four exits with a support person in the front seat—light traffic*
T, S	12	*Driving four exits with a support person in the back seat—heavier traffic*
S	13	*Driving four exits alone—light traffic*
T	14	*Driving four exits alone—heavy traffic*
T, S	15	*Driving six exits with a support person in the front seat—heavy traffic*
S	16	*Driving six exits alone—light traffic*
T	17	*Driving six exits alone—heavier traffic*
T	18	*Driving eight exits alone—heavier traffic*

		Hierarchy for *phobia about getting injections*		
Variable	**Rank**	**Scene**
T	1	*Watching a movie in which a minor character gets a shot*
T	2	*Talking to a friend about her flu shot*
T	3	*Pricking a finger with a pin*
T	4	*Making a doctor's appointment for a nonmedicinal saline injection*
SP	5	*Driving to the medical center*

SP	6	Parking in the medical center parking lot
T, SP	7	Thinking about shots while sitting in the waiting room
SP	8	Entering the treatment room
TP	9	Nurse entering the room with injection materials
TP	10	Nurse filling the syringe
T	11	Smelling alcohol on the cotton ball
TP	12	Seeing the hypodermic poised in the nurse's hand
T	13	Receiving a small saline shot in the right arm
T	14	Receiving a larger saline shot in the left arm
T	15	Receiving a flu shot in the arm
T	16	Having a blood sample taken

Hierarchy for *phobia about being near bees*		
Variable	**Rank**	**Scene**
T	1	Seeing a picture of a bee
TP	2	Planning to practice in the backyard later in the day
SP	3	Standing at the door looking out at backyard
SP	4	Standing outside near the back door—for 1 minute
TP	5	Standing outside, near the back door—3 minutes
SP	6	Standing halfway to the dahlias (where there are lots of bees)—1 minute
TP	7	Standing halfway to the dahlias—3 minutes
SP	8	Standing close enough to hear buzzing—1 minute
TP	9	Standing close enough to hear buzzing—3 minutes
SP	10	Standing next to the dahlias (bees all around)—1 minute
TP	11	Standing next to the dahlias—2 minutes
TP	12	Standing next to the dahlias—5 minutes

PLANNING FOR REAL-LIFE EXPOSURE

To the greatest extent possible, make each scene something you could intentionally do in real life. Consider the fear of snakes, for example. Hierarchy scenes in which you're walking in the woods and see a snake are hard to set up when you're ready to work on your coping skills in vivo. It's better to have scenes in a store that sells snakes, where you get closer and closer to the glass terrariums, eventually touch a snake, then pick it up, and so on.

STARTING TO BUILD YOUR HIERARCHY

To build your hierarchy for your first fear, start by thinking of a scenario in which you experience your feared object or situation in a way that creates almost no anxiety. You can imagine yourself at a distance in space or time, having a support person by your side, or dealing with only mildly threatening aspects of the situation.

Next, imagine the worst possible experience you can imagine having in regard to your feared object or situation. For example, if you're afraid of public speaking, you might imagine giving a long presentation before a large audience. Or if you're afraid of crowded theaters or classrooms where you're far from an exit, you could create a very claustrophobic scene where the room is stuffy and you'd have to step across many people in their seats to get to the exit. Think about the four variables and how you can manipulate them to make the scene as threatening as imaginable. That said, remember to make all of your scenes something you can replicate in real life.

Once you've identified your least and most intense items, write them on a blank sheet of paper.

FILLING IN THE MIDDLE SCENES

Now imagine six to eighteen additional scenes of increasing intensity that are connected to your phobia. At first just brainstorm, thinking of as many scenes as you can, keeping in mind the four variables. Think of varying degrees of temporal and spatial proximity. Try to increase the degree of threat. If you plan to use a support person later, in real-life exposure, build varying levels of support into your hierarchy as well. Write your ideas down as you think of them.

Once you have six to eighteen of scenes, write them down on a separate piece of paper and rank them from least threatening (number 1) to most threatening (the highest number). At this point, you might want to rewrite your items on a new sheet of paper in rank order.

Review your hierarchy and make sure the incremental increase in fear is approximately equal throughout. If some increments are significantly larger than others, you'll need to fill in the gaps with additional scenes. If some increments are too small, delete items or manipulate the variables so they evoke different levels of fear. Keep working on it until the steps are about even.

FINALIZING YOUR HIERARCHY

Write your finalized hierarchy in rank order on a copy of the following hierarchy form, leaving the version in the book blank so you can copy it for use with other phobias. For now, just fill in the "Scene" column. You'll add coping thoughts in step 4. If you need more rows for hierarchy items, simply use another copy of the blank hierarchy form and revise the rank accordingly.

	Hierarchy for _____	
Rank	Scene	Coping thoughts

Step 4: Develop Coping Thoughts

You should develop one or two coping thoughts as you get ready to visualize each new scene in your hierarchy. To do so, briefly visualize the scene, making it as real as possible. Notice what you see, what you hear, and even what you feel physically. Next, listen to your thoughts. What are you saying to yourself about potential dangers or catastrophes that might occur in the scene? Here are some key questions to ask yourself when developing your coping thoughts:

- Do I have a plan to handle this situation? What would I do if the problem I fear occurred?

- How likely are the frightening outcomes that I imagine? Can I estimate the odds against these happening?

- How long would I have to endure the situation if it actually occurred? Sometimes it's enough just to remind yourself, "I can do this; it's only a short time."

- What coping skills do I have to handle this? What relaxation skills can I use? How can I reassure myself? Are there things I can remind myself to do?

The answers to these questions may give you some ideas for coping thoughts to help manage anxiety in that particular scene. You can also consult the following list of generic coping thoughts, which may give you other good ideas:

- This feeling isn't comfortable or pleasant, but I can accept it.

- I can be anxious and still deal with this situation.

- I can handle these sensations.

- This is an opportunity for me to learn to cope with my fears.

- This will pass.

- I'll ride this out. I don't need to let it get to me.

- I deserve to feel okay right now.

- I can take all the time I need to let go and relax.

- I've survived this before, and I'll survive this time too.

- I can do what I have to do in spite of anxiety.

- This anxiety won't hurt me; it just doesn't feel good.

- These are fight-or-flight reactions. They won't hurt me.

- This is just anxiety. I'm not going to let it get to me.

- Nothing serious is going to happen to me.

- Fighting and resisting this isn't going to help, so I'll just let it pass.

- These are just thoughts, not reality.

- I don't need these thoughts. I can choose to think differently.

- This isn't dangerous.

- So what?

Right now, come up with one or two good coping thoughts for the first scene in your hierarchy. Record them in the space provided on the hierarchy form. Because effective coping thoughts may vary depending on the scene, remember to come up with appropriate coping thoughts before working with each new scene in your hierarchy.

Here are some examples of coping thoughts for a few items in a hierarchy devised by Linda, who has a fear of talking to strangers.

Hierarchy for *fear of talking to strangers*		
Rank	Scene	Coping thoughts
4	Driving to a small gathering at a friend's house	Breathe and relax. I'll talk mostly to friends. I can handle strangers if they're with a group of my friends.
7	Standing at the snack table with a stranger	Breathe and relax. I can do this in spite of anxiety.
9	Walking into a party where I know only a few people	Breathe and relax. This is an opportunity to learn to cope. I can ask the standard questions when I talk to strangers.
14	Getting trapped in a boring conversation with a motormouth and wanting to escape	Breathe and relax. I'll excuse myself to go to the bathroom.

Notice that Linda always reminds herself to breathe and relax. This helps her let go of physical tension before moving on to the other coping thoughts. You might experiment and see if this works for you.

Step 5: Conduct Brief Imagery Exposure

The brief exposure sequence has five steps:

A. Relax for ten minutes.

B. Visualize the scene.

C. Rate your anxiety.

D. Relax and use coping thoughts between scenes.

E. Repeat steps B through D until your anxiety declines, then move on to the next scene.

A. RELAX FOR TEN MINUTES

Go through progressive muscle relaxation, cue-controlled relaxation (which includes deep breathing), and visualizing a special scene, somewhere you feel calm and safe. Review the coping statements you've prepared for the scene you're working with.

B. VISUALIZE THE SCENE

Start with the first scene in your hierarchy. Set a timer for sixty seconds, then visualize the scene and stay in it for the full minute. Try to bring it to life. See the situation, hear what's going on, feel any physical sensations. What objects or people are in the scene? What colors do you see? What's the quality of light? Do you smell anything, notice the temperature, or feel anything against your skin? Do you hear anything, such as voices, wind, or a ticking clock? Don't picture yourself being anxious in the scene. If you're in the scene, see yourself as comfortable and confident. If your mind wanders from the scene, refocus and concentrate on the details.

Don't use your coping thoughts or relaxation techniques during the scene; save them for between scenes. If you become so upset that you quit visualizing the scene before sixty seconds have elapsed, do your relaxation exercises and try again. If this happens three times in a row, the scene is too intense. You need to break it down into two or three more manageable scenes in your hierarchy.

C. RATE YOUR ANXIETY

When the timer goes off, leave the scene and rate your anxiety level on a scale of 0 to 10, where 0 is no anxiety and 10 represents the worst fear you've ever felt.

D. RELAX AND USE COPING THOUGHTS BETWEEN SCENES

Between visualizations of your hierarchy items, relax and use your coping thoughts. If the scene evoked only moderate anxiety, you might use cue-controlled relaxation and spend time calming yourself by visualizing your special place. If you experienced a lot of anxiety during a scene, spend some additional time doing progressive muscle relaxation or relaxation without tension. These powerful techniques can help you achieve a deeper level of calm.

E. REPEAT STEPS B THROUGH D UNTIL YOUR ANXIETY DECLINES, THEN MOVE TO THE NEXT SCENE

If your rating was 4 or above, revisit the same scene. Once your rating drops to 3 or lower, move to the next scene in your hierarchy. It usually takes at least two exposures to a scene to fully desensitize to it. However, the lowest-ranked scenes may require only one exposure if your anxiety is quite low from the outset.

Practice daily if at all possible. Your first practice session should last about twenty minutes. Later you can extend your sessions to as much as thirty minutes. The main limiting factor is fatigue. Always stop a session if you begin to feel tired or bored.

Expect to master from one to three hierarchy items during each practice session. When starting a new practice session, always go back to the last scene you successfully completed. This helps you consolidate your gains before facing new items that evoke more anxiety. Continue visualizing and coping with scenes until you've mastered the highest-ranked item in your hierarchy.

Step 6: Conduct Brief Real-Life Exposure

In most cases you can use the same hierarchy to practice in vivo exposure to feared situations. After you've visualized the first three or four scenes in your hierarchy, go back and start conducting real-life exposure to the first scene. The work in your imagination and in real life will reinforce one another.

If some of your items can't be easily practiced in a real-life situation, modify them so they can. Consider the item "Elevator stuck between floors." This is clearly something you can't create on demand. But you can modify it to "Standing in the elevator at the Barclay Building, where the door closes and then the elevator doesn't move for a long time." This isn't the same as being stuck between floors, but it evokes some of the same feelings.

It may be difficult to ensure that real-life situations last exactly sixty seconds. Just be sure to stay in the situation for at least that long, without making an early exit when your anxiety rises.

Example

Jennifer, a product manager for a major apparel firm, had become extremely phobic in meetings where she was expected to speak before the group, particularly when she had to make quarterly product presentations. Her anxiety increased greatly after her most recent presentation when she was criticized for giving a sloppy, disorganized description of her product line and manufacturing plans.

It took Jennifer about three weeks to learn progressive muscle relaxation, relaxation without tension, and cue-controlled relaxation, and to develop an effective special-place visualization. During that time she built the following hierarchy. Although she developed her coping thoughts over time, as she progressed through her hierarchy, we provide them here by way of example. On occasion, a coping thought proved ineffective, so Jennifer crossed it out and replaced it with something new.

Hierarchy for *meetings where I'm expected to speak before a group*

Rank	Scene	Coping thoughts
1	Product-planning meeting scheduled in two weeks	Let go and relax. I've got plenty of time to prepare.
2	Trying to assemble the material I'll need to present, one week before meeting	Let go and relax. Everything will be ready. I know what I need to do.
3	Bringing the presentation home the night before the meeting	Let go and relax. I'll read the presentation if I get nervous and don't trust my memory.
4	Arriving at work on the morning of the ten o'clock meeting	Let go and relax. ~~This is just anxiety, it won't hurt me.~~ I've survived this before; I'll get through it this time.
5	Walking into the meeting, greeting people, stacking papers on the desk in front of me	Let go and relax. I'll ride this through; I'm prepared.
6	Listening to other, very well-prepared product presentations	Let go and relax. ~~I can do what I have to do in spite of anxiety.~~ I've done my best. I accept whatever happens.
7	Introduction of my product line	Let go and relax. I've done my best; I accept whatever happens. I've survived this before.
8	Starting to speak and looking around at all the faces turned expectantly to me	Let go and relax. I can do this; I've done it before. I'm doing my best.
9	Feeling like it just goes on and on and the end is still a long way off; seeing everyone looking intently at me and not knowing what they're thinking	Let go and relax. It's all prepared. Just keep going; you'll get there eventually.
10	A moment of silence at the end before there's any reaction, and not knowing what people think	Let go and relax. Smile at them. I did my best.

Jennifer developed her coping thoughts by imagining the scene first and listening to the scary things she was saying to herself. When she was able to identify the thoughts that were causing her fear, she used the list of key questions to either develop a coping plan or remind herself of some of her coping skills. She also found a number of helpful coping thoughts on the generic list. She used the coping suggestion "Let go and relax" with every scene because it reminded her to release the tension in her body.

Jennifer followed the brief exposure procedure carefully. She found that the first two items were easy and evoked very little anxiety. She felt moderate anxiety with the third scene and had her first experience of marked anxiety with the fourth scene, which she rated at 8 on the scale of 0 to 10. Afterward she did some progressive muscle relaxation and spent extra time with her special place visualization. On her third exposure to the fourth scene, Jennifer was able to experience the scene with only mild anxiety, rating it 2 out of 10, and could move on.

Working in twenty-minute sessions each day, she proceeded through the scenes, alternating between visualizing and relaxing, until she got to the ninth item on her hierarchy, where she experienced high anxiety six times in a row. She decided to break that item down into two separate scenes. The first scene was "Feeling like it just goes on and on and the end is still a long way off." She found herself able to cope with that scene more easily and desensitized to it after three more visualizations. The second part of the scene, "Seeing everyone looking intently at me and not knowing what they're thinking," was more difficult. Twice more she experienced extreme anxiety, but on the third visualization her fear decreased. With four more visualizations, Jennifer was able to experience the scene with very little anxiety.

Jennifer used the same hierarchy and coping thoughts in real life as she prepared for her next product presentation. The realities of her actual work schedule required some deviations from the hierarchy she used for imagery work. For example, at the last minute her presentation was moved to an earlier spot on the agenda, so she didn't have a long period of sitting and listening to others before she had to give her presentation. She covered her surprise and alarm by pouring herself a glass of water, taking a deep breath, and reminding herself, "I've done my best. I accept whatever happens."

The exposure work paid off. Jennifer was able to get through the actual presentation with only mild to moderate anxiety. While she didn't completely eradicate her anxiety, she did achieve something vitally important: developing the ability to cope with feelings of fear so she could continue to meet the challenges of her job.

SPECIAL CONSIDERATIONS

If you worked your way through this chapter because of a phobia but brief exposure doesn't completely resolve your phobia, move on to chapter 14, "Prolonged Exposure," but note that you should only practice prolonged real-life exposure, not prolonged imaginal exposure. If you experience difficulties in practicing brief exposure, they are likely to be due to one of the three common problems: incomplete relaxation, difficulties with visualization, or a poorly constructed hierarchy.

Incomplete Relaxation

If you can't relax at the beginning of a session, try to imagine lying on a soft lawn on a calm summer day, watching clouds slowly floating by. Or imagine watching leaves float by on a broad, slow river. Each cloud or leaf takes some of your muscular tension away with it. You may also want to make an audio recording of your relaxation routine and play it at the beginning of each session or scene.

Difficulties with Visualization

If you find that your visualized scenes seem flat, unreal, and unevocative of the distress you would feel in real-life scenes, you probably have trouble visualizing things clearly. To strengthen your powers of imagination, ask questions of all your senses to make your scenes more vivid.

- **Sight:** What colors are in the scene? What colors are the walls, the landscape, cars, furnishings, or people's clothes? Is the light bright or dim? What details are there—books on the table, pets, chairs, rugs? What pictures are on the walls? What words can you read on signs?

- **Sound:** What are the tones of voice? Are there background noises such as planes, traffic, dogs barking, or music? Is there wind in the trees? Can you hear your own voice?

- **Touch:** Imagine reaching out and feeling things. Are they rough or smooth, hard or soft, rounded or flat? What's the weather like? Are you hot or cold? Do you itch, sweat, or have to sneeze? What are you wearing? How does it feel against your skin?

- **Smell:** Can you smell dinner cooking? Flowers? Tobacco smoke? Sewage? Perfume or aftershave? Chemicals? Decay? Pine trees?

- **Taste:** Are you eating or drinking? Are the tastes sweet, sour, salty, or bitter?

It also helps to go to the real setting of one of your scenes to gather images and impressions and practice remembering those details. Observe the setting, then close your eyes and try to see the scene. Then open your eyes and notice what you missed. Close your eyes and try again. Describe the scene out loud to yourself, or whisper to yourself if others are present. Open your eyes and see what you missed this time, and what you changed in your mind. Close your eyes and describe the scene again, adding sounds, textures, scents, temperatures, and so on. Keep this up until you have a vivid sense picture of the scene.

Poorly Constructed Hierarchy

If you don't experience a reduction in anxiety with repetitions of a particular scene, you probably need to reconstruct your hierarchy with a more gradual gradient.

If you can visualize your scenes clearly and experience little or no anxiety, you probably need to reconstruct your hierarchy with a steeper gradient between scenes or with a greater variety of content in the scenes.

If you can visualize your scenes clearly and experience erratic levels of anxiety, the scenes in your hierarchy are probably not evenly spaced with regard to intensity. Reconstruct the hierarchy and try again.

CHAPTER 14

Prolonged Exposure

Prolonged exposure is a simple technique in which you intentionally imagine a feared situation or entertain an obsessional train of thought. You hold this situation or thought in your mind for a long time, at high intensity and without avoiding or neutralizing the images, until you finally grow bored with the images and they lose their power to upset you. Prolonged exposure provides more desensitization and habituation effects than brief exposure, but it is more difficult, and sometimes people have a hard time tolerating the process.

Prolonged exposure has a long history. In 1967, Thomas Stampfl reported on what he called implosion therapy (Stampfl and Levis 1967). He found that the fears of phobic patients would disappear, or "implode," after they were bombarded with six to nine hours of continuous verbal descriptions of their feared situations. However, most therapists and clients found this technique too time-consuming and exhausting, until Zev Wanderer devised physiologically monitored implosion therapy in the early 1980s. He used blood pressure biofeedback to pinpoint the most disturbing phrases and images in a client's hierarchy of fears. By intensifying the imagery, he reduced the average time needed for an initial exposure session to two hours, and subsequent sessions could be as short as thirty minutes (Wanderer 1991).

Still, this took up quite a few office hours and didn't fit into neat, fifty-minute modules. So he took advantage of another technological aid, the loop tape. He asked clients to record their fearful imagery on a three-minute constant-loop cassette tape while hooked up to a blood pressure monitor. When the monitor indicated that a client had reached a sustained maximum arousal, Wanderer would stop the tape recorder, capturing the loop that elicited the greatest response. The client could then take the tape home and do the actual exposure sessions as homework. Dr. Wanderer later found that many clients could self-monitor their arousal and make their own loop tapes at home.

Psychologists Paul Salkovskis and Joan Kirk (1989) developed a method using a thirty-second loop tape to treat obsessional thinking. They instructed clients to focus on the content of the tape, rather than trying to avoid or neutralize the obsession while they listened to the tape. In the first three editions of this book, we presented a version of these loop tape techniques called flooding.

Prolonged exposure can also be done in vivo (in real life), by finding actual situations in which you can place yourself for an extended period of time. Prolonged exposure to real situations is the treatment of choice for phobias that cannot be resolved by brief imagery or in vivo exposure.

SYMPTOM EFFECTIVENESS

Prolonged imagery exposure is very effective for reducing obsessional thinking that isn't accompanied by compulsive behavior, such as the fear of doing or saying harmful or unacceptable things. It's also used to desensitize people with post-traumatic stress disorder to images of past trauma (Foa, Hembree, and Olaslov Rothbaum 2007).

Prolonged real-life exposure is quite effective for panic or for simple phobias that don't respond to brief exposure, such as fear of snakes, heights, small spaces, freeways, and so on. It is also used to desensitize people to fears associated with obsessive-compulsive disorder, such as fear of contamination or causing harm.

Because prolonged exposure will elevate your blood pressure for an extended period, you shouldn't use this approach if you have high blood pressure or a family history of heart attack or stroke. Prolonged exposure is also contraindicated if there is any chance that you might perform a feared action such as suicide or harming others (McMullin 1986).

TIME TO MASTERY

Prolonged exposure is intense, but it's relatively simple. For prolonged imagery exposure, it will take you about an hour to make a recording and three to ten exposure sessions of at least one hour's duration to reduce your anxiety level to near 0. If you have a hierarchy of feared experiences from chapter 13, you'll repeat this process for each step of the hierarchy.

For prolonged real-life exposure, you will work through each item on your hierarchy by remaining in the feared situation until you feel a significant reduction in distress, and will repeat each exposure until your anxiety is near 0.

INSTRUCTIONS

If you worked through chapter 13, "Brief Exposure," you'll find the approach in this chapter to be somewhat similar, with both approaches using imagined scenes and, later, real-life situations. However, there are some major differences. Prolonged exposure obviously requires longer exposures; it also utilizes an audio recording during imagery-based exposures. And, importantly, prolonged exposure does not make use of relaxation skills or coping statements; in fact, these strategies are prohibited in prolonged exposure.

Prolonged Imagery Exposure

Prolonged imagery exposure is a five-step process:

1. Record intense fear images.

2. Listen to your recording.

3. Rate your discomfort every five minutes.

4. Stop when your peak discomfort is halved.

5. Repeat steps 2 through 4 until your initial discomfort is near 0.

Before you begin the procedure, read all of the instructions and photocopy the Discomfort Rating Chart from step 3.

STEP 1: RECORD INTENSE FEAR IMAGES

You'll need some means of recording your voice, such as a digital recorder or a microphone and recording software on your computer. Sit in a comfortable chair with your recorder handy, along with a pencil and paper in case you need to make a list of your frightening images.

Close your eyes and tune in to your body for a moment to take a baseline reading: How do you feel? How fast and deeply are you breathing? Can you feel your heart beating? How cold or warm are various parts of your body? Do you have any aches or pains, hunger pangs, nausea, or other internal sensations? Notice how you feel now so you'll know more clearly when conditions change in your body later.

You can open your eyes or leave them closed as you ask yourself these questions:

- What is the most important thing I wish to overcome?

- What am I avoiding that I want to approach?

- What do I want to do that I'm afraid of?

- What's holding me back?

- What do I fear will happen to me in this situation?

- What thoughts frequently prey on my mind?

- What worries do I have a hard time putting out of my mind?

When you have a clear idea of the phobia or obsession you want to work on, start your recorder and begin talking about it. If you have a hard time starting to talk, use your pencil and paper to jot down some frightening situations or phrases and then read each scene or thought out loud. Elaborate on each and see how scary it feels.

Describe what you fear in the most vivid detail possible, as if it were actually happening to you. For example, don't describe your fear of heights in an abstract way, as you might relate it to a therapist:

I sometimes get nervous when I'm in a high place. I'm afraid I might fall out the window or over the railing.

Instead, describe what you fear as if it were happening in a movie you're watching:

I walk out onto the observation platform of the Sears Tower. I trip and fall against the railing; it breaks and I plunge over the edge, flailing in the air and screaming my guts out.

Likewise, if you're recording a train of obsessional thoughts, don't be dry and analytical about it:

I can't stop thinking about my baby getting sick.

Instead, describe your worst nightmare as if it were happening in the moment:

Suddenly I realize I haven't fed or changed Sally all day. I rush into her room to find her convulsing in the crib, covered with shit and vomit. I pick up her thrashing body, and it goes limp in my arms. I know she's dead, dead, dead, and it's all my fault.

Don't include any descriptions of avoidance of your fear, such as "I turn away so I won't have to see," "I try not to think about it," "I run from the room," and so on. Likewise, don't describe any neutralizing thoughts. Neutralizing can take several forms. In the case of obsessions, neutralizing can be compulsive mental rituals like counting, repeating nonsense syllables, magical incantations, prayers, or affirmations—anything you typically do in your mind to neutralize the obsessional thoughts.

In the case of phobias, neutralizing might be reminding yourself that your fears are out of proportion—that you know the bridge won't really collapse. Or it might involve using phrases such as "Whatever happens, happens," or "Forget it and let go." Such thoughts may have a coping value in other applications of cognitive therapy, but for prolonged exposure you need to wallow in the worst, craziest, most unrelieved and unmitigated fear images you can muster. Leave yourself no escape and no respite from your fear.

Include sights, sounds, scents, flavors, and physical sensations, such as pain, textures, and temperatures. Using all five senses makes your scene much more vivid. (See "Special Considerations" in chapter 16, "Changing Core Beliefs with Visualization," for more help with creating vivid imagery.)

Keep talking and adding details until you start to get scared. Keep track of your physical reactions. Your breathing should speed up and become more shallow. You might notice that you're breathing from the middle of your chest instead of deeply from your belly. You might start sweating. Your hands may feel clammy and your stomach queasy. You might start to cry or feel like crying. You might tremble or get a headache.

Don't stop talking, even if you're shaking and crying. Keep asking yourself, "What could be worse than what I'm describing?" Use your physical reactions to get yourself just as scared and upset as you can.

When you reach what feels like the peak of your arousal and you can't get any more upset, stop recording. Play back what you recorded and edit it down to two or three minutes of the most upsetting material.

Some people have stage fright when it comes to talking into a recorder, even though there is no audience beyond themselves. If this is the case for you, you may have to practice for a long time before you get a usable recording. You may have to write out a script and read it.

STEP 2: LISTEN TO YOUR RECORDING

Get comfortable in your chair. Have a pencil and a photocopy of the Discomfort Rating Chart handy. Put on earphones if you like. Set your computer or digital recorder to play your scene as a loop, over and over. If your equipment doesn't have this feature, replay it manually. Hit the play button and turn up the volume until it's nice and loud, filling your consciousness and really affecting you.

Listen attentively for at least an hour. Try to stay with the content of your recording to the greatest extent possible. If you're working with obsessive thoughts, avoid neutralizing thoughts or rituals, such as counting, repeating nonsense syllables, saying favorite prayers or affirmations, and the like. If you're working with phobic images, don't argue against them with positive counterstatements like "This could never happen," "It will be over soon," "It wouldn't actually be this bad," and so on.

STEP 3: RATE YOUR DISCOMFORT EVERY FIVE MINUTES

Use a copy of the Discomfort Rating Chart to rate your discomfort from 0 to 10, with 0 representing no discomfort and 10 representing the worst discomfort you've ever felt. Put a check mark or an X next to the appropriate discomfort level at each five-minute interval.

Prolonged exposure is so unpleasant that you'll probably be peeking at your watch or clock frequently enough to know when each five-minute interval is up. If you have trouble keeping track of the time, use a timer to alert you every five minutes.

You're likely to notice that your discomfort rating increases during the first ten to twenty minutes. Don't be discouraged or worry about that; it's normal.

Discomfort Rating Chart

10																		
9																		
8																		
7																		
6																		
5																		
4																		
3																		
2																		
1																		
0																		
Min.	5	10	15	20	25	30	35	40	45	50	55	60	65	70	75	80	85	90

STEP 4: STOP WHEN YOUR PEAK DISCOMFORT IS HALVED

Keep listening to the recording for an hour or until your discomfort has declined to 50 percent of the highest level you reached during the session. Don't quit prematurely. That's a form of avoidance, and it will act like a reward, reinforcing your fear or obsession. It could even make your reaction more intense next time.

STEP 5: REPEAT STEPS 2 THROUGH 4 UNTIL YOUR INITIAL DISCOMFORT IS NEAR 0

Give yourself a few hours or a day to recover, then listen to your recording again, following the directions for steps 2, 3, and 4. The next time you listen to your recording, you'll probably find that your discomfort level is greater at the beginning of the session than it was at the end of your previous session, but not as high as the peak of the previous session. This is a normal discomfort "rebound."

Schedule exposure sessions every day, and keep working with the same recording until you can start a session at a minimal level of discomfort that quickly drops to near 0. For each phobia or obsession, it will probably take from three to ten sessions to get to that point.

If you're using a hierarchy of feared images, once your discomfort with an item is near 0, move up to the next item on your hierarchy. Record this new scene using the most upsetting descriptions possible and proceed in the same way. Below, we've provided a few examples to help you see how the entire process works.

Example

Robert, a mail carrier, had developed a dog phobia as a result of several close calls with large dogs, most recently being attacked by a large Doberman on a front porch. The dog came up the stairs, blocking Robert's exit, and bit him multiple times. He was trapped by the dog for more than ten minutes before the owner called off his animal. He went on leave from the post office and, contrary to his lawyer's advice, decided to work on the phobia himself.

He purchased a small digital recorder and tried to record details of his most feared situation. But his mind kept going blank, and he wasn't able to make the scene very horrible or vivid.

To improve the imagery for his recording, Robert made a list of the most frightening dog images he could think of. Then he closed his eyes and visualized them one at a time, noticing which triggered the most intense fear reactions. The worst scene involved being attacked and dragged down by two German shepherds.

Now he had something to work with. With the recorder running, he elaborated on the scene until he could feel a strong anxiety reaction in his body. Robert was careful to not include any images that involved escape, relief from his fear, coping, or other neutralizing thoughts. For example, at one point he included an attempt to bolt past the dogs to freedom, but then realized his error and edited that scene out. In his final, edited tape, every image maintained the same trapped, terrified experience. Here's the final script that Robert recorded:

> *The German shepherds are lunging, their mouths foaming. Their teeth are red with my blood. One of them has my arm, his teeth deep in my flesh. I try to throw him off, but he's hanging on to my arm, biting deeper. I can feel the teeth crunching the bone. I feel a searing pain in my leg. The other dog has my calf and is trying to pull me down. I feel the dog's hot breath and razor-sharp fangs. I hear ferocious growls. The dogs are lunging, growling, and blocking my way. They want to kill me, rip my throat. They want to pull me down and rip my neck open. My clothes are red, my wounds are gushing blood. They want me down where they can finish me, their jaws crunching my throat, ripping my jugular. Searing pain racks my body; I'm stumbling, ready to fall, knowing I'm going to die.*

Robert's recording worked especially well because it flowed well when the end looped back to the beginning. There wasn't an awkward transition where he had to imagine himself on the ground having his throat crunched and then suddenly on his feet again at the scene's beginning. Robert cleverly got the throat crunching in as a fear about the outcome.

His recording completed, Robert sat in a comfortable chair with earphones. He closed his eyes and listened to the gruesome scene for an hour, working hard to keep his mind focused on the scene. Whenever his thoughts started to drift away from the scene, he forced himself to concentrate on it again. If he had a neutralizing image or thought—for example, knocking the dogs away or hoping that a passerby might help—he quickly shut it out.

Robert charted his anxiety level every five minutes. Here's the chart from his first exposure session. Notice that he had to go longer than an hour to reduce his anxiety to 50 percent of its highest point.

Robert's First Discomfort Rating Chart

	5	10	15	20	25	30	35	40	45	50	55	60	65	70	75	80	85	90
10																		
9			X	X														
8		X			X	X			X									
7							X											
6	X							X		X	X							
5												X	X					
4														X	X			
3																		
2																		
1																		
0																		
Min.	5	10	15	20	25	30	35	40	45	50	55	60	65	70	75	80	85	90

The following three sessions over the next three days were gradually easier. Here's Robert's chart from his fifth and last session. Notice that after brief initial anxiety, Robert experienced no discomfort for the remainder of the session.

Robert's Fifth Discomfort Rating Chart

	5	10	15	20	25	30	35	40	45	50	55	60	65	70	75	80	85	90
10																		
9																		
8																		
7																		
6																		
5																		
4																		
3																		
2		X																
1	X		X	X														
0					X	X	X	X	X	X	X	X						
Min.	5	10	15	20	25	30	35	40	45	50	55	60	65	70	75	80	85	90

Robert's fear of dogs declined to the point where he could walk near a dog park or visit friends who had large dogs. He felt that if he had to, he could even walk his old mail route. Fortunately, his lawsuit netted him a large enough settlement that he could go back to school and train for a different job.

MAY LIN'S TRAUMATIC MEMORIES

May Lin, a thirty-two-year-old cellist, had been mugged at gunpoint three years ago on her way home from a rehearsal. She used prolonged imagery exposure to desensitize herself to her memories of the assault. The computer in her studio was already set up for recording music, so she had a convenient means of making a recording of her feared scene. She consulted the police report of her mugging to remind herself of the details and, after several revisions, came up with this script:

I'm walking into the parking lot and I notice it's darker than usual. I hear glass crunch underfoot and realize that someone has broken the security light. A jolt of adrenaline feels like a punch to my chest. I walk faster toward my car. It's only three rows away but it seems like a mile. A tall guy in a dark sweatshirt looms up in front of me and holds something metallic in my face. It's a gun! He yells like a wild animal. I hug my cello case to my body and turn it away from him. He shoves up against me and I can smell pot and sweat. He grabs my purse and pulls me off balance. I twist so I won't fall on the cello. My purse strap is caught on my arm and tangled up with the cello. I fall and hit my right knee and elbow. He drags me by the purse strap before it comes loose, and I can feel asphalt and broken glass grinding into the flesh of my shoulder. The entire time he's growling like an animal, without words. He runs away with my purse. I wet myself and feel all shaky inside, like I'm going to throw up. My heart is pounding like a hammer in my chest and I taste blood inside my mouth where I've bitten my lip.

May Lin included vivid sights, sounds, smells, tastes, and tactile sensations. She deleted the a sentence that expressed relief that her mugger didn't take her cello because it seemed to lessen the horror of the attack.

She set up her computer to play the recording over and over, and set the alarm on her phone to ring every five minutes. It was very scary to listen to the recording for the first hour. Her fear ratings were up around 9 out of 10 for more than half of the first session. She set aside an hour each morning to listen to her recording and committed to doing it before she practiced the cello. By the eighth morning, her anxiety level never rose above 3, and her anxiety decreased by over 50 percent in only 20 minutes, by which time she found the scene almost boring.

PAUL'S BLASPHEMY OBSESSION

Paul, a very religious person with a deep and long-standing faith, was plagued by obsessional blasphemous thoughts. He had lived with this problem for years and always hoped it would go away, but instead it kept getting worse. He experienced these thoughts increasingly often, and whenever he did, he felt guilty and fearful of eternal damnation. At his therapist's suggestion, he kept a thought journal for several days, writing down all of the upsetting thoughts as they came up. Then he used the list to record a script full of random statements about God, the Devil, and the Bible. On three different occasions he tried to listen to his recording, but he got so upset that he had to stop after a couple of minutes. The material he'd recorded was too daunting for him to tackle all at once. So he divided it into these three sections, from least to most upsetting, and made three different recordings:

Recording 1: *Reading the Bible is a total waste of time. The Bible is a random collection of ancient drivel. It's just a pile of dusty papyrus that somebody found in some dirty old jars in the desert. All the so-called holy books have nothing to do with God's word. They're just pathetic attempts by primitive people to make sense out of a senseless universe. All that stuff about the Apocalypse and the Rapture is just a big horselaugh on the human race.*

Recording 2: *Jesus was just a man. He is not my personal savior. He doesn't know me from Adam. In fact, he doesn't know anyone, because he's dead and gone. He wasn't the son of God. He was just some nutcase in the Middle East, a weirdo who got picked by a crowd of other weirdos as a figurehead for the pile of sanctimonious crap they called a religion. All of modern Christianity today is a sham, just a way for frauds to bilk poor people out of their money, and a way for the powers that be to keep people in line. True believers like me are deluded fools.*

Recording 3: God has left the building. He's not in charge. Considering all the pain and evil and suffering in the world, it's obvious that God has left us. He has abandoned us. He is not watching over us at all. If God happens to glance our way, he just laughs at us and smites somebody down for fun. It would be better if God didn't exist, but it's not that easy. He does exist; he just doesn't care. If anyone is in charge, it's Satan.

Paul averaged six prolonged exposures before he desensitized to each recording. His three weeks of prolonged imagery exposure were grueling, but by the end of that time he could listen to the most upsetting recording with an anxiety level of only 4 out of 10 at the beginning, which dropped to 1 or 2 within ten minutes. Eventually, Paul found that his obsessional thoughts occurred less frequently, didn't last as long, and didn't upset him as they had before he practiced prolonged imagery exposure.

Prolonged Real-Life Exposure

For persistent phobias and avoidant symptoms of post-traumatic stress disorder and obsessive-compulsive disorder, you need to practice prolonged exposure in vivo—out in the real world. Because it isn't practical or safe to plunge yourself into the middle of a dog fight or arrange to be in a real plane crash, you'll have to be creative. It's a good idea to develop a hierarchy of several real situations that range from moderately distressing to very scary. (See chapter 13, "Brief Exposure," for detailed instructions on creating an effective hierarchy.) Then place yourself in each situation, starting with the least distressing, for a prolonged period, until your anxiety level drops to 50 percent of its peak level during a given session. Practice the same exposure daily until your anxiety level is near 0.

When practicing prolonged real-life exposure, follow the same rules as for prolonged imagery exposure:

- Focus on the details that scare you.

- Don't escape by distracting or distancing yourself.

- Don't perform relaxation exercises or calming mental rituals.

- Continuously rate your level of anxiety on the same scale of 0 to 10, where 10 is the worst discomfort you've ever felt. You can use the Discomfort Rating Chart from earlier in the chapter for this.

- Stay in the situation until you experience a significant desensitization effect, where your anxiety declines to half or close to half of its highest level during that session.

Because the details of prolonged real-life exposure vary so widely depending on the person and the phobia or obsession, it's difficult to provide a more precise outline of how to proceed. Therefore, we've provided two examples to help you see how this process works in real life.

CHAVI'S CONTAMINATION PHOBIA

Chavi, a twenty-six-year-old woman with obsessive-compulsive disorder, had debilitating fears related to germs and contamination. Her avoidance had gotten so extreme that it was threatening her job at an optical devices company and her relationship to her girlfriend. She decided to use prolonged real-life exposure for her fear of germs and began by creating a hierarchy of real-life contamination experiences.

Hierarchy for *fear of contamination*	
1	Hold the front closet doorknob firmly, with all five fingers.
2	Touch the floor in the living room with my hand flat on the floor.
3	Sit on the living room floor with the back of my legs in full contact.
4	Touch the stair rail at work, with full hand contact.
5	Touch the floor of my bathroom, far from the toilet, with my hand flat on the floor.
6	Sit on my bathroom floor, with the back of my legs in full contact.
7	Touch my toilet seat, with full hand contact.
8	"Contaminate" my purse by touching it after I touch the toilet, and leave it that way.
9	Sit on a public toilet with bare skin and no paper shield.

Chavi had to make strict rules for herself to prevent subtle forms of avoidance. In addition to including specific instructions about full contact with objects and surfaces, she didn't allow herself to wash her hands immediately after an exposure session and instead waited until just before her next meal. She also didn't allow herself to take any showers except first thing in the morning.

She spent two weeks working through the first four items on her hierarchy and was successful, even though she often felt like she was crawling with germs. Then she freaked out about touching her bathroom floor and stopped practicing prolonged real-life exposure for a month. She had to start over with the first scene, but this time she successfully completed her hierarchy in about six weeks. For the first time in years, Chavi was able to travel and dine out like a normal person, without constant anxiety and without having to hide her old cleaning rituals.

KARA'S PTSD AVOIDANCE

Years ago, Kara, a forty-one-year-old schoolteacher, had participated in a political rally that was broken up by the state police. The police used water cannons and tear gas, and in the resulting chaos, Kara broke her ankle. Yet even after her ankle healed, she was tormented by anything that reminded her of the event. She was terrified by large crowds and loud noises and eventually moved to a small town that was peaceful and safe, but she was still troubled by her memories and found herself avoiding even very safe situations. She had used prolonged imagery exposure to reduce her fear of the original scene at the rally, but she was still very nervous day to day, out in the real world, so she decided to try prolonged real-life exposure. She started by making a hierarchy of scary situations that she could arrange to participate in.

	Hierarchy for *post-traumatic stress disorder*
1	*Walk for an hour downtown on Saturday afternoon.*
2	*Watch a documentary about the revolution in Venezuela.*
3	*Sit in the waiting room of the loud carwash that reminds me of the water cannons.*
4	*Sit for an hour in the central square on Sunday morning when it's crowded.*
5	*Have lunch with Jaco at that noisy sidewalk café.*
6	*Have lunch alone at the sidewalk café.*
7	*Ride the subway at rush hour when it's packed.*
8	*Spend an hour in a crowded dance club.*
9	*Attend the fireworks display at New Year's.*

Kara started with a walk downtown on a busy Saturday afternoon. The noise and people upset her a lot at first, but she kept walking, looking, and listening. Over the course of an hour, her anxiety level peaked at 8, then declined to 2 or 3 in the last fifteen minutes. She continued working through her hierarchy and sometimes had to repeat an activity two or three times before her fear declined to near 0. It took her four months to reach the last item on the hierarchy, and by then it was too late for the New Year's fireworks display, so she substituted a visit to a local theme park that had fireworks every weekend. She went with Jaco on teen night, when the theme park was full of rowdy youths, and was surprised and delighted to find herself actually enjoying the evening.

CHAPTER 15

Testing Core Beliefs

Core beliefs are your most basic assumptions about your identity in the world. For instance, they depict you as beautiful or ugly, worthy or unworthy, lovable or unlovable. These core beliefs are formed mainly during childhood and affect most of your actions as an adult. They determine the degree to which you believe you are safe, competent, powerful, autonomous, and loved; they also establish your sense of belonging and a basic picture of how you will be treated by others.

From these beliefs you create rules that govern your behavior. If the beliefs are positive, the rules telling you how to live will be realistic and flexible. The reverse is also true: negative beliefs yield negative rules that are restrictive and driven by fear.

For example, Bud is an artist who, as a child, believed his parents when they called him stupid. He formed the negative core belief "I am stupid," which in turn produced these negative rules:

- *Don't apply for grants. Who would want my ideas?*

- *Don't do anything mathematical. I don't have the brains.*

- *Don't argue. People will know I'm dumb.*

- *Don't say too much. People will see how little I know.*

Core beliefs and the associated rules are so fundamental to personality that few people are aware of them. Yet every part of your life is dictated by these beliefs and rules, and they have an enormous influence on your automatic thoughts. Bud's automatic thoughts, in any interaction, remind him of his stupidity and lead him to expect negative judgments and rejection: "Boy, was that dumb," "What a stupid remark," "They're wondering if you can even read," "Idiot," "Shut up, you're making a fool of yourself," and so on.

In summary, core beliefs are the foundation of your personality. They are the basis for rules that largely dictate what you can and cannot do and the automatic thoughts that determine how you interpret events in your world. However, you can change negative core beliefs. This chapter will teach you how to identify, test, and modify these beliefs, based on approaches developed by psychologists Aaron Beck and Arthur Freeman (1990), Donald Meichenbaum (1988), Jeffrey Young (1990), and Matthew McKay and Patrick Fanning (1991).

SYMPTOM EFFECTIVENESS

Techniques in this chapter can help you identify your core beliefs, test their veracity, and begin the process of changing beliefs that don't serve you well. This process can relieve worry, depression, perfectionism, procrastination, social phobia, low self-esteem, and shame and guilt.

People who are victims of child abuse, are in crisis, or are addicted to substances should work on core beliefs only with the guidance of a mental health professional.

TIME TO MASTERY

It will take eight to twelve weeks for you to identify your core beliefs, test the validity of one core belief, and then change it and the rules associated with it.

INSTRUCTIONS

Identifying, assessing, and changing your core beliefs is a seven-step process:

1. Identify your core beliefs.

2. Assess their negative impact.

3. Identify rules based on your core belief.

4. Generate catastrophic predictions.

5. Select the rule you want to test.

6. Test your rule.

7. Rewrite your core belief and its rules.

Step 1: Identify Your Core Beliefs

You are probably aware of one or two of your core beliefs. But many of them may not be conscious. To identify core beliefs you may not be aware of, start by keeping track of your automatic thoughts for one week using the Thought Journal from chapter 2, recording your thoughts whenever you experience negative feelings. Anytime you feel anxious, sad, hurt, guilty, and so on, record the experience in your thought journal, along with the automatic thoughts associated with the emotion. If you're unable to make a journal entry right away, just be sure to do so by day's end. Here's an example from Janet, a thirty-one-year-old cashier at a hardware store and a single parent. She struggles with feelings that she's an inadequate mother to her son, Brad, and also has a hard time being assertive with her boyfriend, George.

Janet's Thought Journal

Situation When? Where? Who? What happened?	Feelings One-word summaries Rate 0-100	Automatic thoughts What were you thinking just before and during the unpleasant feeling?
I need to start working on my taxes.	Anxiety 40	I don't understand this. What makes me think I can do this?
The electric screwdriver is lost when I need it.	Anger 50	Every time I go to repair something, I can't find the tools. I need to be more orderly.
I'm cooking and I can't find the pot holder when I need it.	Anxiety 20	This house is a rat's nest. It wouldn't take long to straighten it up. I just put off doing things.
Balancing the checkbook and there isn't enough money to pay the bills.	Anxiety 85	I need to stop spending so much on restaurants or I won't have any money. I have no control over my spending.
I took Brad to the movies after I told him I wouldn't because he wasn't helping around the house.	Anger 35	I'm not a good mother. Image of my mom upset, telling me I'm too soft.

If you can't remember your automatic thoughts, use visualization to help recall details of the situation. Relax your muscles and then picture the event you wish to remember. See the situation and feel the sadness, anxiety, anger, or other difficult emotions. Mentally invoke your other senses to smell, hear, taste, and feel the situation. Then listen carefully to your automatic thoughts and write them in your journal. After you've kept your Thought Journal for one week, you can use the following two techniques—laddering and theme analysis—to reveal core beliefs associated with negative feelings.

LADDERING

Laddering uncovers core beliefs by working down, rung by rung, through the meanings of an automatic thought in your Thought Journal until you reach the core belief underpinning it. Start by selecting any automatic thought from your Thought Journal. Now write, "What if (your thought)? What does this mean?" Answer these questions with beliefs about yourself, rather than descriptions of your feelings. Feelings don't lead to core beliefs, but self-statements do.

Here's what Janet wrote using the statement "I have no control over my spending" from her journal:

What if I have no control over my spending? What does this mean?

It means I'll go broke.

What if I go broke? What does this mean?

It means my life will fall apart.

What if my life falls apart? What does this mean?

It means I can't control my life.

What if I can't control my life? What does this mean?

It means I am helpless.

Here Janet discovered a negative core belief: "I am helpless." This allowed her to challenge the belief to see if it was true.

Now select one statement from your journal and, on a separate piece of paper, use the laddering technique to reveal the core belief that underpins that statement.

THEME ANALYSIS

Theme analysis is another method to unearth core beliefs. Review the problematic situations listed in your Thought Journal, searching for a theme or common thread running through these situations. To see how this works, consider these situations, recorded by Bud, the artist:

- *Applying for a grant*

- *Arranging for a show of my work at a gallery*

- *Being asked to speak in front of the PTA*

- *Being asked for advice by a friend*

- *Driving on the freeway*

When Bud reviewed these situations, he realized that all of them except driving on the freeway reflected anxiety about exposing himself to judgment. He discovered a basic belief that he wouldn't measure up to others' expectations. He felt unworthy.

You can also look for themes in automatic thoughts, rather than situations. When Janet reviewed her Thought Journal, she saw that she was chastising herself repeatedly with statements like "I need to be more orderly," "This house is a rat's nest," and "I just put off doing things." This helped her see that one of her core beliefs was that she was lazy.

Right now, analyze your journal to find your core beliefs. Look for themes that pervade the problematic situations or your thoughts, then write them down.

Step 2: Assess the Negative Impact

If you've identified two or more core beliefs, rank them by negative impact on your work, mood, relationships, health, and ability to enjoy life. Begin working on the belief that has the greatest negative impact, unless there's a compelling reason not to.

Step 3: Identify Rules Based on Your Core Belief

Now that you've identified a core belief that has a strong negative impact on your life, it's time to explore its veracity. Because core beliefs are so subjective, you can't test them directly. But you can test the rules derived from core beliefs.

These rules provide a behavioral blueprint for how you should act, rules designed to help you avoid pain and catastrophe. For example, if you have a core belief that you are unworthy, typical rules might be "Never ask for anything," "Never say no," "Never get angry at anyone," "Always be supportive and giving," "Never make a mistake," "Never be an inconvenience," and so on. The following exercise will help you identify the rules derived from the core belief you're working on.

At the top of a sheet of paper write the core belief you wish to explore and question. Then carefully read through the following Basic Rules Checklist (adapted from McKay and Fanning 1991). For each item ask, "If my core belief is true, what must I do or not do in this situation?" Be honest. Ask yourself, "What do I actually do to cope with my belief? How do I protect myself? What do I avoid? How do I think I'm supposed to act? What are my perceived limits?" As you discover your rules, write them down.

Basic Rules Checklist

- Dealing with other people's…

    Anger

    Needs, desires, or requests

    Disappointment or sadness

    Withdrawal

    Praise or support

    Criticism

- Dealing with mistakes

- Dealing with stress, problems, or losses

- Taking risks, trying new things, facing challenges

- Making conversation

- Expressing your…

    Needs

    Feelings

    Opinions

    Pain

    Hopes, wishes, or dreams

    Limits or saying no

- Asking for support or help

- Being…

    Alone

    With strangers

    With friends

    With family

- Trusting others

- Making friends

    Whom to seek

    How to act

- Finding a sexual partner

    Whom to seek

    How to act

- Being in an ongoing romantic relationship

- Expressing your sexuality

- Working

- Dealing with children

- Dealing with illness or maintaining health

- Engaging in recreational activities

- Traveling

- Maintaining your environment

Using the Basic Rules Checklist for her core belief "I am helpless," Janet discovered these rules:

- *Walk on eggshells to keep George in a good mood.*

- *Don't buy a house.*

- *Don't start conversations at parties.*

- *Don't trust myself with a credit card.*

- *Don't make independent decisions.*

- *Don't go back to school to develop a new career.*

- *Don't try to solve problems.*

Step 4: Generate Catastrophic Predictions

Next, consider the consequences of breaking each rule. You'll probably find that each rule is based on a catastrophic assumption about how things will turn out if you ignore its mandate. This is because you developed these rules to cope with genuine emotional or physical threats. However, these rules may no longer be necessary, and the consequences for disobeying them may no longer be catastrophic or even unpleasant.

For each rule you've listed, write the consequences you believe will occur if you disregard it. Include not only your feelings, but objective consequences you can observe and test. For instance, Janet identified these consequences for breaking the rule "Walk on eggshells to keep George in a good mood":

- *He'll leave me.*

- *He'll take his anger out on Brad.*

- *I'll get upset and he'll hurt me.*

Here are the consequences she foresaw for breaking the rule "Don't try to solve problems":

- *I won't be able to think of any solutions and I'll get depressed.*

- *My solution will be something stupid that won't work.*

- *George will make fun of my solutions.*

Step 5: Select the Rule You Want to Test

Now that you've identified some of the rules associated with a core belief, you're almost ready to start testing them. But first you have to choose which rule to test. There are five guidelines for selecting a good rule to test:

- Choose a rule for which it's easy to set up a test situation. Janet can't test her rule "Don't buy a house" because of the time, energy, and money involved. However, she could easily test the effect of being assertive with her boyfriend. The situation needs to be very specific. For example, Bud can't test his rule "Don't argue." A better choice would be something like "Don't argue with the plumber over the hot water heater bill."

- Choose a rule that allows you to test the underlying core belief directly. If Janet tested the rule "Don't start conversations at parties," she wouldn't be testing her core belief that she is helpless. If, however, she tested the rule "Don't go back to school to develop a new career" or "Don't make independent decisions," the outcome could definitely challenge the core belief.

- The rule should allow for a clear prediction of behavioral responses (yours and others'), not just suggest subjective feelings. In Bud's case, that means predicting how the plumber will respond if he contests the bill.

- The outcome should be relatively immediate. If Janet decided to buy a house to dispute her core belief, she would lose her momentum by the time she found, bought, and moved into a new home.

- Choose a rule that has a relatively low amount of fear associated with it, or a rule that can be tested in gradients, from slightly risky to very risky. Janet could check her rule "Don't go back to school to develop a new career" by enrolling in one short community college course. If successful, she could move on to more challenging state college courses.

Step 6: Test Your Rule

Having selected a rule to test, you need to find real-life situations in which to test it. The following six-step process will help you clarify what you fear will happen if you break your rule and then compare the actual outcome.

A. Identify one relatively low-risk situation in which to make your initial test. Janet decided to enroll in a carpentry class at her local community college because this didn't require a big investment of time or money.

B. Begin a predictions log. Write a specific prediction of what the catastrophic outcome will be, including people's behavioral responses, based on your core belief. Using Bud's example, he predicts that the plumber will mock him and refuse to do any more work for him. You can include feelings in your prediction, but only in addition to observable results.

C. Make a contract with yourself to break your rule. Commit to testing your rule in a specific time, place, and situation. If possible, enlist a support person. Inform your support person of your plans and commit to reporting the results of your test to that person.

D. Create a script of your new behavior. Visualize what you'll do. Role-play a test with a friend, or make an audio recording of a dry run of your test. To avoid incurring the very consequences you wish to avoid, check that your tone of voice and body language aren't cold, frightened, or otherwise negative.

E. Test your new behavior and collect data. In your predictions log, write the outcomes of your test. Write which specific parts of your predictions occurred and which did not. If you're uncertain about how people reacted to your test, ask them about it. Here are some questions you might try:

- "Did you have any reaction to what I said?"

- "I had the impression that you might be feeling _____ when I said _____. Was there anything to that?"

- "Is it okay with you that I _____?"

Write the answers to these questions in your predictions log, along with the other data you collected. How did others who were present look during the test? What was said? What happened?

F. Select more situations in which to test your rule and repeat steps B through E for each test. Choose situations that gradually heighten your risk. As you obtain more positive outcomes to tests in which you break your rules, your core belief will be modified.

Bud tested his rule "Do not argue" many times. His predictions log listed his expectations, followed by what actually happened: people's reactions and his responses. He discovered that 80 percent of the time people listened to his arguments with respect, and that 60 percent of the time people actually altered their behavior as a result of his argument. He was surprised that people only got irritated or disregarded his argument 20 percent of the time. He noted that although some people attacked him personally when he argued with them, his successes helped him be resilient in response to those attacks.

With time, Bud's test situations became more spontaneous. He actively took on situations he previously would have avoided. You should experience something similar. With time and success, you'll begin to look for opportunities to break the rules. Occasional setbacks are almost inevitable, but the data in your predictions log will allow you to take an objective view of those setbacks.

Step 7: Rewrite Core Beliefs and Develop New Rules

After you've tested your rules sufficiently and recorded your data in your predictions log, rewrite your core belief. Generalize the information in the log, but also include specific facts that support your generalization and help cement it into a new core belief. For example, Janet rewrote a core belief about being a poor mother to say, "I am usually a skillful mother. I am loving and self-disciplined as a mom, especially when I'm not tired from work." Bud wrote his new core belief like this: "I'm smart enough and can interact with people well. Most people respond with respect when I assert my ideas."

Next, use your revised core belief to write new rules. Use "I" language and the present tense, and write your new rules as affirmations, rather than as commands or restrictions. If possible, include predictions with the rules, written in the future tense. Here are the new rules Bud came up with:

- *I am able to argue my position well, especially if I think before I speak.*

- *I can accept criticism from people I respect without feeling stupid.*

- *I can think about people's objections and decide for myself what is correct.*

- *I am able to brainstorm ideas with supportive people and feel accepted.*

When you write your new rules, they may seem to belong to another person, someone more positive than you've seen yourself as being. Working on your core beliefs can change you dramatically. For this reason, you may not be sure of the validity of your new rules. This is okay. You can confirm that your new rules are valid with an evidence log, in which you record interactions, events, conversations— anything that will support your new rules and core beliefs. This will strengthen your new core beliefs. Whenever situations arise that support your new rule, record what happened and what it means. Here are some examples from Bud's evidence log:

What happened: *I played a trivia game at a party, and although I didn't win, I answered as many questions as Sam and Cindy.*

What it means: *I can hold my own in games that require thinking.*

What happened: *I asked Sal for more advertising for my show. I prepared what I was going to say, and I said it. I sounded knowledgeable, and Sal budgeted more money for the show.*

What it means: *If I script difficult tasks in advance, I can do as well as the next person.*

If you don't remember to write in your log, try setting an alarm to go off every three hours as a reminder. When the alarm goes off, review the previous three-hour period for situations to record in your evidence log. Carry your log with you, or keep notebooks at work, in your car, or wherever else you might have the opportunity to use them. Before going to sleep, review your day for additional items to record in your evidence log.

Actively try to verify and thereby strengthen your new belief by testing its rules in a specific arena. Select a low-risk arena at first. Perhaps you might test the rules just with a supportive friend, or just in the morning, or just at the coffee shop. Later, when the consequences become less threatening and you are more comfortable with your new belief, you may extend the risk and widen the arena.

Example

Sandra, an emergency dispatcher, wanted a higher-paying job in the same field, but she was afraid to train and apply for another position. She decided to try changing some of her core beliefs to help her overcome her reticence.

She kept a Thought Journal and explored its meaning through laddering and theme analysis. She discovered that she felt incompetent and unsafe. She decided that her lack of security ("I'm not safe") had the greatest negative impact on her life and that she would attack this core belief first.

She generated several rules from this core belief, including one she decided to test: "Don't ever question your boss, because you'll lose your job." She scripted her first test of this rule with help from her husband, and then she told her boss she needed relief during the busiest hours of the evening.

She was pleasantly surprised that her boss accommodated her request for relief during busy times and proceeded to riskier tests. Finally, she rewrote her core belief as "I am reasonably safe at work because I am skillful and appreciated to the point that my boss will accommodate my requests."

Sandra searched for opportunities to test her new core belief and its rules. Eventually she took special training and requested a transfer within her department. In the long term, she plans to attend nursing school.

CHAPTER 16

Changing Core Beliefs with Visualization

If you worked through chapter 2, "Uncovering Automatic Thoughts," you probably identified several automatic thoughts that reflect some of your deeply held core beliefs. Likewise, if you worked through chapter 15, "Testing Core Beliefs," you probably identified several core beliefs that have a negative impact on your life. Core beliefs have their roots in childhood experiences. You can probably remember holding these beliefs since you were anywhere from four to twelve years old. In this chapter, you'll learn a powerful technique for changing those core beliefs by visualizing your inner child. It is taken in large part from an earlier book by Matthew McKay and Patrick Fanning: *Prisoners of Belief* (1991).

Psychologically speaking, it isn't true that you can't change the past. Although you can't alter what happened to you or what you did, you can use inner-child visualizations to restructure your memories so they cause you less pain and interfere less with your present life. This technique works because your unconscious mind doesn't believe in time.

To your unconscious mind, things that happened when you were six months old can be just as important and immediate as things that happened yesterday. Deep inside, your entire infant personality survives in detail. This inner infant has no knowledge of any older versions of you. It remains an infant, with an infant's needs, abilities, and understanding of the world.

Likewise, you have a two-year-old toddler inside of you, with a two-year-old's self-centered and contrary feelings. There are countless versions of you, of all ages from birth to your present age.

The inner child is more than an interesting metaphor. It explains why grown adults sometimes act childishly or immaturely: A stressful event is reminiscent of a childhood trauma and awakens a younger version of themselves. Then they react as if they were still that same age, be it two or five or ten years old.

Painful feelings you experienced as a child can return to haunt you in the form of negative thoughts about yourself. Unmet needs from early times may still drive you to this day.

SYMPTOM EFFECTIVENESS

Abundant case reports indicate that inner-child visualizations can alter negative core beliefs, reduce depression, raise low self-esteem, and relieve pervasive feelings of shame and guilt. However, no major study has been undertaken to date on the effectiveness of inner-child visualizations.

TIME TO MASTERY

This chapter provides guidance on inner-child visualizations for six different developmental stages. If you work on one developmental level per day, it will take you about a week to record guided imagery tailored to your core beliefs and memories. For maximum effectiveness, practice inner-child visualizations two or three times a day, for ten to twenty minutes a day. You will start to experience a shift in awareness from the very start, and will see significant results within several weeks as you listen to your recordings, refine their imagery, and explore different core beliefs.

INSTRUCTIONS

Inner-child visualizations are an aspect of an approach known as reparenting, in which you work with your inner child to resolve old painful feelings and meet old needs symbolically. This work is often part of 12-step recovery programs for adult children of alcoholics or victims of childhood sexual or physical abuse. These powerful techniques also work well for those who struggle with long-standing negative core beliefs about themselves or the world.

Different core beliefs are formed at different times. The approach in this chapter uses visualizations divided into developmental stages outlined by John Bradshaw (1990). But no two people's experiences are identical, and your experience may not match the stages presented here. If you find this to be the case, simply adjust the visualization to match the ages that correspond to your early traumas.

When you visualize your inner child, you imagine that you, a wise, experienced adult, are visiting yourself as a child during a particularly hard time—a specific scene that you feel may have contributed to one of your negative core beliefs. Impart to your younger self the wisdom you've acquired and the skills you've developed to deal with hard times. Specifically, counter the negative belief that was formed in that early childhood scene with a more positive and accurate belief. In your imagination, actually become the perfect parent or friend you needed at the time but didn't have.

Your unconscious mind doesn't believe in reality any more than it believes in time. That is, it doesn't distinguish between actual experience and dreams or fantasies. The good advice and support that you give your inner child in your imagination, years after the fact, can be processed, stored, and used by your unconscious just as if you had received it at the time of the trauma in question. The fact that you have two contradictory versions of the same memory doesn't bother your unconscious because it doesn't insist on the kind of logic that your conscious mind requires.

Success with these visualizations requires that you be able to relax physically, releasing muscular tension throughout your body. If you have trouble doing this, you'll find instructions for several effective methods in chapter 5, "Relaxation."

This technique will work best if you record the visualization instructions, altering them as needed to fit your history and automatic thoughts. As you record, speak slowly and clearly, with frequent pauses.

The visualizations in this chapter can be a very powerful emotional experience. If you begin to feel overwhelmed by your feelings at any time during a visualization, open your eyes and stop at once. Don't continue until you have discussed it with a trusted friend or a mental health professional. This is especially important if you have a history of serious mental illness. If you were physically, sexually, or emotionally abused as a child, you should consult with a mental health professional before doing inner-child work.

Don't try to do all of the following visualizations in one session. Do one or two a day so you'll stay fresh. This will also ensure that you have enough time to absorb the results and allow the emotional impact to subside.

Your Infant Visualization

Lie on your back with your legs and arms uncrossed. Close your eyes and relax using your favorite relaxation method.

Imagine that within you is a parklike landscape with paths, woods, meadows, buildings, streams, and fountains. Within this park you can find all the times of your life, all the selves that you have been at all ages and in all places. Your inner world contains all that has ever happened to you and all that you have ever thought or dreamed about.

Imagine that you are walking down a path in your park. This path cuts through time. You can visit any time in your past just by strolling along this path. As you saunter along, you notice a structure off in the distance. You approach and realize that it's the place where you lived as an infant. If you don't actually recall your first home, just imagine it however seems right.

Enter the home and go to the room where you slept as an infant. Again, if you don't remember what it looked like, that's okay. Go into the room and find a crib or bed. Go to it and see a sleeping baby. This is you as an infant. Study the baby's tiny fingers, little mouth, and wispy hair. Notice the color and texture of the blanket. What is the baby wearing? The more details you add, the more real this moment will become for you.

Imagine that the baby wakes up and starts crying. See your mother, father, or whoever took care of you coming into the room. That person can't see the adult you; you're invisible. Watch your caregiver coping poorly with your needs: being cross and angry, being rough or not cuddling your infant self, trying to feed you when you really need to be changed, trying to change you when you just want company, and so on. See and hear your infant self fretting and fussing.

Now have your caregiver leave the room. Your infant self starts crying again. This time, pick your infant self up. Cuddle and hug your infant self. Offer some milk from a bottle.

Soothe your infant self with the following phrases, rephrasing them if you like and adding any alternative statements that feel right to you. Observe how the baby's crying stops and is replaced by calm and contentment:

- *Welcome to the world.*

- *I'm glad you're here.*

- *You're special and unique.*

- *I love you.*

- *I'll never leave you.*

- *You're doing the best you can to survive.*

Next, change your point of view and experience the whole bedroom scene again, this time imagining that you are your infant self: imagine that you're sleeping, that you wake up crying, and that your caregiver comes in and fails to help, and then feel more calm as your adult self comforts you.

Take just as much time and lavish an equal amount of detail on this second scene. When you're finished and you're ready, open your eyes and take a break. This is a good visualization to do when you feel overwhelmed, helpless, or insecure.

Your Toddler Visualization

Relax in a quiet place and see yourself on the path that leads to your inner child. This time, spend a few moments fixing details in your mind: the scents, sights, sounds, and tactile sensations of your inner world. Notice what kind of trees there are and what kind of soil is underfoot.

Next, visualize one of the earliest scenes you can remember. Pick a time when you were one to three years old. If you have no memories from that time, you can make up a scene from stories family members have told you or from family photographs. Imagine a time when you were unhappy, when something happened that hurt you. Maybe you broke something, someone abandoned or lost you, something was taken away, or you were spanked or scolded.

See yourself in that situation. How are you dressed? What color is your hair? How long is it? Notice the expression on the face of your inner toddler.

Watch the painful scene begin. See how upset your inner child becomes, noticing all the details.

When the scene concludes, take your toddler self aside, into another room or some other safe place. Introduce yourself and comfort your inner child with the following statements, rephrasing them if you like and adding any alternative statements that feel right to you:

- *I am you. I'm from the future when you're all grown up.*

- *I've come to help you, to be with you whenever you need me.*

- *I love you.*

- *There's never been another kid like you.*

- *I like you just the way you are.*

- *I'll never leave you.*

- *You're acting normally for a child your age.*

- *It's not your fault. You have no choice in the matter.*

- *It's perfectly all right to explore.*

- *I'll protect you while you learn about the world.*

- *You have a right to say no.*

- *It's okay to be angry or scared or sad.*

Hug your younger self and promise to return whenever needed. Say good-bye, then turn and leave the room.

Now switch your point of view. Relive the scene from the point of view of yourself at age two or three. Include all of the actions, sights, sounds, and smells. Listen to your older, wiser self and be comforted.

End the session whenever you're ready and take a break. This is a good visualization to do whenever you feel confused, abandoned, put down, or shamed.

Your Preschooler Visualization

Get relaxed in a quiet place and sink into your inner world. Explore the path back through time until you come to the place where you lived when you were four, five, or six, before you entered the first grade. Pick a time when you were frightened and unhappy. Maybe you had a fight with your cousin, your father came home drunk, your mom got hysterical, you got lost at the county fair, or the bully at day care threatened or attacked you.

See your preschool self in that scene. Watch without being seen. How tall are you? Are you skinny or plump? What are you wearing? Are there any favorite toys around? What color are your eyes? How is your skin tone? Are you fresh and rosy from a bath, hot and dusty from playing outdoors?

As the traumatic scene unfolds, notice how scared or confused your preschool self is. Notice how your inner child tries to understand and make things right, despite not having sufficient skills and knowledge to do so.

When the painful scene is over, take your inner child to a safe place and sit down together. Put your arm around your younger self and explain that you're visiting from the future and that your younger self can count on you. Say the following statements to your inner child, rephrasing them if you like and adding any alternative statements that feel right to you:

- *I love you.*

- *You're the only one like you in the world.*

- *I like you just the way you are.*

- *You're doing your very best.*

- *You simply don't have much power to change what's going on.*

- *It's not your fault.*

- *I'll help you figure out how to protect yourself.*

- *It's okay to cry.*

- *You're good at thinking for yourself.*

- *You're good at imagining things.*

- *I'll help you separate what's real from what's imaginary.*

- *You can ask for what you want.*

- *It's okay to ask me any questions.*

Try to sense how your inner child is interpreting the event that just happened. What does the child believe is going on? What does it mean to the child about his or her worth, lovability, safety, belonging, and so on? The child is confused and trying to make sense of things. Offer an explanation to your inner child that leaves him or her innocent and blameless for what happened. If there's a positive way to interpret the child's behavior, offer that now. Hug your inner child, say you will see him or her again soon, and leave.

Now change your point of view and relive the painful scene from the point of view of yourself as that child. Really experience the shame, anger, confusion, or fear. If you don't experience the feeling, you won't get the full benefit of the visualization. Listen carefully to your older self and know that you were not to blame, that you were doing your best.

Next is a step that you haven't done in previous inner-child visualizations: Relive the painful scene from your child's point of view once again. But this time, experience it as if you know your future self and already understand the positive messages your future self has given. This time, you know what you didn't know before: that it's all going to turn out okay, that you will survive, that it's not your fault, and so on.

This time, feel less pain in the scene. If it feels right, you can change the memory and react differently than you did in real life. For example, if you were lost at the fair, instead of sitting down and crying you might find an adult and ask for help. Or if you were scared and alone in your room listening to your parents fight, you might imagine yourself singing songs to drown out their words.

Whatever you do, don't blame yourself for not reacting differently at the time. You really were doing the best you could. Also, don't change the actions of others in your scene. Even in imagination it's important to remember that you can't change other people's behavior; you can only change your own.

When you're ready, end the scene and take a break. You can repeat this visualization several times, covering a variety of difficult memories you have from this time in your life. This is a good exercise to do whenever you feel dependent, ashamed, or guilty.

Your School-Age Child Visualization

This visualization follows the same pattern as the previous one. Get relaxed and imagine a scene from ages seven through ten: maybe you were humiliated in front of the whole second grade, your father didn't show up for the soccer championship, or something happened that made you feel stupid or clumsy or inadequate. Relive the painful memory, first watching the scene unfold from the point of view of your future self.

At the end of the scene, take your school-age self aside. Say the following statements to yourself, rephrasing them in your own words if you like and adding any alternative or balancing thoughts that you've found particularly useful in the earlier chapters of this book.

- *The way you are at school is okay.*

- *I'll stand up for you.*

- *It's fine to try out new ideas and ways of doing things.*

- *You can make your own decisions.*

- *It's okay to disagree.*

- *You can trust your feelings.*

- *It's okay to be afraid.*

- *We can talk about anything.*

- *You can choose your own friends.*

- *How you dress is your business.*

- *You're acting normally for your age.*

- *You have no real choice in this matter. There's nothing else you could do. You're doing the best you can to survive.*

As you did during the preschooler visualization, try to sense how your inner child is interpreting the difficult event. Understand what it means to your child in terms of his or her lovability, control, safety, and so on. Again, offer an explanation that leaves your inner child innocent and blameless for the event. And if there is a positive way to interpret the child's behavior, offer that now.

Repeat the scene two more times, first from the point of view of your school-age self, feeling all the old painful feelings but having the help and support of your future self at the end of the scene. Then relive the scene as your school-age self but with your future skills and knowledge. This time you can change how your school-age self reacted in the scene if you wish; just don't change the actions of others in the scene.

When you're ready, end the visualization and take a break. Congratulate yourself for bringing your inner child to life and renewing yourself in this way. You can repeat this visualization for a variety of school-age memories that you have identified as contributing to your present negative beliefs and automatic thoughts. This is a good visualization to do whenever you feel discouraged about your own competence.

Your Adolescent Visualization

This visualization follows the same pattern as the previous one. This time, get relaxed, enter your past, and visit a painful event from your adolescence—roughly ages eleven through fifteen. For most people, this is an era with plenty of turmoil—rebellion against parents, conflicts at school, intense and stormy peer relationships, new and powerful sexual feelings—with many related painful events to choose from.

First observe the memory you've chosen from your adult point of view, watching the events unfold. Then take your adolescent self to a safe place and share the following statements in your own words, adding any alternative statements that you've found helpful in previous visualizations:

- *You can find the right person to love.*

- *You can find something meaningful to do in life.*

- *It's okay to disagree with your parents.*

- *You are becoming an independent person.*

- *You can safely experiment with sex.*

- *It's okay to feel confused and lonely.*

- *You have lots of new and exciting ideas about life.*

- *It's okay to be wrapped up in yourself now.*

- *It's normal to be ambivalent.*

- *It's all right to feel embarrassed and awkward.*

- *It's fine to masturbate.*

- *No matter how far out you go, I'll be here for you.*

- *You're acting normally for your age.*

- *Often you have no real choice in the matter.*

- *You're doing the best you can to survive.*

Afterward, share your adult, reasonable beliefs with your adolescent inner child. Again, offer an explanation that leaves your younger self blameless for the events. Look for a positive way to interpret the adolescent's behavior.

As before, relive the scene from your adolescent point of view twice: once to feel the original pain with your future self there, and once as an adolescent with your future skills and knowledge, perhaps changing your behavior and responding differently than you did in the actual event.

Take a break when you're done. You can repeat this exercise to heal a variety of painful memories from your adolescent years. This is a good visualization to do anytime, but especially if you are feeling confused about sex or are in conflict with authority.

Your Young-Adult Visualization

Following the same steps as in the previous visualization, visit a painful scene from your young adulthood. After viewing the scene, confer with your young-adult self and share the following statements in your own words, adding any alternative statements that you've found helpful in previous visualizations:

- *You will learn how to love and be loved.*

- *I know you will make a difference in the world.*

- *You can be a success on your own terms.*

- *You're acting normally for your age.*

- *You're doing the best you can to survive.*

- *Often you have no choice in the matter.*

Again, offer an explanation for the painful event that takes a compassionate view of your young-adult self. Look for a positive way to interpret your young-adult behavior.

Then experience the memory from your young-adult point of view, with all the frustrations and pain you can remember, but with your future self there to help. Finish by reliving the scene again as your young-adult self, but with your future skills and knowledge. Let yourself act differently if you wish.

Come back to the present knowing that you can handle adult life on your own terms. You can revisit scenes from your young-adult life to heal a variety of memories that have contributed to your automatic thoughts. This is a good visualization to do anytime you have familiar feelings of confusion over work, money, or love.

Example

Pam was a clerk in a grocery store who was in therapy because of persistent depression, low self-esteem, and a pervasive sense of shame. Some of her key automatic thoughts were "I'm a failure," "scatterbrain," and "wimp," usually accompanied by an image of herself as a skinny, short, insignificant little girl.

She did inner-child visualizations off and on for several weeks. A couple of scenes were particularly powerful. In one, she visited her school-age inner child on a day in late July. She was eight, playing in the backyard with strict instructions from her mom not to leave the backyard. She snuck into the front yard to get the sprinkler, leaving the gate open. At that moment, her mom let out the dog, who dashed out of the gate and into the street. Pam started chasing the dog and almost got hit by a passing car.

Her mother dragged Pam out of the street and into the house and threw her in a closet, screaming all the way: "I thought I told you to stay in the back. What the hell are you thinking of? You stupid idiot, you let the dog out and nearly got the both of you killed. You stay in there and don't move a muscle." Her mom left to catch the dog.

Pam's adult self came into the closet and said, "Calm down, Pammy. It's going to be all right. I'm your future self. I've helped you before, and I'll help you again. I love you. You were doing your best. You just forgot to close the gate. That's normal for someone your age."

She reinterpreted the behavior of her school-age self: "You were just trying to get the sprinkler and cool off. It's good to try to help yourself." She also explained her mother's agitation: "Mom isn't mad at you because you're stupid. She was really afraid. She thought you were going to get run over, and it scared her."

Pam relived the scene again, from her younger self's point of view, feeling the fear and shame intensely, and then feeling very comforted by her older self. Then she experienced the scene yet again, reliving the memory with the benefit of her adult self's knowledge and skills.

Pam's other powerful scene was from her adolescent years. When she was sixteen a popular boy gave her a lift home. On the way he pulled over near the cemetery, a notorious spot for parking and necking. Pam was afraid to rebuff him and allowed him to kiss her and fondle her breasts. When he tried to go further, she started crying. He drove recklessly away in silence and dropped her off at her house. The next day he acted like he didn't even know who she was and called her a "skinny little stick" in front of his friends.

Pam visualized her adult self taking her adolescent self aside. "Listen," she told herself, "you're not what other people call you. It's okay to be a virgin. It's okay to be afraid and take it slow. I'm here to tell you that you will survive. This guy isn't important—you are. Soon you'll feel more comfortable and confident."

When Pam relived the scene from the point of view of her adolescent self, she felt strong waves of shame and humiliation. She wanted to hear the words of her adult self over and over: that it was okay, that she wouldn't be a frightened virgin forever, that she would have friends, that it was okay to be different. Then she visualized the scene a third time, again from the point of view of her adolescent self, but this time armed with her adult knowledge and skills. She changed the plot by telling the guy to keep his creepy hands off her, getting out of the car, and taking a bus home. When he taunted her in the schoolyard, she just smiled and gave him the finger.

Talking Back

If your childhood trauma includes parents or other caregivers who abused or neglected you, you can talk back to them as part of your inner-child visualizations. The following approach is based on a role-playing exercise developed by Jeffrey Young (1990).

You can talk back in two ways. The first way is to visualize yourself as a child talking back to adults who mistreated you:

- *You're not treating me right.*

- *You have no right to do this.*

- *This is your problem, not mine.*

- *It's not my fault.*

- *You're asking too much from me.*

The second way to talk back is to visualize your adult self stepping into a scene to address the person abusing or neglecting your younger self:

- *You're mistreating your child.*

- *This is wrong.*

- *It's your fault, not the child's.*

- *Back off.*

You can create an alternative scenario in which your adult self rescues your inner child from the scene, stops the abuse, chases away or hits the abuser, or in some other way intervenes directly in the situation.

SPECIAL CONSIDERATIONS

If you have difficulty visualizing, try the following simple exercise: Close your eyes and recall something very familiar. Choose something neutral or pleasant, such as your bedroom decor, what you had for breakfast this morning, or a pleasant experience, whether recent or from your childhood. Imagine it in as much detail as possible. Beyond visual stimuli, such as shapes, colors, and lighting, also pay attention to scents, tastes, textures, temperature, sounds, and physical sensations. If you can't feel these sense impressions in your mind, just describe them to yourself verbally. As you practice mentally describing something very familiar to you, you will gradually improve your powers of imagery.

If you have trouble creating strong visual images, you probably have a well-developed memory that favors another sense, such as smell, touch, or hearing. If this is true, recall an experience by tuning in to whatever sense is easiest for you. Impressions of the other senses will gradually arise if you keep practicing with your favored sense. For more help with visualizing, see "Visualization Skills," in chapter 5.

CHAPTER 17

Stress Inoculation for Anger Control

Anger is one of the most devastating and physically harmful emotions. Stress inoculation training was extended to the treatment of anger by Raymond Novaco in 1975. In his book *Anger Control: The Development and Evaluation of an Experimental Treatment*, he makes a strong case for the proposition that the source of all anger is what you think about a situation.

Provocations don't make you angry; hurtful, attacking statements don't make you angry; and stressful and overwhelming situations don't make you angry. Trigger thoughts are what turn painful and stressful situations into anger. Trigger thoughts blame others for deliberately and needlessly causing you pain and see others as breaking rules of appropriate or reasonable behavior. If you decide that people are deliberately harming or attacking you and that you are a victim of their unreasonable behavior, your trigger thoughts act like a match to gasoline.

You aren't helpless when provocations occur. Anger need not be automatic. Stress inoculation teaches you how to relax away your physical tension while developing effective coping thoughts to replace old trigger thoughts that provoked anger.

In recent years, cognitive behavioral practitioners and researchers have found that it's best to avoid the use of coping thoughts during exposure. However, stress inoculation for anger control is the exception to this rule. In an anger-provoking situation, the goal of exposure is not to accept and tolerate the anger, but to actively develop coping skills that can help you counter trigger thoughts.

SYMPTOM EFFECTIVENESS

Numerous studies have demonstrated the effectiveness of stress inoculation for anger control (for example, Novaco 1987). Other studies have shown that the combination of relaxation skills and coping thoughts provides an effective anger management treatment (Hazaleus and Deffenbacher 1986).

TIME TO MASTERY

Developing the relaxation skills for stress inoculation will take two to four weeks. Once you've mastered those skills, you could successfully complete a visualized anger hierarchy in a week or less.

Applying your new coping skills to real-life situations that might provoke anger takes longer. You'll need to take advantage of situations as they spontaneously they arise, using them as a laboratory to experiment with relaxation skills and coping thoughts. Real-life anger management may require two to six months of hard work before your new skills become automatic and can be used reliably whenever you're provoked.

INSTRUCTIONS

There are five steps in stress inoculation for anger control:

1. Learn relaxation skills.

2. Build an anger hierarchy.

3. Develop coping thoughts for hierarchy items.

4. Practice anger coping skills with imagery.

5. Practice your coping skills in real life.

Step 1: Learn Relaxation Skills

If you haven't done so already, you need to master four skills described in chapter 5, "Relaxation": progressive muscle relaxation, relaxation without tension, cue-controlled relaxation, and visualizing a peaceful scene. Don't proceed past step 3 until you've practiced all of these procedures.

Step 2: Build an Anger Hierarchy

Get a blank piece of paper and begin writing down as many anger-provoking situations as you can think of. Think of a full range of situations, from minor irritations to things that make you blow your top. This list should include at least twenty-five. If you can't think of that many, try breaking some of your anger episodes into separate items corresponding to how things escalated between you and any other people involved.

STARTING TO BUILD YOUR HIERARCHY

Once your list is complete, take a fresh piece of paper and write the least anger-provoking item at the top. At the bottom of the page, write the item associated with the greatest anger.

FILLING IN THE MIDDLE SCENES

Now it's time to select six to eighteen items of graduated intensity that you can fill in between your lowest and highest anger scenes. You might want to assign rankings on the first list you wrote, then rewrite the list in rank order.

Review your hierarchy to make sure the incremental increase in anger is approximately equal throughout. If some increments are significantly larger than others, you'll need to fill in these gaps with additional scenes. If some increments are too small, delete or revise items so they evoke different levels of anger. Keep working on it until the steps are approximately even. Here's an example, constructed by Celeste, a retired legal secretary who struggles with anger, particularly toward her husband.

Celeste's Anger Hierarchy	
Rank	**Scene**
1	*The cleaning lady banging into the hardwood baseboards with the vacuum*
2	*Reading about the national debt*
3	*A friend being very bossy and hurrying me while eating just because she's through with her meal*
4	*Watching people speed in their cars and feeling upset about the possibility of being hit*
5	*Telephoning customer service and being shifted from one person to another and finally being cut off*
6	*My husband storing our old car in the garage, blocking cabinets I want to use*

7	A friend getting angry, withdrawing, and pouting when anyone is late
8	My husband making me repeat questions many times before answering, and seeming to deliberately tune me out
9	My sister prodding for details about personal affairs and then blabbing to others
10	Reading an article in the paper about the government giving money to other countries and spending on pork-barrel legislation while taxes keep going up
11	My husband going to a party in an old shirt when I've gone to the trouble to dress up for the occasion
12	My in-laws demanding help with an elderly relative while I'm rushed and in the middle of planning a dinner party
13	My husband leaving things lying around the living room every day so I have to pick them up
14	My elderly sister eating continually and gaining weight against her doctor's orders, which makes me worried and angry
15	My husband spending money to buy steak for "the boys" but not taking me out to a nice restaurant
16	A part-time employer is cool and gives no commitment about the availability of future work.
17	My husband splurging on fine liquors and crazy gadgets for his camera while things need fixing around the house
18	My husband staying up late to watch TV and then not wanting to do anything the next day
19	Expected to cook an elaborate meal at the end of the day when I feel tired. Treated coolly if I refuse.
20	My husband spending so much time at his parents' house on his days off that we can't spend any time together.

FINALIZING YOUR HIERARCHY

Write your finalized hierarchy in rank order on a copy of the following hierarchy form, leaving the version in the book blank so you can copy it for use with other phobias. For now, just fill in the "Scene" column. You'll add coping thoughts in step 4. If you need more rows for hierarchy items, simply use another copy of the blank hierarchy form and revise the rank accordingly.

Anger Hierarchy

Rank	Scene

Step 3: Develop Coping Thoughts for Hierarchy Items

You should develop two or more coping thoughts as you get ready to visualize each new scene in your hierarchy. To do so, briefly visualize the scene, making it as real as possible. Notice what you see, what you hear, and even what you feel physically. Next, listen to your trigger thoughts. Are you blaming others for deliberately harming or hurting you? Do you see their behavior as wrong and bad, as violating basic rules of conduct?

If your trigger thoughts involve blame, here are some suggested coping responses to control your anger:

- I may not like it, but they're doing the best they can.

- I'm not helpless. I can take care of myself in this situation.

- Blaming just upsets me. There's no point in getting mad. Don't assume the worst or jump to conclusions.

- I don't like what they're doing, but I can cope with it.

If your triggers involve broken rules, where others seem to be violating standards of reasonable behavior, some of the following coping thoughts may be helpful:

- Forget "shoulds." They only upset me.

- People do what they want to do, not what I think they should do.

- No one is right or wrong; we just have different needs.

- People change only when they want to.

- No one's bad. People do the best they can.

Some of the best coping thoughts simply remind you to not get upset. They affirm that you can stay calm and relaxed in the face of irritation. Here are some general coping thoughts for dealing with anger:

- Take a deep breath and relax.

- Getting upset won't help.

- Just as long as I keep my cool, I'm in control.

- Easy does it. There's nothing to be gained by getting mad. I'm not going to let them get to me.

- I can't change others with anger; I'll only upset myself.

- I can find a way to say what I want to without anger.

- Stay calm—no sarcasm or attacks.

- I can stay calm and relaxed.

- Stay cool and don't make judgments.

- No matter what's said, I know I'm a good person.

- I'll stay rational. Anger won't solve anything.

- Their opinion isn't important. I won't be pushed into losing my cool.

- It's just not worth it to get so angry.

- This is funny if I look at it that way.

- Anger means it's time to relax and cope.

- Maybe they want me to get angry. I'm going to disappoint them.

- I can't expect people to act the way I want them to.

- Stay cool. Take it easy.

- I can manage this. I'm in control.

- I don't have to take this so seriously.

- I have a plan to relax and cope.

If none of the coping thoughts from these lists feels right to you, come up with your own. Or you can combine elements from different coping thoughts into something that feels more useful. Some of the best coping thoughts involve a specific plan for handling a situation: stating your wants clearly, saying no, finding an alternative way to meet your needs, and so on. A good plan in a problematic situation can make you feel less helpless. And when you experience yourself having more control, you're likely to feel less angry.

Now it's time to distill the two or three best coping thoughts for the first scene in your hierarchy. Write them in the space provided on the hierarchy form. You'll do this for each succeeding scene you come to. Here's an example of some coping thoughts from Celeste's hierarchy.

Celeste's Anger Hierarchy		
Rank	**Scene**	**Coping thoughts**
3	A friend being very bossy and hurrying me while eating just because she's through with her meal	Don't take her too seriously. It's a shame she acts this way; I can relax even if she can't. Easy does it. There's no point in getting mad.
8	My husband making me repeat questions many times before answering, and seeming to deliberately tune me out	No one's bad. People do the best they can. I don't know why he's like that, but I won't let it upset me. Getting upset is bad for my health.
13	My husband leaving things lying around the living room every day so I have to pick them up	I'm not helpless. I can assert myself. I'll have him pick his things up before we sit down to watch television. Stay calm. It's no big deal.
17	My husband staying up late to watch TV and then not wanting to do anything the next day	I'll do something with a friend. He can stay home. No one is right or wrong; we just have different needs. Let it go. That's just him.

Step 4: Practice Anger Coping Skills with Imagery

Applying anger coping skills with imagery is a six-step process. Here's an outline of the sequence:

A. Relax for ten to fifteen minutes.

B. Visualize the scene.

C. Start to cope.

D. Rate your anger.

E. Relax between scenes.

F. Repeat steps B through E until your anger declines, then move on to the next scene.

A. RELAX FOR TEN TO FIFTEEN MINUTES

Go through progressive muscle relaxation, cue-controlled relaxation (which includes deep breathing), and visualizing a special place, somewhere you feel calm and safe. Briefly review the coping statements you've prepared for the scene you're working with.

B. VISUALIZE THE SCENE

Start with the first scene in your hierarchy. Try to bring the scene alive. See the situation, hear what's going on, feel the growing tension on a physical level. Remember your trigger thoughts. Remind yourself of the unfairness, wrongness, or outrageousness of the offense. When you really feel the anger, go on to step C.

C. START TO COPE

Once the visualized scene is clear in your mind and you feel angry, immediately begin relaxing and using coping thoughts. We recommend that you use cue-controlled relaxation at this point because it's the quickest stress-reduction strategy. All you have to do is take a few deep breaths and use your cue word or phrase.

As you cope physically using cued-controlled relaxation, try to recall your coping thoughts. Say them to yourself while continuing to visualize the scene. Keep coping and visualizing the provocative situation for about sixty seconds.

D. RATE YOUR ANGER

Using a scale of 0 to 10, where 0 is no anger and 10 represents the worst rage you've ever felt, rate the anger you experienced in the scene just before you shut it off. This is a good time to spend a moment evaluating your coping thoughts. If any have proved ineffective, stop using them. If none of them work, go back to the general list of coping responses and find one or two others to experiment with. If you've been using coping thoughts from the lists and they haven't worked, perhaps try coming up with a few of your own. Those you develop yourself are likely to be a better fit for you.

E. RELAX BETWEEN SCENES

Always relax between visualizations of your hierarchy items. If the scene evoked only moderate anger, you might use cue-controlled relaxation and spend time calming yourself by visualizing your special place. If a particular scene really upset you or you had difficulty reducing your anger during a scene, try progressive muscle relaxation or relaxation without tension before reentering the scene.

F. REPEAT STEPS B THROUGH E UNTIL YOUR ANGER DECLINES, THEN MOVE TO THE NEXT SCENE

If your rating was 2 or above, revisit the same scene. If you rated your anger at 0 or 1, move to the next scene in your hierarchy. Practice daily if at all possible. Your first practice session should last fifteen to twenty minutes. Later you can extend your sessions to as much as thirty minutes. The main limiting factor is fatigue. If you get tired and have difficulty visualizing a scene, it's best to postpone practice until you're more alert.

Expect to master from one to three hierarchy items during each practice session. When starting a new practice session, always go back to the last scene you successfully completed. This helps you consolidate your gains before facing new items that evoke more anger. Continue visualizing and coping with scenes until you've mastered the highest-ranked item in your hierarchy.

Step 5: Practice Your Coping Skills in Real Life

Because anger-provoking situations tend to arise unpredictably, it's hard to schedule real-life practice for your new coping skills. If your hierarchy includes items that occur frequently or predictably, you'll find many opportunities to practice. The key to real-life practice of your relaxation skills and coping thoughts is to recognize the first signs of anger. The earlier you intervene with cue-controlled relaxation and helpful coping thoughts, the more likely you are to maintain control.

If you're entering a situation where an anger response seems likely, prepare your coping thoughts in advance and commit to using cue-controlled relaxation at the first touch of anger. By now, with all of your imagery-based practice with your hierarchy, you've hopefully "overlearned" cue-controlled relaxation. It should be getting increasingly automatic and easy to do.

If you have difficulty remembering to use relaxation and coping thoughts during a particular situation, set aside some time to visualize the scene and practice coping with it, using the same procedure as in step 4. Extra practice with an imagined scene can make you more prepared and better able to remember to use your skills when that situation next shows up in real life.

Example

Sam, a middle-aged college professor, had a long-standing anger problem that was affecting both his job and his relationship with his wife, Jill. Most upsetting were situations where he felt treated with disrespect.

While learning his relaxation skills, Sam also began developing his hierarchy. He started by listing as many anger situations as possible, including everything from slightly annoying items to situations where he inevitably blew up. Then he identified the scene that produced the least anger: "Jill doesn't get up for the phone. I have to drop what I'm doing and get it." He also identified a recent situation that had absolutely enraged him: "A student tells me my class is full of 'unnecessary rhetoric.'"

With the extremes in place, Sam filled in eight middle items on his hierarchy. Sometimes it was hard to tell which of two items was more annoying, and he had to adjust his arrangement a few times. In fact, the very act of creating a hierarchy proved upsetting, and Sam threw it in the trash at one point. Here's Sam's hierarchy, including all of the coping thoughts he eventually developed for each scene. You may notice that Sam mostly used coping thoughts from the recommended list, but sometimes he included his own ideas for coping with particular situations. Because tension in his body seemed to be a major trigger for anger, Sam often used reminders to physically relax. When coping thoughts proved ineffective, he replaced them with something new from the lists or came up with something of his own.

Sam followed the stress inoculation procedure carefully, beginning each session with progressive muscle relaxation, cue-controlled relaxation, and his special-place visualization. During scenes he used cue-controlled relaxation to achieve quick muscle release.

Sam worked hard at visualizing the items on his hierarchy until he felt truly angry, and then he initiated his coping responses. The scene that proved to be the worst problem was item 9, "Jill says you fucked up… " He had to repeat the scene five times before he was able to reduce his anger to 1 on the scale of 0 to 10. When he started practicing the next day, Sam found that he was back up to level 5 with the scene. He had to visualize and cope in the scene three more times before he was finally able to achieve zero anger.

In real-life anger management, Sam used cue-controlled relaxation and several general coping thoughts to handle the most provocative situations. If these proved inadequate and he relapsed into an anger response, he rehearsed the scene by visualizing it and practicing more specific coping thoughts.

Sam's Anger Hierarchy		
Rank	Scene	Coping thoughts
1	Jill doesn't get up for the phone. I have to drop what I'm doing and get it.	Forget "shoulds." They only upset me. Easy does it. Take a big breath. If I don't want to get up, I'll let the answering machine take the call.
2	Jill complains that we never talk.	No one is right or wrong; we just have different needs. I can't fix this with anger. I'm doing the best I can.
3	Jill tells me to drive faster because we're late.	Stay calm—no attacks. Easy does it. Take a big breath. She's embarrassed when she's late, that's all.
4	The department head assigns me to a classroom that's in one of the temporary bungalows.	I can cope with this. The actual room is okay. People do what they want, not what I want.

5	Jill tells me at the last minute about social events without any consideration for my schedule.	Stay calm—no attacks. State my position clearly: that I won't go if I hear about it at the last minute. I don't like it, but she's doing her best.
6	The department head gets a complaint and pressures me to raise a student's grade.	Breathe and stay calm. Forget "shoulds." We just have different needs. He has pressure from above. He's in a bind.
7	They give me two students who barely speak English—what is this?	Breathe and stay calm. I can cope with this. I'll send them to tutoring. Forget the damned "shoulds."
8	Jill doesn't like something I say, so she turns her back and holes up in her office.	Breathe and relax. She's doing the best she can. This will blow over like always. Don't take it so seriously.
9	Jill says, "You fucked up," pointing her finger at me.	Breathe and relax. I can't change this with anger. I'll just make it worse. Tell her we'll talk later when we're calm.
10	A student tells me my class is full of "unnecessary rhetoric."	Don't say anything you'll regret. I can't fix this with anger. Breathe, relax, and answer rationally.

SPECIAL CONSIDERATIONS

If you experience difficulties in practicing stress inoculation, they are likely to be in one of the three common problem areas: incomplete relaxation, difficulties with visualization, or deeply ingrained behavior patterns.

Incomplete Relaxation

If you can't relax at the beginning of a session, try to imagine lying on a soft lawn on a calm summer day, watching clouds slowly floating by. Or imagine watching leaves float by on a broad, slow river. Each cloud or leaf takes some of your muscular tension away with it. You may also want to make an audio recording of your relaxation routine and play it at the beginning of each session or scene.

Difficulties with Visualization

If you find that your visualized scenes seem flat, unreal, and unevocative of the distress you would feel in real-life scenes, you probably have trouble visualizing things clearly. To strengthen your powers of imagination, ask questions of all your senses to make your scenes more vivid.

- **Sight:** What colors are in the scene? What colors are the walls, the landscape, cars, furnishings, or people's clothes? Is the light bright or dim? What details are there—books on the table, pets, chairs, rugs? What pictures are on the walls? What words can you read on signs?

- **Sound:** What are the tones of voice? Are there background noises such as planes, traffic, dogs barking, or music? Is there wind in the trees? Can you hear your own voice?

- **Touch:** Imagine reaching out and feeling things. Are they rough or smooth, hard or soft, rounded or flat? What's the weather like? Are you hot or cold? Do you itch, sweat, or have to sneeze? What are you wearing? How does it feel against your skin?

- **Smell:** Can you smell dinner cooking? Flowers? Tobacco smoke? Sewage? Perfume or aftershave? Chemicals? Decay? Pine trees?

- **Taste:** Are you eating or drinking? Are the tastes sweet, sour, salty, or bitter?

It also helps to go to the real setting of one of your scenes to gather images and impressions and practice remembering those details. Observe the setting, then close your eyes and try to see the scene. Then open your eyes and notice what you missed. Close your eyes and try again. Describe the scene out loud to yourself, or whisper to yourself if others are present. Open your eyes and see what you missed this time, and what you changed in your mind. Close your eyes and describe the scene again, adding sounds, textures, scents, temperatures, and so on. Keep this up until you have a vivid sense picture of the scene.

Deeply Ingrained Behavior Patterns

If you repeatedly struggle with an anger-provoking situation that involves a familiar sequence of responses (for instance, fights about money with your spouse or about homework with your children), we encourage you to read chapter 18, "Covert Modeling." This is an excellent technique for developing and rehearsing new behavior patterns.

CHAPTER 18

Covert Modeling

Covert modeling is an effective way of altering an existing negative sequence of thinking and behavior by learning a new pattern and substituting it. You can probably think of a number of behavior patterns that you find unsatisfactory and want to change. You may want to improve your performance at work, in a personal relationship, or at school. You might have fallen into some routine that you don't like, such as sitting in front of the TV with a can of beer instead of playing with your kids. Maybe you find yourself repeatedly coming home tired at the end of a long work day and getting into an argument with your spouse. Or perhaps you feel bored and uncommunicative every time you go to visit your in-laws. Some situations may provoke so much anxiety that you avoid them entirely: taking tests, going to the doctor, being in enclosed or crowded rooms, being alone, dealing with new situations, speaking before others, and so on.

Likewise, there are probably some new patterns of behavior that you'd like to add to your repertoire that might not require any change in your existing behavior. You may want to learn assertiveness skills to aid you in looking for a new job, asking for a raise, or dating again after a divorce. Covert modeling can be useful for learning new behavior patterns, as well.

One of the most effective ways of learning to perform a new behavior is by observing and imitating someone else doing it successfully. An aspiring musician may learn to perform on stage by watching his favorite artists on television or at concerts and then modeling his act on theirs. In social-skills training, shy individuals often watch videotapes of people who initiate and maintain conversations and then imitate those videotaped models.

Unfortunately, good models are not always readily available when you need them. However, in 1971 psychologist Joseph Cautela found that you can learn new behavior sequences by imagining people, including yourself, performing the desired behavior successfully. He called his technique covert modeling. Covert modeling allows you to identify, refine, and mentally practice the necessary steps for completing a desired behavior. Once you feel confident imagining yourself doing a particular sequence, you can more effectively perform it in real life.

In the classic covert modeling method, you first imagine someone very different from yourself performing the desired behavior. Then you imagine someone similar to yourself and, finally, visualize yourself in action. In actual practice, most people skip the dissimilar and similar models and simply imagine themselves performing the new behavior.

Joseph Cautela stressed the importance of seeing your models struggling with and eventually overcoming difficulties rather than succeeding perfectly on the first try. This advice has stood the test of time. More recently, cognitive therapists have refined the technique by adding analysis of negative automatic thoughts associated with old, unsuccessful behavior and composing new, more positive thoughts to go with the new behavior.

SYMPTOM EFFECTIVENESS

Covert modeling can be used to improve any already existing behavior sequence or to learn a new behavior sequence. It is helpful in reducing avoidance behavior associated with phobias and performance anxiety and in increasing assertive behavior. Covert modeling can be used to reduce bad habits, interpersonal conflict, or anger.

If you can't create clear and detailed mental images, covert modeling will probably be of little help to you. However, vivid visual imagery isn't absolutely necessary. If you are able to form strong physical or auditory impressions, you can probably use this technique successfully.

One study found that guided behavior rehearsal—actually experiencing a feared situation—was more effective than covert modeling in reducing avoidance behavior (Thase and Moss 1976). Unfortunately, avoidance behavior does not always lend itself to rehearsing in real life, making covert modeling a useful alternative.

TIME TO MASTERY

You should see results after four fifteen-minute sessions. Personal preference will determine how quickly you begin to implement your new behavioral sequences in real life.

INSTRUCTIONS

Covert modeling is an eight-step process:

1. Develop visualization skills.

2. Write out your problem behavior.

3. Write out your desired behavior.

4. Imagine the context.

5. Imagine performing the desired behavior.

6. Role-play the desired behavior.

7. Prepare coping statements.

8. Perform the desired behavior in real life.

Throughout this section, we've used examples from Kira, a divorced mother, to help illustrate the process. She experiences a lot of anger and resentment toward her ex, Jerry, but recognizes that she needs to find better ways of handling their interpersonal conflicts so they can work together on issues related to raising their seven-year-old son, Danny.

Step 1: Develop Visualization Skills

Sit down in a comfortable, quiet place where you won't be interrupted for about fifteen minutes. Close your eyes and scan your body for tension, then relax using your favorite practice from chapter 5. After you've let go of the tension in your body, take a few deep breaths, focusing on your breathing and allowing yourself to become more and more relaxed.

With your eyes closed, practice recalling what the room you're sitting in looks like. What are the major furnishings in the room? How are they positioned? What are their colors, textures, and shapes? What are the walls, ceiling, and floor like? What are the decorations? What's on the tables or desks?

After imagining the room, open your eyes and see how much detail you captured. Repeat this exercise until you're satisfied with your imagery of the room. You may want to try this exercise in a variety of settings to further develop your ability to visualize.

Next, imagine a spot out in nature in your mind's eye. Hear the leaves rustling in the gentle, warm breeze. Notice the rough, mottled bark of the trees and their shining green leaves. Feel the earth beneath you and notice its color and texture. Listen to the water flowing nearby and the birds flitting from branch to branch. Smell the various scents that fill this natural place. Feel the pleasantly warm sun through the trees. Allow yourself to fantasize what your eyes, ears, nose, and skin would tell you about the spot in as much detail as possible. Then imagine that an old friend walks up to you through the trees and greets you. What does he or she look like? What does he or she have to say? What does your friend's voice sound like? What do you have to say?

Once you've developed some facility in imagining scenes using sight, sound, smell, and feeling, you're ready to move on to step 2. It isn't necessary that your images be as clear as a motion picture, but they should be as vivid as practice can make them.

Step 2: Write Out Your Problem Behavior

Write out your problem behavior and thoughts as a sequence of separate steps. If you're learning an entirely new behavior, skip this step and move on to step 3. Kira decided that she wanted to start with the critical, defensive remarks she typically made when her ex-husband, Jerry, brought their son home on Sunday nights after their weekend together. Here's how she described her old behavioral sequence:

A.   *I start looking out the window and watching the clock around 6:00 p.m., thinking, "I know he'll be late. He's so inconsiderate."*

B.   *At 7:30 they drive up, half an hour late. I'm seething, thinking, "Danny will be tired and all wound up. I'll never get him to bathe and get to bed on time."*

C.   *I open the door before they get to it and say, "You're late."*

D.   *Jerry explains why they're late, whatever the excuse is.*

E.   *I shoo Danny inside and stand on the porch arguing with Jerry about our visitation schedule. I'm thinking what an irresponsible, uncaring jerk he is.*

F.   *I have to ask Jerry for money because he's almost always late with child support. I assume that he's going to get mad.*

G.   *He begrudgingly gives me the money and stomps off. I go inside, thinking, "This is awful. This stinks. I hate him." I look and act angry.*

H.   *Danny is inside, looking scared and sad.*

I.   *I feel guilty for arguing in front of him. I think, "I'm a bad mom. I can't manage my life."*

Step 3: Write Out Your Desired Behavior

Next, write out your desired new behavior in that same situation. You need not use the same number of steps or divide them at similar points. It's likely that the further you go with the sequence, the more the steps will diverge. Here's what Kira came up with. Note that while her behaviors are different, the events she's responding to stay much the same. For example, Jerry still arrives late, and she still requests money that Jerry is obligated to contribute.

A.   *I do the laundry, weeding, or paperwork, keeping busy so I'm not just waiting around watching the clock. I think, "They'll get here when they get here. The important thing is to stay calm."*

B.   *At 7:30 they drive up and I think, "I've really missed Danny. I hope he had a nice time with his dad."*

C. *I keep doing what I'm doing and wait for them to come to the door. I answer the door and give Danny a big hug. Then I say, "Hi, you guys. How was your weekend?"*

D. *They come in and I smile while they tell me about their weekend. I still feel a bit angry that Jerry is late but think, "Keep smiling. Don't make this an unpleasant transition for Danny."*

E. *I tell Danny to go unpack his bag and get ready for a bath.*

F. *I wait for Danny to leave the room before I ask Jerry for the money he owes me. I tell myself to stay calm and just say things clearly and evenly.*

G. *If we have a serious conflict brewing, I tell Jerry I'll call him tomorrow, and then I say good-bye.*

H. *When Jerry leaves, I go help Danny with his stuff. I resist the urge to quiz him about what he ate, how late he stayed up Saturday night, and so on. I try to find out what he did that he really enjoyed over the weekend.*

Step 4: Imagine the Context

Practice imagining the context in which the problem behavior occurs. Hold this clear image twice, for fifteen seconds each time. Here's what Kira came up with to describe waiting for Jerry and Danny to arrive on Sunday evenings:

I imagine the clock on the wall, the deepening twilight, and the view out the front window. I feel it getting cooler and hear the neighbor's dog barking and the stereo playing softly in the background.

Step 5: Imagine Performing the Desired Behavior

Imagine yourself performing the desired sequence of behavior and thoughts, with difficulty at first, then successfully. Visualize the successful sequence at least twice. An option is to make an audio recording of the desired sequence, pausing after each step so you can visualize yourself performing the new behavior. Then you can listen with your eyes closed, visualizing the desired sequence as often as it takes to feel confident in your ability to actually do it. Here's what Kira recorded:

I see myself in cutoffs and a T-shirt, sitting at the dining room table sorting papers. (pause) I hear Jerry and Danny on the porch. (pause) They knock and I run to let them in. (pause) I greet them with a hug for Danny and a smile, and they tell me about the weekend enthusiastically. (pause) When Danny leaves the room, I ask Jerry for the money he owes me. (pause) He makes excuses and I start to lose my cool. (pause) I tell myself, "We'll solve this eventually. It will be okay." (pause) I calm down and tell him I don't have time to go into it tonight and that I'll call him when Danny's at school.

Step 6: Role-Play the Desired Behavior

The next two steps are optional . If you're ready to try the desired behavior in real life, go on to step 8. But if you feel the need for more preparation, the next two steps will help increase your confidence and enhance your chances of success.

There are several ways to role-play your desired behavior. You can rehearse it in front of a mirror. You can take both parts of a dialogue by sitting in a chair and saying what you would say, then shifting to another chair and saying what the other person would say, then shifting back to your chair to respond, and so on. Another method is to rehearse the scene with friends who play the roles of significant characters while you play yourself, making the scene as realistic as possible. Finally, you can record yourself practicing saying what you want to say loud and then play it back to get used to hearing yourself say assertive things.

Because Kira still felt uncertain about her ability to keep her anger in check, she decided to role-play by practicing saying key statements in front of a mirror. Here are the statements she came up with:

- *Hi! How was your weekend?*

- *Why don't you two say good-bye while I make some tea?*

- *Sweetie, go unpack your bag and get ready for your bath.*

- *Jerry, October's child support was due Friday.*

- *I have to insist that you bring Danny back by seven. He needs a predictable routine so he can settle in, get a bath, and get to bed in time to be fresh for the new school week.*

- *This isn't a good time to talk. I'll call you tomorrow around noon.*

Step 7: Prepare Coping Statements

Even after practicing your desired behavior, you might have some pessimistic thoughts that could inhibit you from applying your desired behavior in real-life situations. If so, compose a couple of all-purpose coping statements that you can use to remind yourself to relax and follow your plan. Statements for relaxing might be "Stay calm," "Just breathe slowly," "Keep cool," "I can relax and focus," and so on. Statements to help you stick to your plan might be "Take one step at a time," "I've prepared for this," "Just follow the plan," "I can do this," and so on.

Step 8: Perform the Desired Behavior in Real Life

Here's where all of your hard work pays off: Now you're ready to perform the desired new behavior in real life. You have a detailed plan and know just what to do. If everything doesn't go exactly as you wish or if you fall back into old behaviors, remember that changing old habits takes time. Congratulate yourself for sticking with your plan, keep practicing, and rest assured that continued practice, in both imagination and real life, will enhance your success.

Kira worked on all of the preceding steps over the course of the week so she could implement her new behavior the next Sunday. She was pleased at how well things worked out. Even though Jerry brought Danny home forty-five minutes late, full of junk food and exhausted, she didn't lose her cool. She stayed focused on making it a smooth transition for Danny. She held off on her critical remarks until Danny was out of earshot, and even then she made her point calmly and took care of business without her usual bitterness and rage. What could have been a screaming match ended up being a relatively quiet negotiation, and she wasn't nearly as upset afterward. She had a nice evening with her son and he got to bed on time.

Examples

Covert modeling can take endless forms. To help round out your understanding of the process, we've provided two more examples to help you see how it works.

FRANK AND SHARON

Frank and his twelve-year-old daughter, Sharon, had a good relationship until they began to quarrel over her math homework. Frank resolved to use covert modeling to change this problem behavior.

Step 1: Frank practiced creating imagery in his mind. He chose calming scenes from nature for their added relaxation value.

Step 2: Frank described his problem behavior and his thoughts in sequential order and included descriptions of his daughter's behavior as well:

A. *I'm watching television while Sharon is playing in her room.*

B. *At 9:30 she asks for help with a math problem.*

C. *I say, "Sure," and we sit down at her desk together.*

D. *I have to read the whole chapter in order to understand the problem.*

E. *It's after 10:00 (her bedtime) before we figure out the first problem, and there are four equally hard problems to go.*

F. *I think, "This isn't fair."*

G. *I start to feel testy and ask her why she didn't start earlier, and she says that I don't want to help her anyway.*

H. I think, "She's totally irresponsible, dumping it all on me."

I. I start to get loud, and she starts to cry.

J. Her crying gets worse, and I tell her I'm going to figure out the other four problems by myself.

K. She stays up for half an hour while I'm trying to do the problems, and I finally insist that she go to bed.

Step 3: Frank wrote out his desired new behavior as follows:

A. I set up a rule that Sharon can't ask for help with her homework after 9:00.

B. I also tell her that that I won't help her after 10:00, and if her homework isn't finished by 10:00, she'll have to go to school with it incomplete.

C. I check in with her at intervals during the evening to see how she's doing on her homework.

D. When I think she's being unfair and irresponsible, I remind myself that she's only twelve, and that it's my job to set limits and help her structure her evening.

E. I help her until 9:45 and then tell her I'm feeling pressured and will only do one more problem. I also joke about not wanting to burn the midnight oil with her again.

F. If I notice that I'm getting loud, I take a deep breath and lower my voice. To further calm down, I get some juice and cool off in the kitchen.

G. If Sharon cries, I give her a hug, tuck her into bed, and remind her that we don't do homework after her bedtime.

Step 4: Frank imagined the context as his daughter's desk in her room. He clearly visualized this setting twice, for fifteen seconds each time.

Step 5: Frank chose to imagine performing the desired behavior while sitting on the sofa in the living room after Sharon went to bed. He made a point of relaxing before he started imagining. He took three slow breaths and told himself to relax and notice the tension draining out of his body. He ran through the desired behavioral sequences in his mind, seeing and hearing himself succeed only after struggling through the usual problems.

Step 6: After practicing step 5 for about fifteen minutes a day for four days, Frank decided to role-play the desired behavior. He practiced with his wife, asking her to play Sharon's role.

Step 7: Frank decided to use three coping statements when he talked to Sharon. For relaxation, he would use "Breathe and relax." To help him stick to his plan, he would use "Keep it simple and sensible" and "Use a gentle voice."

Step 8: With his confidence bolstered by his imagery-based practice, role-playing, and coping statements, Frank carried out his new behavior sequence in real life. He and Sharon had a few tearful bedtimes, but over time she learned to get her work done earlier and Frank kept his cool.

SANDRA AND HER BOSS

It had never occurred to Sandra to ask for a raise until her friend Jan, who held the same level clerical position in another department, asked for and got a substantial salary increase. Since asking for a raise was an entirely new behavior for Sandra, she skipped step 2. Writing out her desired behavior produced a long script because there were at least two confrontations involved and several different ways her boss might react. After several revisions, this is what she settled on:

A. *I approach my boss in the staff lounge.*

B. *I have difficulty getting his attention but finally do.*

C. *I ask for fifteen minutes of his time in the next couple of days to discuss a raise.*

D. *He tries to put me off and says to contact his secretary. I have to repeatedly ask for and finally get him to commit to a time to meet.*

E. *I tell myself, "Be persistent."*

F. *At the appointed time, I walk into his office and greet him.*

G. *I sit in the blue chair he reserves for guests.*

H. *We make some small talk about the weather and how busy the office has been.*

I. *I explain that I'm here to request a 10 percent raise.*

J. *I mention my good performance record and how long I've been working at the same salary level.*

K. *He looks displeased and replies that the department isn't doing well and we all have to learn to live with less.*

L. *I think, "I deserve this. Don't give up."*

M. *I point out that it would be more cost-effective to give me a raise than to train a new employee to take over my responsibilities.*

N. *He continues to be negative.*

O. *I take a deep breath and remind myself to be strong and calm, and that I deserve the raise.*

P. *I say that if I can't get the raise I deserve, I'll start looking for a new job.*

Q. *He offers a 5 percent raise.*

R. *I stick to my demand and remind myself and him that I'm competent and experienced.*

S. *He eventually agrees after seeing that I won't be budged.*

T. *I thank him, make sure to ask when the raise goes into effect, and walk out of his office feeling elated.*

Sandra practiced visualizing the staff lounge and her boss's office until she could clearly imagine the sights and sounds in each. Then she visualized herself going through all the steps of asking for and getting a 10 percent raise. After practicing in her imagination four times, she felt that she had the behavioral sequence firmly in her mind.

Sandra role-played the scene with her husband playing the role of her boss. Her husband made a point of being a particularly tough boss to talk to. Because she was still very nervous about asking for the raise, Sandra came up with some coping statements. She wrote them on an index card and kept it in the middle drawer of her desk at the office. Over the next few days, she referred to it frequently to counteract her negative thoughts about asking for a raise.

With all of this preparation, and armed with her coping statements, Sandra felt ready to approach her boss. The next time she saw him in the lounge, she asked him for a meeting. Then she presented her case. Her boss was a tough negotiator, but they eventually settled on an 8 percent raise.

CHAPTER 19

Covert Sensitization

Destructive habits are among the greatest sources of painful emotions. These are your vices—things you have learned to do that feel good in the moment, but for which you later pay dearly. In fact, this is the hallmark of destructive habits: short-term gain coupled with long-term loss. There is pleasure, for example, in a three-hour martini lunch. It's a nice way to unwind, hold tension at bay, and socialize. Unfortunately, a habit of three-hour martini lunches wastes time and may leave you quite dysfunctional for the rest of the afternoon. As a consequence, you suffer *more* stress as you try to catch up on missed work while wrestling with alcohol-induced weariness. Likewise, if you gorge nightly right up to and including the chocolate mousse, over the months you'll be sad to observe your slow evolution into a blimp. Or if you frequently indulge in your love of shopping, you'll eventually have to face those ever-mounting credit card balances and finance charges.

Covert sensitization was developed and popularized by psychologist Joseph Cautela (1967) as a treatment for destructive habits. It's called covert because the basic treatment takes place inside your mind. The theory behind covert sensitization is that behaviors that become strong habits do so because they are consistently reinforced by a great deal of pleasure. So one way to eliminate the habit is to begin associating the behavior with a very unpleasant imagined stimulus. As a result, your old habit no longer evokes images of enjoyment and instead becomes associated with something noxious and repulsive. This association is formed by pairing pleasurable images associated with your habit with imagery involving unpleasant stimuli, such as nausea, physical injury, social ostracism, or some other painful experience. Covert sensitization can help you remove most, if not all, of the habit's appeal.

Once your formerly pleasurable habit has become painful to you, you can escape the unpleasantness by imagining doing something more appropriate that's associated with enjoyable feelings. For example, once you've connected the image of nightly gorging with nausea, you can replace it with the image of enjoying lighter, healthier food and pair that image with feelings of strength, well-being, and relaxation.

SYMPTOM EFFECTIVENESS

Covert sensitization has had significant success in the treatment of bad habits. It is effective in treating sexual deviations such as sadistic fantasies, pedophilia, and exhibitionism. It has also been used to reduce stealing, fingernail biting, compulsive gambling, compulsive lying, and compulsive shopping. It has been helpful in curtailing use of nonaddictive drugs such as marijuana.

Covert sensitization has been used with mixed results for alcohol, obesity, and smoking problems. It's not effective in treating alcoholism per se, but it has been used to treat a habit of alcohol indulgence on particular occasions and in particular environments. The previously mentioned martini lunch at a favorite watering hole can lose its appeal with covert sensitization. Although this approach isn't the final answer to obesity, covert sensitization can be used to treat a weight problem that's exacerbated by a few particular foods or a certain eating environment. Overall, research evidence indicates that it isn't particularly effective with smoking.

In short, covert sensitization is effective when the habit is confined to a particular substance, setting, or situation. It isn't very effective with generalized habits such as smoking and compulsive eating or drinking. The reason appears to lie in the word "sensitization." You become sensitized to something unpleasant, which you associate with your habit in particular settings and situations. Sensitization to one particular food, drink, or setting does not seem to generalize. It is nearly impossible to become sensitized to all food, all drink, or all situations associated with compulsive eating, drinking, and smoking, explaining why the technique is less effective with such pervasive habits.

TIME TO MASTERY

The first step in covert sensitization is learning progressive muscle relaxation and then shorthand muscle relaxation, from chapter 5. You can master progressive relaxation in less than a week. After that, you'll begin to see results from the covert sensitization procedure within two weeks.

INSTRUCTIONS

Using covert sensitization for bad habits is a seven-step process:

1. Learn progressive muscle relaxation.

2. Analyze your destructive habit.

3. Create a hierarchy of scenes in which you enjoy your habit.

4. Create an aversion scene.

5. Combine pleasurable and aversive scenes.

6. Alter the aversive scene.

7. Practice covert sensitization in real life.

Step 1: Learn Progressive Muscle Relaxation

The first step in covert sensitization is relaxing. Progressive muscle relaxation, outlined in chapter 5, "Relaxation," is the quickest and most effective way to let go of muscular tension. Practice progressive muscle relaxation twice daily until you can perform the technique in fifteen minutes, then practice shorthand muscle relaxation, also in chapter 5. Once you've mastered the shorthand procedure, you'll will be capable of deep muscle relaxation throughout your entire body in less than two minutes.

Step 2: Analyze Your Destructive Habit

Next, spend some time thinking about the particulars involved in your bad habit. What environment are you typically in when you engage in the habit? Who is with you? How do you set the situation up? What's the first thing you do as you prepare to launch into your old habit?

Marcos, a housepainter who was becoming too stout to climb scaffolding, analyzed the conditions under which he tended to gorge himself. He shopped once a week and usually spent that evening watching television and making endless raids on the icebox. He continued eating until he had polished off the cinnamon bread, ice cream, and fruit pies—his favorite snacks. He also gorged at an Italian restaurant a block from his house and a nearby McDonald's. As he analyzed his gorging habit, he realized he was always alone on these occasions because he was embarrassed about friends observing his bingeing. He also noticed that he usually had skipped lunch and felt terribly hungry before bingeing. The first thing he did before gorging was think of all the wonderful foods he had in the icebox or peruse the menu with a sense of excitement as he searched for the most filling meal.

Step 3: Create a Hierarchy of Scenes in Which You Enjoy Your Habit

Make a short list of five to ten scenes in which you enjoy your destructive habit. Rank them from least to most pleasurable, and assign pleasure ratings on a scale from 1 to 10. If your destructive habit is overeating, you could base your hierarchy on a few of your favorite foods, always being certain to include the settings in which they are consumed. Below, you'll find a blank form to copy and use for your pleasure hierarchy. But first, review the following examples to get an idea of the different ways you might construct your hierarchy. Here's the pleasure hierarchy Marcos came up with, which is fairly straightforward.

Pleasure *1-10*	Scene
1	*Leaving work and thinking about a big dinner*
3	*Shopping for favorite snacks*
5	*Snacking on fruit pies while at home watching TV*
6	*Snacking on ice cream while at home watching TV*
8	*Snacking on cinnamon bread while at home watching TV*
10	*Eating a huge, spicy meal at my favorite Italian restaurant when I feel very hungry*

Your hierarchy might contain scenes revolving around anticipation of or preparation for the destructive habit, as in this hierarchy created by a compulsive shopper.

Pleasure *1-10*	Scene
1	*Depositing my paycheck and thinking about a favorite department store, imagining the clothes racks and display cases*
2	*Looking through mail-order catalogs for ideas about things to buy*
4	*Fantasizing about new clothes while making dinner*
5	*Walking around a big department store*
6	*Selecting clothes to try on*
7	*Impulsively splurging on a gift*
9	*Getting something really exciting, like a new stereo or TV*
10	*Getting my purchase home to be tried out or tried on*

Another way of creating a pleasure hierarchy is to focus on various elements of the situation. For example, a teacher found himself smoking a lot of marijuana in the hour after he got home from his last class. Here's his hierarchy, which consists of the routine steps he took in preparing and smoking a joint.

Pleasure 1-10	Scene
1	Getting stash box, papers, and matches out of bookcase
3	Sitting in my reclining chair and spreading out a newspaper to catch excess
5	Putting on earphones to listen to music and rolling the joint
7	Lighting up and taking the first hit
8	Smoking the joint, spacing out, and having to relight it
9	Feeling stoned
10	Spacing out and forgetting about everything

Now it's your turn. When developing your pleasure hierarchy, write it out completely. The items in the examples are abbreviated, but yours should be much more detailed. You might include where you are, who you're with, what you're doing, what you're thinking, and what's going on inside your body. Here's a detailed item from the hierarchy of a compulsive gambler:

The cards are dealt and I pick them up one by one. I feel excited and nervous. I'm at Jack's house, at the kitchen table with the green felt tablecloth. A couple of strangers are there, but it's mostly the same crowd. The fifth card goes around, and we're ready for the first bets. I'm to the left of the dealer; I bet a buck.

The more detail you have, the easier it will be to imagine the scene. If you have difficulty getting a mental image of an item in your hierarchy, spice it up with a variety of sense impressions. In addition to what you imagine seeing, imagine how it smells, what you hear, whether you feel warm or cold, and so on.

When creating your hierarchy, make sure the pleasure rating of your first item is no more than 1 or 2. In other words, select something barely pleasurable to start off with, then work your way up to number 10, the most intensely delightful aspect of your habit. Try not to let more than two points separate consecutive items.

Pleasure 1-10	Scene

Step 4: Create an Aversion Scene

To create an aversion scene, you'll need to come up with something you find deeply repulsive or frightening to think about. Choose from the following list. You may find it helpful to first rate each for the degree of repulsion or fear you experience when simply imagining the item.

- Open wounds

- Crawling insects

- Dead people

- Raging fire

- Getting teeth drilled

- Nausea or throwing up

- Thunder

- Throwing up in public

- Looking down from high places

- Having a heart attack

- Falling

- Physical injury

- Getting an injection or having blood drawn

- Fainting

- Vast open space

- Looking foolish

- Tight, confined spaces

- Snakes

- Dead animals

- Spiders

- Rejection or ostracism by friends

- Blood

- Rejection or ostracism by strangers

- Severe criticism

Nausea is the most commonly used aversive item for covert sensitization. Social ostracism and rejection have also been used extensively. The item should be sufficiently aversive that thinking about it generates strong bodily sensations. Really *feeling* your repulsion or fear bodily is crucial to the success of this procedure. For example, the thought of nausea should be accompanied by a very specific memory of something that really nauseated you, until you begin to actually feel nauseous.

Step 5: Combine Pleasurable and Aversive Scenes

Once you're able to clearly imagine and experience the aversive item and a memory or scene associated with it, you can begin pairing it with items on your pleasure hierarchy. Here's an example showing how Marcos, the housepainter, worked on the fifth item in his hierarchy: snacking on cinnamon bread. He began by sitting in his favorite chair and using shorthand muscle relaxation to let go of all of the tension in his muscles. When he felt relaxed, he began imagining his combined scene:

I'm relaxed. The TV is on. There's a blue glow. I'm slumped in my chair and think of getting a little something to eat. I go into the kitchen and butter five pieces of cinnamon bread. It looks delicious. As I bring the first slice to my mouth, I start to feel queasy. It's like that time I ate the bad crab. Suddenly I feel sick to my stomach. I start to take a bite but everything I ate earlier comes up and I vomit all over myself. I throw the bread in the garbage and open a window. Immediately I feel relief. While I'm breathing the fresh air, the nausea goes away.

Here are precise instructions for how to pair each item of your pleasure hierarchy with the aversive scene:

1. Start with a detailed description of that particular item on the hierarchy, including your enjoyment of it.

2. Introduce the aversive item, in vivid detail, so you no longer feel any pleasure in whatever you were just enjoying.

3. Imagine yourself feeling better as soon as you stop whatever you were doing.

Write out this type of three-step scenario for each item on your hierarchy. You can do this on another blank copy of the pleasure hierarchy or, if you need more space, on a separate piece of paper. The aversive scene should be as disgusting as possible and full of detail so it completely eradicates any experience of pleasure. Be sure to eliminate the aversive item as soon as you stop engaging in your formerly pleasurable habit. Let yourself have immediate feelings of relief, comfort, and relaxation.

When you've rewritten all of the items in your hierarchy to include the aversive scene, you can begin practicing covert sensitization. Read over the first item in your hierarchy until you have it clearly in mind. Close your eyes and relax using progressive muscle relaxation or shorthand muscle relaxation. Relaxation helps you form clearer images. When the tension is out of your body, imagine the first item, starting with the pleasurable aspect. Notice what you see, smell, and hear. Notice everything you're doing. Then move right into the aversive experience and stay with it until you feel uncomfortable and repulsed. Remember to imagine feeling better as soon as you stop engaging in the behavior associated with your habit.

Using this procedure, practice visualizing each item in your hierarchy three to five times before going on to the next item, and limit yourself to one or two items per day. Over a period of approximately one week, you can complete the entire hierarchy.

Step 6: Alter the Aversive Scene

Now you'll change the scene so that you avoid vomiting, being ostracized, or whatever you've chosen for an aversion by not engaging in your destructive habit. At the first sign of feeling queasy, put the food down, get up and leave the bar, quit the card game, and so on, and imagine yourself starting to feel better. Here's how Marcos rewrote the fifth item of his hierarchy to reflect this change:

I'm relaxed. The TV is on. There's a blue glow. I'm slumped in my chair and think of getting a little something to eat. I go into the kitchen and butter five pieces of cinnamon bread. I start to bring a piece to my mouth, but I have that queasy feeling and put the bread down right away. I immediately feel relieved and relaxed again.

Go through your hierarchy again and revise all of the items so you avoid the aversive item rather than experiencing it. As you did the first time you worked through your hierarchy, practice each item three to five times before going on to the next one, and limit yourself to one or two items per day.

Step 7: Practice Covert Sensitization in Real Life

Once you've mastered covert sensitization with imagined scenes, practice the procedure in the presence of tempting objects or situations at times when your desire to engage in your habit is low. As you become more confident about controlling a destructive habit, you can begin using covert sensitization when the temptation is stronger. For example, if you've been working on controlling cravings for pastries, you might walk past a bakery window when you aren't very hungry and practice covert sensitization while you look in. Later, when you're more sure of yourself, you can go down to the bakery just before breakfast and repeat the procedure.

SPECIAL CONSIDERATIONS

If you have difficulty visualizing or feeling a physical reaction to an aversive stimulus, you can provide yourself with an aversive stimulus in real life by actually smelling rotten meat, rotten eggs, or ammonia. You can also try holding your breath, doing push-ups, or making harsh, unpleasant sounds.

As you practice covert sensitization, always time the nausea or other aversive stimulus to coincide exactly with the moment you begin to engage in the destructive habit. Cut off the aversive stimulus as soon as you abandon the destructive habit.

The effects of covert sensitization can be strengthened with booster sessions. If you start feeling impulses to engage in your destructive habit again, or if mild impulses become stronger or more frequent, go through your hierarchy again and resensitize yourself to the aversive scenes.

CHAPTER 20

Problem Solving

Problems that elude solution result in chronic emotional pain. When your usual coping strategies fail, a growing sense of helplessness makes the search for novel solutions more difficult. The possibility of relief seems to recede, the problem begins to appear insoluble, and anxiety or despair can increase to crippling levels.

In 1971, psychologists Thomas D'Zurilla and Marvin Goldfried described a problem as a failure to find an effective response. For example, the fact that a person can't find one of his shoes in the morning is not in itself a problem. It becomes a problem only if he neglects to look under the bed, where the shoe is most likely to be found. If he looks in the sink, the medicine cabinet, and the garbage disposal, he is beginning to create a problem—his response is not effective in finding the missing shoe. In this chapter, we'll outline a problem-solving strategy that will help you generate effective solutions to any type of problem.

SYMPTOM EFFECTIVENESS

Problem solving is effective for reducing anxiety associated with procrastination and the inability to make decisions. It is useful for relieving feelings of powerlessness or anger associated with chronic problems for which no solution has been found. It is helpful as part of the treatment for worry, depression, bad habits, procrastination, immobilization, and interpersonal conflicts.

Problem solving is not recommended for the treatment of phobias or conditions of global, free-floating anxiety.

TIME TO MASTERY

Problem-solving techniques can be put into effect the same day they are learned. After several weeks of practice, applying the steps becomes largely automatic.

INSTRUCTIONS

The problem-solving strategy we'll outline in this chapter is a seven-step process:

1. State the problem.

2. Outline your goals.

3. List the alternatives.

4. Evaluate the likely consequences of promising strategies.

5. Identify the steps for implementing your strategy.

6. Try your solution.

7. Evaluate the results.

Step 1: State the Problem

The first step in problem solving is to identify the problem situations in your life. People normally experience problems in areas such as finances, work, social relationships, and family life. The checklist on the following pages will help you identify the area in which you operate least effectively and have the most problems. This is the area you'll concentrate on as you develop problem-solving skills.

After each situation listed, check the box that best describes how much it interferes with your life:

• None: doesn't apply to you or doesn't bother you

• Little: mildly affects your life and is a small drain on your energy

• Moderate: has a significant impact on your life

• Major: greatly disrupts your day-to-day existence and has a strong negative impact on your sense of well-being

If you have trouble determining how significant a given situation is for you, imagine yourself in that situation. Include lots of sights and sounds and actions to make it seem real. In that situation, do you feel angry, depressed, anxious, or confused? These are red flag emotions and indicate that you're probably in a situation that is a problem for you—something about the way you're responding to the situation isn't working for you.

Problem Checklist

	Interference			
Health	None	Little	Moderate	Major
Difficulty sleeping				
Weight problems				
Feeling physically tired and run-down				
Stomach trouble				
Chronic physical problems				
Difficulty getting up in the morning				
Poor diet and nutrition				
Finances				
Difficulty making ends meet				
Insufficient money for basic necessities				
Increasing amounts of debt				
Unexpected expenses				
Too little money for hobbies and recreation				
No steady source of income				
Too many financial dependents				
Living Situation				
Bad neighborhood				
Too far from work or school				
Too small				
Unpleasant conditions				
Things in need of repair				
Poor relationship with landlord				
Work				
Monotonous and boring work				
Poor relations with boss or supervisor				
Being rushed and under stress				
Wanting a different job or career				

	None	Little	Moderate	Major
Needing more education or experience				
Fear of losing job				
Not getting along with coworkers				
Unemployment				
Unpleasant conditions				
Needing more freedom at work				
Psychological				
Having a particular bad habit				
Religious problems				
Problems with authority				
Competing goals or demands				
Obsession with distant or unobtainable goals				
Lack of motivation				
Feeling very depressed at times				
Feeling nervous at certain times				
Feeling blocked from attaining goals				
Feeling angry a lot				
Worrying				
Recreation				
Not having enough fun				
Ineptitude at sports or games				
Too little leisure time				
Little chance to enjoy art or self-expression				
Little chance to enjoy nature				
Wanting to travel				
Needing a vacation				
Inability to think of anything fun to do				
Social Relationships				
Timidity or shyness				
Not having many friends				

	None	Little	Moderate	Major
Too little romantic contact				
Feeling lonely				
Not getting along well with certain people				
A failed or failing love affair				
Feeling left out				
Lack of love and affection				
Vulnerability to criticism				
Wanting more closeness to people				
Not being understood by others				
Not knowing how to converse well				
Not finding the right partner				
Family				
Feeling rejected by family				
Discord with partner at home				
Not getting along with one or more children				
Feeling trapped in a painful family situation				
Insecurity and fear of losing partner				
Inability to be open and honest with family members				
Desire for sexual contact with someone other than partner				
Conflict with parents				
Having interests different from partner's				
Interference by relatives				
Marriage or relationship breaking up				
Children having problems at school				
Sick family member				
Excessive quarreling at home				
Anger or resentment toward partner				
Irritation with habits of family members				
Worry about family members				

Other

If particular situations not listed above interfere with your life moderately or in a major way, write them here.

_____

_____

_____

Now review the checklist and figure out which general category causes the most interference in your life. From that area, pick one of the situations that you ranked as causing moderate or major interference.

Make a copy of the following Problem Analysis Worksheet, leaving the version in the book blank so you can use it for other problems in the future. Use the worksheet to analyze the situation you've chosen. Try to put at least one word in each blank. If you need more space, use a separate sheet of paper.

Describing the situation in terms of who, what, where, when, how, and why will help you better understand your problem. It will also help you uncover many details that you might not otherwise consider. Take your time. Describing the details of your behavior and feelings and what you want is also important because this information provides clues for generating solutions later. (An example from Jane, the mother of a rebellious twelve-year-old son, follows the blank form.)

Problem Analysis Worksheet

Situation (from the checklist of problems or described briefly in your own words): _____

_____

_____

Who else is involved? _____

_____

What happens? (What is done or not done that bothers you?) _____

_____

_____

Where does it happen? _____

_____

When does it happen? (What time of day? How often? How long does it last?) _____

_____

How does it happen? (What rules does it seem to follow? What moods are involved)? _____

_____

Why does it happen? (What reasons do you or others give for the problem at the time?) _____

_____

What do you do? (What is your actual response to the problem situation?) _____

_____

_____

How do you feel? (Angry? Depressed? Anxious? Confused?) _____

_____

What do you want? (What things do you want to change?) _____

_____

_____

Jane's Problem Analysis Worksheet

Situation (from the checklist of problems or described briefly in your own words):   *Not getting along with my son*

Who else is involved?   *Twelve-year-old son, Jim*

What happens? (What is done or not done that bothers you?)   *He won't do chores, like take out the garbage, water the garden, or set the table.*

Where does it happen?   *At home, especially in the family room in front of the TV*

When does it happen? (What time of day? How often? How long does it last?)   *Afternoon and evening, for about two hours, nearly every day*

How does it happen? (What rules does it seem to follow? What moods are involved?)   *The more I remind him of chores, the more sullen he gets. He just sits there while I get madder, then does his chores resentfully after I threaten him with no TV.*

Why does it happen? (What reasons do you or others give for the problem at the time?)   *He's going through a stage. I expect too much. He doesn't care how I feel.*

What do you do? (What is your actual response to the problem situation?)   *I suffer in silence, then remind, then nag, then yell and threaten.*

How do you feel? (Angry? Depressed? Anxious? Confused?)   *Angry at Jim; feel he doesn't care about me; feel stressed and upset.*

What do you want (What things do you want to change?)   *I want Jim to obey me.*

Step 2: Outline Your Goals

Having completed your Problem Analysis Worksheet, it's time to set one or more goals for change. Examine your response to the problem: what you do, how you feel, and what you want. These statements are particularly helpful for developing specific goals. Use the following space to record up to three goals to address the problem you analyzed:

Goal A: _____

Goal B: _____

Goal C: _____

Jane was struck by how many ineffective methods she used to get Jim to obey, and also by how she kept using these methods even though they weren't working. But the problem was greater than Jim's resistance. Jane was concerned about how angry and stressed she felt during her interactions with her son. She needed to calm down. And she was aware that much of her upset stemmed from a growing sense that Jim didn't care about her. This feeling needed to change as well. Jane decided to set the following three goals to address her concerns:

Goal A: *Develop an effective strategy to get Jim to cooperate.*

Goal B: *Feel calmer.*

Goal C: *Feel more cared for by Jim.*

Step 3: List the Alternatives

In this phase of problem solving, you brainstorm to create strategies that will help you achieve your newly formulated goals. In 1963, Alex Osborn, an author who wrote several books on creative thinking, outlined a technique for brainstorming that has stood the test of time. It has four basic rules:

- **Criticism is ruled out.** This means that you write down any new idea or possible solution without judging it as good or bad. Evaluation is deferred to a later decision-making phase.

- **A freewheeling approach is welcomed.** The crazier and wilder your idea is, the better. Following this rule can help lift you out of mental ruts. You may suddenly break free of your old, limited view of the problem and see it in an entirely different light.

- **Quantity is best.** The more ideas you generate, the better your chances are of having a few good ones. Just write them down, one after another, without thinking a lot about each idea. Don't stop until you have a good, long list.

- **Combine and improve items.** Go back over your list to see how some ideas might be combined or improved. Sometimes two pretty good ideas can be joined into one even better idea.

Brainstorming should be limited to general strategies for achieving your goal. Before figuring out the nuts and bolts of specific actions, you need to decide on a good overall strategy. You'll work out the details of how to implement your strategy in step 5.

Use the following form to list ten alternative strategies for accomplishing each of your goals. It's important not to give up the search for alternative strategies too quickly. Your tenth idea may be the best one. And don't feel limited to ten. If you come up with more strategies, list them on a separate piece of paper. (An example from Jane follows the blank form.)

Alternative Strategies Lists

Goal A: _____

    1. _____

    2. _____

    3. _____

    4. _____

    5. _____

    6. _____

    7. _____

    8. _____

    9. _____

  10. _____

Goal B: _____

    1. _____

    2. _____

    3. _____

    4. _____

    5. _____

    6. _____

    7. _____

    8. _____

    9. _____

  10. _____

Goal C: _____

1. _____

2. _____

3. _____

4. _____

5. _____

6. _____

7. _____

8. _____

9. _____

10. _____

Alternative Strategies Lists

Goal A: _Develop an effective strategy to get Jim to cooperate._

1. _No TV for Jim until his chores are done._
2. _Give Jim a larger allowance and tie it to the chores._
3. _Blow up Jim's computer._
4. _Let Jim keep his room any way he wants. Limit chores to common areas._
5. _Explain expectations for chores in the morning before school._
6. _Keep a chore chart._
7. _Give a reward each week for completed chores (credits toward a video game?)._
8. _If chores aren't done by a specific time, take away Jim's phone for the rest of the day._
9. _If Jim doesn't do chores, he has to make his own lunch._
10. _Computer privileges depend on finishing chores._

Goal B: _Feel calmer._

1. _No matter what, stop yelling._
2. _Rest whenever I start feeling upset or angry._
3. _Blow up the TV—the noise drives me crazy._
4. _Have my husband do the disciplining._
5. _Take a week off and go to the mountains._
6. _Get a massage._
7. _Take a course in relaxation._
8. _Exchange massages with my husband after the kids are in bed._
9. _Take Valium._
10. _Start to swim again._

Goal C: _Feel more cared for by Jim._

1. _No matter what Jim does or doesn't do, stop yelling at him._

2. _Talk to Jim instead of blasting him._

3. _Have my husband do the disciplining._

4. _Spontaneously hug Jim two or three times a day._

5. _Reward him with a hug when he actually does a chore._

6. _Praise Jim a lot._

7. _Ask Jim about school and check in with him at least once a day._

8. _If he doesn't obey, take a few minutes with him and find out if anything's wrong._

9. _Remember that it's more important to me to share good feelings with Jim than to have him do his chores every day. Put a sign on my mirror to help remind me._

10. _Explain my problems to him and ask for his help._

Ultimately, Jane decided to combine some of her ideas. For example, she combined three items under goal A: No computer, phone, or TV for Jim until he finished his chores. And under goal C she combined checking in with Jim once a day with explaining her problems and asking for his help.

Step 4: Evaluate the Likely Consequences of Promising Strategies

By now you should have several goals, each with at least ten possible strategies for accomplishing it. The next step is to select the most promising strategies and consider the consequences of putting them into action. For some people, this process of weighing consequences happens automatically as soon as they think of a possible strategy. Others ponder the consequences more slowly. Whichever is true of you, it will be helpful to do this step thoroughly and conscientiously.

Use the following Evaluating the Consequences form to practice weighing the consequences more deliberately. Make a copy and leave the version in the book blank so you can use it for strategies in the future. To begin, pick the goal that's most attractive to you. For example, Jane chose feeling more cared for by her son because she was starting to realize this was probably the root of her problem. Go over the list of strategies you came up with for that goal and cross out any obviously bad ideas. Where possible, combine several strategies into one. Try to reduce your list to three strategies representing your best ideas.

List these three strategies in the spaces provided on the worksheet. Under each strategy, list any negative and positive consequences you can think of. How would putting that strategy into action affect what you feel, need, or want? How would it affect the people in your life? How would it change their reaction to you? How would it affect your life right now, next month, or next year? Take some time to come up with both positive and negative consequences for each possible strategy.

When you have the major consequences listed, review each one and ask yourself how likely it is to occur. If the consequence is very unlikely, cross it out; you're telling yourself horror stories or being overly optimistic. Then score the remaining consequences as follows:

- If the consequence is predominantly personal, give it 2 points.

- If the consequence predominantly affects others, give it 1 point.

- If the consequence is predominantly long-range, give it 2 points.

- If the consequence is predominantly short-range, give it 1 point.

Note that a consequence can be both personal and long-range (total score of 4), have a long-range effect on others (total score of 3), and so on.

Add up the scores for each strategy to see whether the positive consequences outweigh the negative. Then select the strategy for which the positive consequences most outweigh the negative consequences. (An example from Jane follows the blank form.)

Evaluating the Consequences

Strategy:

Positive consequences	Score	Negative consequences	Score
Total:		Total:	

Strategy:

Positive consequences	Score	Negative consequences	Score
Total:		Total:	

Strategy:

Positive consequences	Score	Negative consequences	Score
Total:		Total:	

Evaluating the Consequences for Jane's Goal C

Strategy: *Have my husband do the disciplining.*

Positive consequences	Score	Negative consequences	Score
I'll be more relaxed.	3	My husband may be reluctant.	2
I'll have more time.	2		
I'll have a better relationship with my son.	3		
Total:	8	Total:	2

Strategy: *Check in with Jim once a day; explain my problems to him and ask for his help.*

Positive consequences	Score	Negative consequences	Score
We might understand each other better and feel closer.	4	Jim still won't do his chores consistently.	3
Jim won't feel so pressured.	2	Telling Jim my problems might burden him or make him feel guilty.	3
I'll have more time.	2		
Total:	8	Total:	6

Strategy: *No matter what, stop yelling.*

Positive consequences	Score	Negative consequences	Score
It will be quieter.	3	Jim still won't do his chores.	2
I won't hurt Jim's feelings as much.	2	My frustration will build.	4
Total:	5	Total:	6

Step 5: Identify the Steps for Implementing Your Strategy

Now you need to decide on the steps you'll take to put your strategy into action. When Jane evaluated the consequences, the strategy of having her husband, Isaac, do the disciplining seemed by far the best choice, so she came up with the following four steps to put it into action:

1. *Discuss the subject with Isaac after Jim goes to bed on Tuesday.*

2. *Take five minutes after work each day to discuss with Isaac how well Jim is doing his chores.*

3. *Have Isaac spend time with Jim each evening with a focus on how well Jim is doing on his chores.*

4. *Use the time I used to spend disciplining to do something nice for Isaac, like bake a special dessert or give him a back rub.*

You may have trouble thinking of concrete behavioral steps. If so, try using brainstorming to develop a list of alternative steps. Then explore the likely consequences of the steps using the technique you learned for selecting your overall strategy.

Step 6: Try Your Solution

Actually trying out your solution is the hardest step, since you now have to act, but it also has the potential to be highly rewarding. You've selected some new responses to an old situation. Now it's time to put your decisions into effect.

Step 7: Evaluate the Results

Once you've tried the new response, observe the results. Are things happening as you predicted? Are you satisfied with the outcome, meaning the new response is helping you reach your goal? If not, return to your alternative strategies list. You can either select different strategies from the list or come up with new ideas. Then repeat steps 4 through 7.

Example

Al, a forty-three-year-old product manager for a plastics company, had become increasingly dissatisfied with his job. He was bored with overseeing the production of the same packaging components over and over. Six months previously the company had switched to new computer-aided design software, and Al had become fascinated with it. He hatched the idea of cutting back on his hours at work in order to return to school for classes in computer-aided design.

Al's boss took a dim view of his plan, and they had several confrontations about the issue. Al felt resentful and became inattentive to his duties on the production line, which provoked yet more confrontations with his boss. Here's how Al applied the problem-solving strategy in this chapter to his problem.

Step 1: State the problem. Here's how Al described his problem: *My job is boring. I want to go to school and switch careers. I have poor relations with my boss. I want to take time off to attend school, but my boss won't let me.* Al then completed a Problem Analysis Worksheet, spelling out the who, what, where, when, how, and why of his situation. He also looked carefully at his response to the problem:

- What I do: *Ask the boss for time off, get turned down, complain, and take it out on my fabricators by being grumpy and forgetting details.*

- How I feel: *I feel angry, frustrated, and "dissed" by my boss.*

- What I want: *To feel less bored by what I'm doing.*

Step 2: Outline your goals. After looking carefully at his Problem Analysis Worksheet, Al developed three goals: having a better relationship with his boss, enjoying his job more, and learning more about computer-aided design.

Step 3: List the alternatives. Here are some of the alternative strategies that Al came up with for achieving each of these goals:

- *Having a better relationship with my boss*

  - *Get involved in creating the new line of slim DVD cases.*

  - *Stop complaining and picking fights.*

  - *Quit, go to school, and support myself with some online scam.*

- *Enjoying my job more*

  - *Develop more personal relationships with coworkers.*

  - *Attend the retirement and birthday lunches at work.*

- *Learning more about computer-aided design*

  - *Experiment with and learn everything about software at work.*

  - *Take one night class.*

  - *Negotiate with my boss for one morning per week off for a class.*

Step 4: Evaluate the likely consequences of promising strategies. Al crossed off several obviously bad alternatives, such as quitting outright. For the remaining options, he considered the consequences in terms of long- versus short-range outcomes and outcomes for himself versus others. This showed him that his best options were to get involved in the new product line, stop complaining, and concentrate on his relationships with coworkers. His intention was to improve his relationship with his boss to the point where he could resume negotiations about getting some time off.

Step 5: Identify the steps for implementing your strategy. Since all of these strategies involved changing habitual ways of behaving, Al felt a bit stymied as to how to implement them. So he did some more brainstorming to develop some concrete steps to follow day by day.

Step 6: Try your solution. Al put his plans into effect and committed to sticking with his new approach for five weeks.

Step 7: Evaluate the results. Al was gratified to find that his relationship with his boss did indeed improve. And because he was busy and not fighting with his boss, he enjoyed his job more. Eventually he and his boss agreed on a two-week trial in which Al took a couple of hours off Tuesday morning to research continuing education options. When his boss saw that Al could still serve all of his customers well and fulfill his other job responsibilities, he agreed to let Al take that time off on a regular basis so he could take a computer-aided design class at the local junior college.

SPECIAL CONSIDERATIONS

Some people feel a little overwhelmed by the complex steps involved in problem solving. Their response is "Do I really have to do all that?" The answer is yes, the first time, especially if you've been stuck in a problematic situation for a while. Your old, habitual solutions haven't worked. You need to follow each step of the technique to identify and then achieve your goals. Later, you can tailor the process to fit your particular style, and much of it will have become automatic.

CHAPTER 21

When It Doesn't Come Easy

Each of the techniques in this book is designed to change the way you habitually react to things. However, your old ways of reacting have been with you a long time. They're familiar and therefore difficult to change. This chapter takes a look at why old habits are hard to part with, even when they clearly contribute to your pain.

Cognitive behavioral therapy isn't a "talking cure" like traditional psychoanalysis. In this approach, change doesn't arise from a series of insights gained during analysis, conversation, rumination, or merely reading about your problem. It happens because you do something. You must actually fill out the worksheets in this book and diligently practice the various exercises.

If you find yourself skipping practice sessions or just going through the motions halfheartedly, ask yourself these questions:

- Why am I doing these exercises?

- Are they really important to me?

- What am I doing or what would I like to be doing instead of these exercises?

- Is this alternative activity more important to me than doing the exercises?

- Can I schedule my life so that I can do both?

- If I don't do the exercises now, exactly when and where will I do them next?

- What would I have to give up if I succeeded with my exercises?

- What would I have to confront if I succeeded with my exercises?

COMMON DIFFICULTIES

A common roadblock to successful use of cognitive behavioral techniques is an untrained imagination. Here are some strategies for strengthening your ability to imagine:

- Focus on senses other than sight when you do visualizations. Create mental sense impressions of sound, touch, taste, and smell. For instance, if you're trying to imagine your kitchen, the visual impressions may be very hazy to you. But you can focus your imagination on the smells of food cooking, the taste of a cold soda, the temperature of the room, the texture of the wooden table-top, the feel of the tiles beneath your bare feet, and so on.

- Record a detailed description of the scene you want to practice imagining.

- Draw a picture of the scene you want to practice imagining as a way of tuning in to the visual details. Notice which objects and details give the scene its unique identity.

Another major obstacle is simply not believing that a technique or exercise will work. Failure to believe is a cognitive problem. You repeat discouraging statements to yourself, such as "I'll never get better," "This won't work," "These sorts of things don't help me," "I'm too stupid," or "Somebody has to show me how." One of the basic tenets of this book is that you believe what you repeat to yourself. If you say any negative statement often enough, you'll act in such a way as to make it true for you. This book will be of little or no value until you overcome the belief that it cannot help you. To work on this issue, commit to a specific period of focused effort: two weeks, one week, even one day. Then evaluate any change in your problem at that time. If you've made a little progress, if the symptom is less painful or frequent, commit to continuing your work with the book for a second period of time.

Boredom is frequently a barrier to success with cognitive behavioral work. Many of these techniques are boring. But they work. Practicing them becomes a trade-off: a few weeks of occasional boredom in exchange for years of freedom from unwanted symptoms. This is the choice you may have to make every day when you do these exercises.

Fear of novelty is a well-documented obstacle to successful treatment. Your worldview changes when you realize that you have the power to change how you think and therefore how you feel. You can no longer see yourself as a helpless victim of good and bad fortune; you become an active creator of your own experience. When you give up a symptom, your life changes. Many people would rather hold on to a familiar though painful symptom than adjust to a new life without it.

Just following new directions may provoke anxiety. The directions may not quite fit your needs. They may be too detailed, cumbersome, or rigid. They may be insufficiently detailed. Either way, bear in mind that the directions are intended to provide a general outline; adjust them to fit your individual needs.

Poor time management is a major roadblock to success. People who give up after half learning a technique often explain that they were overscheduled and didn't have time to use the technique. Here the real problem is usually one of priorities. Other things simply had a higher priority. After-work drinks, errands, long phone calls, television, or surfing the Internet came first. You need to schedule your work with this book just as you do other important parts of your day. Write down the time and place and keep the commitment just as you would an appointment with a friend.

Another difficulty, often overlooked, is success that comes too rapidly. In this case, there's a danger that you may think, "That was a snap to get over. Maybe it wasn't a problem after all. I don't have to worry about that anymore." Minimizing a symptom's significance in this way lays the groundwork for a setback. The symptom may gradually reemerge in your patterns of behavior, perhaps without your immediate awareness. To avoid this, continue using the techniques you've learned in this book for a while after you're free of symptoms. If symptoms do reoccur, immediately revisit the relevant chapters and work through them again.

WHAT'S YOUR EXCUSE?

When you miss an exercise, how do you justify it to yourself? Typical reasons include "I'm too tired today," "I'm too busy," "Missing once won't hurt," "It's too boring," "I feel okay today, so I don't need to do the exercise. "My family needs my help," and "This isn't going to work anyway."

Many of these excuses are partially true: You do in fact feel busy or tired, somebody may need your help, and missing a single session probably won't hurt. What isn't true is the implication that being rushed or tired or feeling the weight of obligations prevents you from working with this book. The complete truth would be, for example, "I'm tired. I could do the exercise, but I choose to focus on the needs of my family today."

What's important is that you take responsibility for your decision to choose one activity over another rather than pretend that you're the passive victim of circumstance. You need to honestly assess your priorities. If your psychological health isn't a very high priority, then you probably won't make sufficient time to master any of the techniques in this book.

Most people's excuses fall back on a favorite theme, and it often sounds a lot like this: "I'm indispensable. Things will fall apart without me." For example, Kaitlyn, an insurance executive, had difficulty delegating responsibility. She believed that only she could do the job right and that the slightest mistake would bring about her downfall. As a result, her desk was piled high with a dozen half-finished tasks and projects. She was stuck in this situation because of her belief that any time she took to work on her exercises would make her fall hopelessly behind at work. Her priorities were successful businessperson first, healthy human being second. This belief had exhausted her and prevented her from trying to solve her problems.

The excuses you use to justify not taking the time to master a technique are likely to be the same ones you have used for years to perpetuate old habits. These excuses are based on faulty premises.

MAKING A CONTRACT

Often it isn't enough to make agreements with yourself to master a particular technique. After a time you slack off and return to old behavior patterns. If you're typical, your commitment to yourself doesn't have the same power as commitments you make to other people. Nobody else feels disappointed or concerned when you fail yourself. Nobody else knows about it.

If you have a tendency to start and not finish things, help ensure your success with the approaches in this book by making a contract with someone who knows and cares about you. Make sure you select someone whose good opinion you value, someone you don't want to let down. Use the contract form that follows or a similar document to formalize the agreement. Both of you should sign it and keep copies.

If concern about failing this person isn't sufficient to motivate you, write a penalty clause into the contract. For example, failure to keep your commitment might obligate you to donate fifty dollars to a candidate or cause you strongly disagree with. Failure might obligate you to clean out the weeds in your backyard or put off buying a new TV. If your penalty clause includes a donation, have your friend hold the check in a stamped, addressed envelope, to be mailed if you fail to fulfill the contract.

Official Contract

I have decided to deal with my problem of _____

by using techniques in this book, specifically chapter(s) _____

I am making a commitment to _____ (support person's name) to

undertake the following: practicing _____ (technique) _____ times

per day/week for _____ days/weeks.

I will evaluate my improvement only at the end of this period.

I will immediately notify the above-mentioned person of any failure to uphold this commitment.

_____   _____
(signature)   (date)

I commit myself to taking this work seriously, and I will periodically check with _____

(your name) as a reminder that your progress is important to me.

_____   _____
(support person's signature)   (date)

WHEN SYMPTOMS PERSIST

Occasionally you won't be able to get rid of an unwanted symptom, even after working with the techniques in this book conscientiously and practicing them regularly. There are several common reasons why this may occur: misdiagnosis, misplaced emphasis, and secondary gains from symptoms.

Misdiagnosis

It's possible that you're working on anger when your real problem is fear, or treating depression when your main goal should be quitting alcohol or other drugs. Perhaps an underlying physical issue is responsible for your problem.

To help determine whether you're working on the correct problem, revisit chapter 1 and carefully read the description of each problem. Alternatively, you may wish to work with a mental health professional to determine which treatment program outlined in chapter 1 is most appropriate for you. Also consider getting a thorough medical checkup.

Misplaced Emphasis

There are three broad avenues of approach in cognitive behavioral therapy: the physical, the cognitive, and the behavioral. Physical approaches are primarily relaxation techniques such as those you learned in chapter 5: progressive muscle relaxation, breathing exercises, and the like. Cognitive approaches include uncovering and restructuring automatic thoughts, mindfulness, defusion, visualization, and so on. Behavioral techniques involve problem solving, getting mobilized, and exposure to phobic situations.

If you've been doing mostly one kind of work, shift your emphasis to another avenue of approach and see if that provides better symptom control. For example, if you've mostly worked with cognitive approaches, shift to more physical or behavioral techniques.

Secondary Gains from Symptoms

Oddly enough, many people are attached to their symptoms. These symptoms may serve an important function in their lives. For example, your fears may relieve you of social obligations that you find unpleasant and do so in a way that allows you to avoid taking responsibility for disappointing others.

A simple way to determine if you receive such secondary gains from your symptoms is to keep a log of when your symptoms occur and what activities (or would-be activities) surround them. For instance, you might discover that you thought you were nervous in all social settings, but you're actually nervous only when people flirt with you. Your nervousness has functioned to say, "I'm not available."

Often the secondary gain of a symptom dates back to a specific event or situation. Ask yourself when your symptoms first began. They may have been an appropriate and adaptive response to a stressful situation. For example, a young teacher was anxious whenever she was a passenger in a car. She had experienced the symptom since childhood, when she was frequently driven by her intoxicated father. If she became sufficiently frightened and noisy, her father would quickly take her home. In that childhood context, expressing her anxiety helped her escape an objectively dangerous situation.

Another possibility is that you share a symptom with an important person in your life as part of your identification with that person. For example, you may share with your father a belief that people are victims of circumstances, accompanied by a feeling of depression and helplessness. As a result, any new challenge you encounter brings up expectations of failure and the opportunity to reinforce your worldview. Ask yourself who in your family shares your symptoms, then examine that person's belief system and compare it with your own. The easily seen speck in someone else's eye may help you begin to notice the beam in your own.

Getting Help

If your symptoms persist, consult a mental health professional. The old patterns and beliefs that produce symptoms can be difficult to identify. A professional can help you uncover your psychological culprits. And even when you know that certain patterns and beliefs are maladaptive, it can be hard to give them up precisely because they are so familiar. A professional can help you outline and implement a treatment program and provide support when the going gets tough.

PERSISTENCE PAYS OFF

Persist. Don't give up. Your ability to heal yourself by modifying your thoughts and feelings is a tremendous power. You can change what you think and therefore what you feel. You can change the structure of your life by altering the structure of your mind. You can take away your pain. "It's supposed to be a professional secret," Albert Schweitzer once remarked, "but I'll tell you anyway: We doctors do nothing. We only help and encourage the doctor within."

References and Resources

Astin, J. A. 1997. "Stress Reduction through Mindfulness Meditation: Effects of Psychological Symptomatology, Sense of Control, and Spiritual Experiences." *Psychotherapy and Psychosomatics* 66(2):97-106.

Barlow, D. H., and M. G. Craske. 1989. *Mastery of Your Anxiety and Panic.* Albany, NY: Graywind.

Beck, A. T. 1976. *Cognitive Therapy and the Emotional Disorders.* New York: International Universities Press.

Beck, A. T., G. Emery, and R. Greenberg. 1985. *Anxiety Disorders and Phobias.* New York: Basic Books.

Beck, A. T., and A. Freeman. 1990. *Cognitive Therapy of Personality Disorders.* New York: Guilford Press.

Beck, A. T., A. J. Rush, B. F. Shaw, and G. Emery. 1979. *Cognitive Therapy of Depression.* New York: Guilford Press.

Benson, H. 1975. *The Relaxation Response.* New York: Morrow.

Bourne, E. J. 1995. *The Anxiety and Phobia Workbook.* 2nd ed. Oakland, CA: New Harbinger.

Bradshaw, J. 1990. *Homecoming.* New York: Bantam.

Brown, T. A, R. M. Hertz, and D. H. Barlow. 1992. "New Developments in Cognitive-Behavioral Treatment of Anxiety Disorders." In vol. 2 of *American Psychiatric Press Review of Psychiatry*, edited by A Tasman. Washington, DC: American Psychiatric Press.

Cautela, J. 1967. "Covert Sensitization." *Psychological Reports* 20(2):459-468.

Cautela, J. 1971. "Covert Modeling." Paper presented at the fifth annual meeting of the Association for the Advancement of Behavior Therapy, Washington, DC.

Clark, D. 1989. "Anxiety States." In *Cognitive Behavior Therapy for Psychiatric Problems*, edited by K. Hawton, P. M. Salkovskis, J. Kirk, and D. Clark. Oxford: Oxford University Press.

Craske, M. G., and D. H. Barlow. 2008. "Panic Disorder and Agoraphobia." In *Clinical Handbook of Psychological Disorders: A Step-by-Step Treatment Manual*, edited by D. H. Barlow. New York: Guilford Press.

Cuijpers, P., A. van Straten, and L. Warmerdam. 2007. "Behavioral Activation Treatments of Depression: A Meta-analysis." *Clinical Psychology Review* 2 7(3):318-326.

Davis, M., E. R. Eschelman, and M. McKay 1995. *The Relaxation and Stress Reduction Workbook*. 4th ed. Oakland, CA: New Harbinger.

Deffenbacher, J. L., D. A. Story, R. S. Stark, J. A. Hogg, and A. D. Brandon. 1987. "Cognitive-Relaxation and Social Skills Interventions in the Treatment of General Anger." *Journal of Counseling Psychology* 34(2):171-176.

D'Zurilla, T. J., and M. R. Goldfried. 1971. "Problem Solving and Behavior Modification." *Journal of Abnormal Psychology* 78(1):107-126.

Eifert, G. H., and J. P. Forsyth. 2005. *Acceptance and Commitment Therapy for Anxiety Disorders: A Practitioner's Treatment Guide to Using Mindfulness, Acceptance, and Values-Based Behavior Change Strategies*. Oakland, CA: New Harbinger.

Eifert, G. H., M. McKay, and J. P. Forsyth. 2006. *ACT on Life Not on Anger: The New Acceptance and Commitment Therapy Guide to Problem Anger*. Oakland, CA: New Harbinger.

Ellis, A., and R. Harper. 1961. *A Guide to Rational Living*. North Hollywood, CA: Wilshire Books.

Emmelkamp, P. M. G. 1982. *Phobic and Obsessive-Compulsive Disorders: Theory, Research, and Practice*. New York: Plenum.

Foa, E., E. Hembree, and B. Olaslov Rothbaum. 2007. *Prolonged Exposure Therapy for PTSD: Emotional Processing of Traumatic Experience, Therapist Guide (Treatments That Work)*. Oxford: Oxford University Press.

Freeman, A., J. Pretzer, B. Fleming, and K. Simon. 2004. *Clinical Applications of Cognitive Therapy*. New York: Plenum.

Greenberger, D., and C. Padesky. 1995. *Mind Over Mood: Change How You Feel by Changing the Way You Think*. New York: Guilford Press.

Hackmann, A., D. Clark, P. M. Salkovskis, A. Well, and M. Gelder. 1992. "Making Cognitive Therapy for Panic More Efficient: Preliminary Results with a Four-Session Version of the Treatment." Paper presented at World Congress of Cognitive Therapy, Toronto.

Hayes, S. C., and Smith, S. 2007. *Get Out of Your Mind and Into Your Life: The New Acceptance and Commitment Therapy*. Oakland, CA: New Harbinger.

Hayes, S. C., K. D. Strosahl, and K. G. Wilson. 1999. *Acceptance and Commitment Therapy: An Experiential Approach to Behavior Change*. New York: Guilford Press.

Hazaleus, S., and J. L. Deffenbacher. 1986. "Relaxation and Cognitive Treatments of Anger." *Journal of Consulting and Clinical Psychology* 54(2):222-226.

Horney, K. 1939. *New Ways of Psychoanalysis.* New York: Norton.

Jacobson, E. 1929. *Progressive Relaxation.* Chicago: University of Chicago Press.

Kabat-Zinn, J. *Full Catastrophe Living.* New York: Delta, 1990.

Kabat-Zinn, J., L. Lipworth, R. Burney, and W. Sellers. 1986. "Four-Year Follow-Up of a Meditation-Based Program for the Self-Regulation of Chronic Pain: Treatment Outcomes and Compliance." *Clinical Journal of Pain* 2(3):159-173.

Kabat-Zinn, J., A. O. Massion, J. Kristeller, L. G. Peterson, K. Fletcher, L. Pbert, W. Linderking, and S. F. Santorelli. 1992. "Effectiveness of Meditation-Based Stress Reduction Program in the Treatment of Anxiety Disorders." *American Journal of Psychiatry* 149(7):936-943.

Kabat-Zinn, J., E. Wheeler, T. Light, A. Skillings, M. Scharf, T. G. Cropley, D. Hosmer, and J. Bernhard. 1998. "Influence of a Mindfulness-Based Stress Reduction Intervention on Rates of Skin Clearing in Patients with Moderate to Severe Psoriasis Undergoing Phototherapy (UVB) and Photochemotherapy (PUVA)." *Psychosomatic Medicine* 60(5):625-632.

Kaplan, K. H., D. L. Goldenberg, and M. Galvin-Nadeau. 1993. "The Impact of a Meditation-Based Stress Reduction Program on Fibromyalgia." *General Hospital Psychiatry* 15(5):284-289.

Kristeller, J. L., and C. B. Hallett. 1999. "An Exploratory Study of a Meditation-Based Intervention for Binge Eating Disorder." *Journal of Health Psychology* 4(3):357-363.

Linehan, Marsha. 1993. *Cognitive-Behavioral Treatment of Borderline Personality Disorder.* New York: Guilford Press.

Maletzky, B. 1973. "Assisted Covert Sensitization: A Preliminary Report." *Behavior Therapy* 4(1):117-119

McKay, M., and P. Fanning. 1991. *Prisoners of Belief.* Oakland, CA: New Harbinger.

———. 1992. *Self-Esteem.* 2nd ed. Oakland, CA: New Harbinger.

McMullin, R. E. 1986. *Handbook of Cognitive Therapy Techniques.* New York: W. W. Norton.

Meichenbaum, D. 1977. *Cognitive Behavior Modification.* New York: Plenum.

———. 1988. "Cognitive Behavior Modification with Adults." Workshop for the First Annual Conference on Advances in the Cognitive Therapies: Helping People Change, San Francisco.

Novaco, R. 1975. *Anger Control: The Development and Evaluation of an Experimental Treatment.* Lexington, MA: D. C. Health.

O'Leary, T. A., T. A. Brown, and D. H. Barlow. 1992. "The Efficacy of Worry Control Treatment in Generalized Anxiety Disorder: A Multiple Baseline Analysis." Paper presented at the Meeting of the Association for Advancement of Behavior Therapy, Boston.

Osborn, A. F. 1963. *Applied Imagination: Principles and Procedures of Creative Problem Solving.* 3rd ed. New York: Scribner.

Ovchinikov, M. 2010. "The Relationship of Coping Profiles and Anxiety Symptoms after Self-Help ACT Treatment." Dissertation, the Wright Institute.

Rackman, S. J., M. Craske, K. Tallman, and C. Solyom. 1986. Does Escape Behavior Strengthen Agoraphobic Avoidance? A Replication. *Behavior Therapy* 1 7(4):366-384.

Saavedra, K. 2007. "A New Mindfulness-Based Therapy for Problematic Anger." Dissertation, the Wright Institute.

Salkovskis, P. M., and J. Kirk. 1989. "Obsessional Disorders." In *Cognitive Behavior Therapy for Psychiatric Problems*, edited by K. Hawton, P. M. Salkovskis, J. Kirk, and D. Clark. Oxford: Oxford University Press.

Speca, M., L. Carlson, E. Goodey, and M. Angen. 2000. "A Randomized, Wait-List Controlled Clinical Trial: The Effect of a Mindfulness Meditation-Based Stress Reduction Program on Mood and Symptoms of Stress in Cancer Outpatients." *Psychosomatic Medicine* 6 2(5):613-622.

Stampfl, T. G., and D. G. Levis. 1967. "Essentials of Implosion Therapy: A Learning-Theory-Based Psychodynamic Behavior Therapy." *Journal of Abnormal Psychology* 7 2(6):496-503.

Thase, M. E., and M. K. Moss. 1976. "The Relative Efficacy of Covert Modeling Procedures and Guided Participant Modeling on the Reduction of Avoidance Behavior." *Journal of Behavior Therapy and Experimental Psychiatry* 7 (1):7-12.

Titchener, E. B. 1916. *A Text-Book of Psychology.* New York: Macmillan.

Wanderer, Z. 1991. *Acquiring Courage.* Oakland, CA: New Harbinger. Audio recording.

Weekes, C. 1997. *Peace from Nervous Suffering.* New York: Bantam.

Wolpe, J. 1958. *Psychotherapy by Reciprocal Inhibition.* Stanford, CA: Stanford University Press.

———. 1969. *The Practice of Behavior Therapy.* Oxford: Pergamon Press.

Young, J. 1990. *Cognitive Therapy for Personality Disorders: A Schema-Focused Approach.* Sarasota, FL: Professional Resource Exchange.

Zettle, R. D. 2007. *ACT for Depression: A Clinician's Guide to Using Acceptance and Commitment Therapy in Treating Depression.* Oakland, CA: New Harbinger.

Matthew McKay, PhD, is a professor at the Wright Institute in Berkeley, California. He has authored and coauthored numerous books, including *The Relaxation and Stress Reduction Workbook*, *Self-Esteem*, and *Your Life on Purpose*. His books combined have sold more than three million copies. McKay received his PhD in clinical psychology from the California School of Professional Psychology. In private practice, he specializes in the cognitive behavioral treatment of anxiety and depression.

Martha Davis, PhD, was a psychologist in the department of psychiatry at Kaiser Permanente Medical Center in Santa Clara, CA, where she practiced individual, couple, and group psychotherapy for more than thirty years prior to her retirement. She is coauthor of *The Relaxation and Stress Reduction Workbook*.

Patrick Fanning is a professional writer in the mental health field. He is coauthor of many self-help books, including *The Relaxation and Stress Reduction Workbook*, *Self-Esteem*, and *The Self-Esteem Companion*.

Index

A

abdominal breathing, 60–61

acceptance and commitment therapy, 128, 153

action plans: for hot thoughts, 55; for limited thinking patterns, 45; for problem solving, 270; for values-based behavior, 154–164

activities: mastery, 139, 145–147; pleasure, 138, 143–145; prediction ratings for, 147–149; recording and rating, 138–142; reviewing your ratings for, 149–151; selecting and scheduling, 142–147

activity scheduling, 137–151; effectiveness of, 137–138; special considerations for, 151; steps in process of, 138–151; time to mastery of, 138

addictions, 9, 196, 244. *See also* destructive habits

adolescent visualization exercise, 214–215

adrenaline, 88, 89

age-specific visualization exercises, 209–216; adolescent visualization, 214–215; infant visualization, 209–210; preschooler visualization, 211–213; school-age child visualization, 213–214; toddler visualization, 210–211; young-adult visualization, 215–216

aggression. *See* anger

agoraphobia, 6; panic disorder and, 4, 6; treatment plan for, 6, 12–13

alcoholism, 244

alternative strategies lists, 263–266

anger: rating levels of, 227, 228; theme related to, 20; treatment plan for, 9, 12–13, 219–231; trigger thoughts as source of, 219

anger control, 219–231; coping thoughts for, 224–226; effectiveness of, 220; example of using, 228–230; hierarchy of scenes for, 221–223; real-life practice of, 228; relaxation skills and, 220, 227; sequence for practicing, 226–228; special considerations about,

230–231; stress inoculation for, 219–231; time to mastery of, 220

Anger Control: The Development and Evaluation of an Experimental Treatment (Novaco), 219

Anger Hierarchy form, 221–222, 223

anxiety: medical checkups for, xii; physiological symptoms of, 71; rating levels of, 79, 82, 99–100, 176; stress inoculation and, 165–166; systematic desensitization and, 165; theme related to, 20; thoughts maintaining, 88–89; worry as symptom of, 2. *See also* panic; worry

anxiety disorders, 12–13

anxiety-maintaining thoughts, 88–89

audio recordings: of breath control exercises, 91, 92; of coping imagery narratives, 107, 110; of intense fear images, 183–185; of progressive muscle relaxation, 62; of visualization instructions, 209

automatic thoughts, 15–25; characteristics of, 18–21; core beliefs and, 199; counting, 25; effect of uncovering, 16; feelings caused by, 15–16; listening to, 21; negative feedback loop of, 16–17; recording in Thought Journal, 22–24; time to mastery of, 16

aversive scenes: combining with pleasurable scenes, 249–250; creating/imagining, 248–249; process of altering, 250–251

avoidance: mild forms of, 10; panic disorder and, 4; worry behavior and, 80

awfulizing: automatic thoughts and, 19; filtering and, 29. *See also* catastrophizing

B

bad habits. *See* destructive habits

balanced/alternative thoughts: for hot thoughts, 53, 54; for limited thinking patterns, 38–42

Barlow, David, 99

Basic Rules Checklist, 199–201

Beck, Aaron, 18, 28, 47, 196

behavioral problems: anger control and, 231; covert modeling and, 233–242; treatment plans for, 12–13; worry control and, 80–83

beliefs: core, 195–205; therapy techniques and, 274; worry related to, 73

Benson, Herbert, 59, 61

black-and-white thinking, 29

Body Scanning practice, 118–119

booster sessions, 251

boredom, 274

Bradshaw, John, 208

brainstorming, 261–262

breath: counting, 117; labeling, 117–118

Breath of Life (Masi), 91

breathing techniques: abdominal breathing, 60–61; mindfulness practice and, 116–118; panic disorder and, 91–92

brief exposure, 165–180; choosing fears for, 167–169; coping thoughts for, 174–175, 176; effectiveness of, 166; examples of, 175, 177–179; hierarchy of scenes for, 169–173, 180; real-life situations and, 172, 177–179; relaxation training and, 167, 176; sequence for conducting, 175–177; special considerations for, 179–180; techniques leading to, 165–166; time to mastery of, 166. *See also* prolonged exposure

C

catastrophizing, 30, 33; alternative responses to, 40–41; core beliefs and, 201; exercises for identifying, 33–38; panic sequence and, 88; risk assessment and, 73

Cautela, Joseph, 233, 234, 243

checking behaviors, 82

chest pain/pressure, 90

childhood trauma: inner-child visualizations for, 208–215; shame arising from abuse and, 8; talking back exercise for, 217

Cognitive Behavior Modification (Meichenbaum), 165

cognitive behavioral therapy: contracts used in, 275–277; difficulties encountered in, 274–275; importance of practice in, 273; why it works, 2

cognitive restructuring, 92–98

Commitment to Value-Based Action Worksheet, 161–164

community life and citizenship, 155

conflict, interpersonal, 12–13

consequences: evaluating in problem solving, 267–269; predicting catastrophic, 201

contracts, 275–277

Conveyer Belt exercise, 121–122

coping: cognitive statements for, 109–110; imagery for, 105–113; with panic, 85–104

coping imagery, 105–113; benefits of, 105; effectiveness of, 106; examples of using, 108, 111–113; narrative writing and, 107; real-life situations and, 111; rehearsing the sequence of, 110; relaxation skills and, 106–107, 109, 110; steps in process of, 106–111; strategy planning and, 109–110; stress points and, 107–108; time to mastery of, 106

coping statements: anger control and, 224–226; brief exposure and, 174–175, 176; coping imagery and, 109–110; covert modeling and, 238

core beliefs, 195–205; assessing negative impact of, 199; catastrophic assumptions and, 201; effectiveness of changing, 196; example of working with, 204–205; explanation of, 195–196; identifying, 197–199; inner-child visualizations and, 207–208; rewriting, 203–204; rules based on, 199–203; time to mastery of, 196

counting: breaths, 117; thoughts, 25

covert modeling, 233–242; coping statements in, 238; effectiveness of, 234; examples of using, 239–242; explanation of, 233–234; real-life performance of, 238–239; role-playing in, 238; steps in process of, 234–239; time to mastery of, 234; visualization and, 235, 237

covert sensitization, 243–251; aversive scenes and, 248–251; effectiveness of, 244; explanation of, 243–244; habit analysis and, 245; pleasure hierarchy and, 245–248, 249–250; real-life practice of, 251; relaxation skills and, 245; special considerations for, 251; steps in process of, 244–251; time to mastery of, 244

Craske, Michelle, 99

cue-controlled relaxation, 64–65, 106, 167

D

deep breathing, 60–61

defusion, 127–135; effectiveness of, 128; example of using, 134–135; explanation of, 127–128; instructions for practicing, 128–134; special considerations about, 135; time to mastery of, 128

depersonalized feelings, 90

depression: immobilization and, 137; theme related to, 20; treatment plan for, 6–7, 12–13

depressive disorders, 12–13

desensitization: interoceptive, 99–104; systematic, 165, 166

destructive habits: analysis of, 245; covert sensitization and, 243–251; treatment plan for, 9–10, 12–13, 243–251

Discomfort Rating Chart, 185–186

distancing exercises, 132–134

dizziness, 90

D'Zurilla, Thomas, 253

E

Ellis, Albert, 18, 31, 47

emotions. *See* feelings

Evaluating the Consequences form, 267–269

evidence log, 204

excuses, 275

exposure: brief, 165–180; interoceptive, 99–101; prolonged, 181–193; real-life, 172, 177–179, 191–193; worry, 77–80

Exposure Hierarchy and Anxiety Intensity Chart, 101–102, 104

F

fainting, 90

family issues, 155, 257

Fanning, Patrick, 196, 207

Fear Assessment Worksheet, 168

fears: exercise for assessing, 167–169; hierarchy of scenes related to, 169–173, 180; recording images evoking, 183–185; stress inoculation and, 165–166; systematic desensitization and, 165. *See also* phobias

feedback loop, 16–17

feelings: physiological component of, 17; thoughts as cause of, 15–16

fight-or-flight symptoms, 12–13, 87–88

filtering, 28–29, 32; alternative responses to, 38–39; exercises for identifying, 33–38

financial problems, 255

flooding technique, 182

forms, charts, and worksheets: Anger Hierarchy form, 221–222, 223; Basic Rules Checklist, 199–201; Commitment to Value-Based Action Worksheet, 161–164; Discomfort Rating Chart, 185–186; Evaluating the Consequences form, 267–269; Exposure Hierarchy and Anxiety Intensity Chart, 101–102, 104; Fear Assessment Worksheet, 168; Important Life Domains and Key Values form, 156–157; Intentions and Interior Barriers form, 158–160, 161; Interoceptive Assessment Chart, 100; Pleasure Hierarchy form, 246–247, 248; Probability Form, 93–98;

Problem Analysis Worksheet, 258–260; Problem Checklist, 255–257; Risk Assessment Worksheet, 73–76; Treatment Planner, 12–13; Weekly Activity Schedule, 140–142

Freeman, Arthur, 196

friendships, 155

G

generalized anxiety disorder, 2

goals for change, 261

Goldfried, Marvin, 253

Greenberger, Dennis, 43

guided behavior rehearsal, 234

guilt, 8, 12–13

H

habits, bad. *See* destructive habits

Hayes, Steven, 127

health issues, 155, 255

heartbeat, rapid, 89

hierarchies: of anger situations, 221–223; of panic sensations, 101–102; of pleasure, 245–248; of threatening scenes, 169–173, 180; of worries, 78

hierarchy worksheets, 170–171, 173, 221–222

Horney, Karen, 32

hot thoughts, 47–58; action plan for, 55; anger as result of, 219; balanced/alternative thoughts for, 53, 54; evidence for/against, 50–53; example of working with, 55–57; special considerations for, 57–58; Thought and Evidence Journal for, 48–58; time to mastery of, 48

hyperventilation, 60, 90, 91

I

idiosyncratic thoughts, 20

imagery: coping, 105–113; of fears, 183–185. *See also* visualization immobilization: treatment plan for, 12–13, 137–151. *See also* activity scheduling

implosion therapy, 181

Important Life Domains and Key Values form, 156–157

in vivo exposure, 191

infant visualization exercise, 209–210

Inner Shuttling exercise, 121

inner-child visualizations, 207–218; age-specific exercises, 209–216; core beliefs and, 207–208; effectiveness of, 208; example of using, 216–217; instructions for, 208–209; special considerations about, 218; talking back exercise, 217; time to mastery of, 208. *See also* visualization

Inner-Outer Shuttle exercise, 119–120

intentions, values-based, 158–161

Intentions and Interior Barriers form, 158–160, 161

Interoceptive Assessment Chart, 100

interoceptive desensitization, 99–104; desensitization process, 102–103; exposure hierarchy, 101–102; initial exposure, 99–101; in real-life settings, 104

interpersonal conflict, 12–13

intimate relationships, 154

J

Jacobson, Edmund, 61

K

Kabat-Zinn, Jon, 115

Kirk, Joan, 182

L

labeling: breaths, 117–118; thoughts, 130

laddering process, 198

learning: of automatic thoughts, 21; values related to, 154

letting-go exercises, 130–131

light-headedness, 90

limited thinking patterns, 27–45; action plans for, 45; balanced/alternative thoughts for, 38–42; effect of challenging, 28; exercises for identifying, 33–38; Thought Journal used for, 42–45; time to mastery of, 28; types of, 28–33

Linehan, Marsha, 138

listening to automatic thoughts, 21

living situation issues, 255

loop tapes, 181–182

low self-esteem, 7–8, 12–13

M

magnifying, 31, 33; alternative responses to, 41; exercises for identifying, 33–38

mantras, 117, 132

Masi, Nick, 91

mastery activities, 139, 145–147

McKay, Matthew, 196, 207

medical checkups, xii

meditation, 115, 116, 129

Meichenbaum, Donald, 165, 196

mental health professionals, 279

mild avoidance, 10, 12–13

mind reading, 30, 33; alternative responses to, 40; exercises for identifying, 33–38

Mindful Focusing exercise, 129–130

mindfulness, 115–125; breathing and, 116–118; effectiveness of, 115–116; example of using, 124–125; explanation of, 115; instructions for practicing, 116–124; observing your body, 116–120; observing your thoughts, 120–124; time to mastery of, 116; Wise Mind Diagram and, 122–124

mindfulness-based stress reduction (MBSR), 115

minimizing, 31

misdiagnosis, 278

misplaced emphasis, 278

mobilization. *See* activity scheduling

modeling. *See* covert modeling

muscular tension: progressive relaxation of, 61–64; treatment plan for, 12–13

"musterbation" thinking pattern, 31

N

narrative writing, 107

National Institute of Mental Health, 137

negative core beliefs, 12–13

negative feedback loop, 16–17

negative label repetition, 132–133

Novaco, Raymond, 219

novelty, fear of, 274

O

obesity, 244

objectifying thoughts, 133

observation: of body processes, 116–120; of thoughts, 120–124, 128–130

obsessional thinking: prolonged exposure for, 182, 190–191; treatment plan for, 5, 12–13

Osborn, Alex, 261

overestimating risk, 72–73, 74, 92

overgeneralization, 29–30, 32; alternative responses to, 39–40; exercises for identifying, 33–38

overlearning, xi, 106, 228

P

Padesky, Christine, 43, 47

panic: breaking the cycle of, 89; sequence in process of, 86–89; symptoms related to, 85, 87–88, 89–90. *See also* anxiety; worry

panic disorder: agoraphobia and, 4, 6; treatment plan for, 3–4, 12–13, 85–104; understanding panic and, 86–90

panic disorder treatment, 85–104; breath control training, 91–92; cognitive restructuring, 92–98; effectiveness of, 85; interoceptive desensitization, 99–104; main components of, 86; Probability Form, 93–98; time to mastery of, 86

parenting role, 154

peaceful scene visualization, 65–67

perfectionism: treatment plan for, 4–5, 12–13; worry control and, 82

persistence, 279

personal history, 72

personalization, 27, 31, 33; alternative responses to, 41; exercises for identifying, 33–38

phobias: brief exposure and, 169; hierarchy of scenes related to, 169–173, 180; prolonged exposure and, 182, 192; stress inoculation and, 165–166; systematic desensitization and, 165; treatment plan for, 5–6, 12–13. *See also* fears

physical abuse, 8, 208

physical checkups, xii

physical self-care, 155

physical stress, 12–13

physiology: of anxiety, 71; of feelings, 17; of panic, 87–88, 89–90

pleasure activities, 138, 143–145

pleasure hierarchy: combining aversive scenes with, 249–250; creating, 245–248

polarized thinking, 29, 32; alternative responses to, 39; exercises for identifying, 33–38

post-traumatic stress disorder, 193

predictions: of catastrophic consequences, 201; of outcomes, 73; of pleasure/mastery, 147–149

predictions log, 202, 203

preschooler visualization exercise, 211–213

Prisoners of Belief (McKay and Fanning), 207

probability estimation: panic disorder and, 92–98; worry and, 72–73

Probability Form, 93–98

Problem Analysis Worksheet, 258–260

problem behavior. *See* behavioral problems

Problem Checklist, 255–257

problem solving, 253–272; action steps for, 270; analyzing problems for, 258–260; effectiveness of, 253; evaluating the consequences of, 267–269; example of applying, 270–272; identifying problems for, 254–258; listing alternatives for, 261–266; observing the results of, 270; outlining goals for, 261; special considerations for, 272; steps in process of, 254–270; time to mastery of, 254; trying out solutions for, 270

procrastination, 11, 12–13

progressive muscle relaxation (PMR), 61–64; brief exposure and, 167; covert sensitization and, 245; instructions for practicing, 62–63; shorthand method of, 64; without contracting, 64

projection, 30

prolonged exposure, 181–193; effectiveness of, 182; examples of using, 187–191, 192–193; historical development of, 181–182; rating discomfort from, 185–186; real-life situations and, 191–193; recording fear images in, 183–185; steps in process of, 183–187; time to mastery of, 182. *See also* brief exposure

psychological problems, 256

public statements, 20

R

ratings: anger, 227, 228; anxiety, 79, 82, 99–100, 176; discomfort, 185–186; pleasure and mastery, 138–142, 147–149

rational emotive therapy, 47

real-life situations: anger control in, 228; brief exposure in, 172, 177–179; coping imagery in, 111; covert modeling in, 238–239; covert sensitization in, 251; interoceptive desensitization in, 104; prolonged exposure in, 191–193

recordings. *See* audio recordings

recreation and leisure issues, 155, 256

relaxation response, 59, 61

relaxation training, 59–67; abdominal breathing and, 60–61; anger control and, 220; brief exposure and, 167, 176; coping imagery and, 106–107, 109, 110; covert sensitization and, 245; cue-controlled relaxation, 64–65; effectiveness of, 59–60; incomplete relaxation and, 230; progressive muscle relaxation, 61–64; relaxation without tension, 64; time to mastery of, 60; visualizing peaceful scenes, 65–67; worry control and, 72, 78

reparenting approach, 208

risk assessment: estimating probability in, 72–73, 92–98; panic disorder and, 92–98; predicting outcomes in, 73; worksheet used for, 73–76; worry control and, 72–76

Risk Assessment Worksheet, 73–76

role-playing: covert modeling and, 238; inner-child visualization and, 217

rules based on core beliefs, 199–204; catastrophic predictions and, 201; identifying, 199–201; rewriting, 203–204; selecting to test, 201–202; testing, 202–203

S

Salkovskis, Paul, 182

school-age child visualization exercise, 213–214

Schweitzer, Albert, 279

secondary gains, 278–279

selective abstraction, 21

self-esteem issues, 7–8, 12–13

self-talk, 18

sensitization. *See* covert sensitization; desensitization

sexual abuse, 8, 208

sexual deviations, 244

shame, 8, 12–13

shorthand muscle relaxation, 64

shorthand thoughts, 18–19

"shoulds", "oughts", "musts": alternative responses to, 42; automatic thoughts and, 19; exercises for identifying, 33–38; limited thinking patterns and, 31–32, 33; list of common and unreasonable, 32

social life, 155

social phobia, 6, 12–13

social relationship problems, 256–257

solving problems. See problem solving

spaciness, 90

spirituality, 155

spontaneous thoughts, 19

Stampfl, Thomas, 181

stress: mindfulness for reducing, 115; symptoms of, 85, 89; treatment plans for, 12–13

stress inoculation: anger control and, 219–231; development of, 165–166

stress points, 107–108

suicidal thoughts, 6

symptoms: minimizing the significance of, 275; reasons for persistence of, 278–279

systematic desensitization, 165, 166

T

talking back, 217

thanking your mind, 132

theme analysis, 198–199

themes: automatic thoughts and, 20–21, 199; focusing on opposite of, 39

Thought and Evidence Journal, 48–58

Thought Journal: automatic thoughts and, 22–24; core beliefs and, 197; hot thoughts and, 48–58; limited thinking patterns and, 42–45

thoughts: anxiety-maintaining, 88–89; automatic, 15–25; catastrophic, 88; coping, 174–175; counting, 25; defusing from, 127–135; distancing from, 132–134; feedback loop related to, 16–17; feelings caused by, 15–16; hot, 47–58; labeling, 130; letting go of, 130–131; limited patterns of, 27–45; listening to, 21; objectifying, 133; observing, 120–124, 128–130; obsessional, 5; recording, 22–24; suicidal, 6; trigger, 47, 219

time management, 274–275

Titchener, Edward, 132–133

toddler visualization exercise, 210–211

traumatic memories: inner-child visualizations for, 208–217; prolonged exposure for, 189–190

Treatment Planner, 11–13; how to use, 11; treatment chart, 12–13

treatment plans, 2–13; for anger, 9; for bad habits, 9–10; for depression, 6–7; for low self-esteem, 7–8; for mild avoidance, 10; for obsessional thinking, 5; for panic disorder, 3–4; for perfectionism, 4–5; for phobias, 5–6; for procrastination, 11; for shame and guilt, 8; for worry, 2–3

trigger thoughts, 47, 219. See also hot thoughts

tunnel vision, 28–29

V

values-based action, 153–164; clarifying values for, 154–157; committing to, 161–164; creating intentions for, 158–160; effectiveness of, 153; life review for, 158; time to mastery of, 154; visualization of, 160

visualization: anger control and, 227; brief exposure and, 167, 176; core beliefs and, 207–208; covert modeling and, 235, 237; guidelines for, 66; of peaceful scenes, 65–67; relaxation training and, 65–67; strengthening your capacity for, 180, 218, 231, 274; values-based intentions and, 160; worry control and, 78–79. See also imagery; inner-child visualizations

W

Wanderer, Zev, 181
Weekes, Claire, 89
Weekly Activity Schedule, 140–142
weight problems, 244
White Room exercise, 120–121
White Room Meditation exercise, 129
Wise Mind Diagram, 122–124
Wolpe, Joseph, 165
work and career issues: problem checklist for, 255–256; values related to, 155
worksheets. *See* forms, charts, and worksheets
worldview changes, 274

worry: cyclical pattern of, 70–71; hierarchy of, 78; panic sequence and, 87; problem indicators for, 69; treatment plan for, 2–3, 12–13. *See also* anxiety; panic
worry control, 69–83; effectiveness of, 70; example of using, 83; exposure technique for, 77–80; preventing worry behavior, 80–83; relaxation skills and, 72, 78; risk assessment and, 72–76; time to mastery of, 70
worry exposure, 77–80
writing: narrative, 107; Thought Journal, 22–24

Y

Young, Jeffrey, 196, 217
young-adult visualization exercise, 215–216

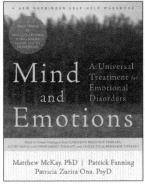

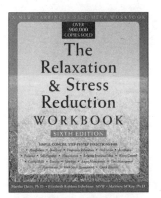

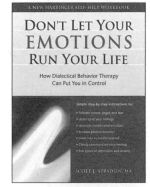